# DILEMMAS
## OF A
# TRADING NATION

For a quarter century since the fall of the Berlin Wall, the world has enjoyed an era of deepening global interdependence, characterized by the absence of the threat of great power war, spreading democracy, and declining levels of conflict and poverty. Now, much of that is at risk as the regional order in the Middle East unravels, the security architecture in Europe is again under threat, and great power tensions loom in Asia.

The Geopolitics in the 21st Century series, published under the auspices of the Order from Chaos project at Brookings, will analyze the major dynamics at play and offer ideas and strategies to guide critical countries and key leaders on how they should act to preserve and renovate the established international order to secure peace and prosperity for another generation.

# DILEMMAS

## OF A

# TRADING NATION

## JAPAN AND THE UNITED STATES IN THE EVOLVING ASIA-PACIFIC ORDER

## MIREYA SOLÍS

Brookings Institution Press
*Washington, D.C.*

The Brookings Institution is a private nonprofit organization devoted to research, education, and publication on important issues of
domestic and foreign policy. Its principal purpose is to bring the
highest quality independent research and analysis to bear on current
and emerging policy problems. Interpretations or conclusions in
Brookings publications should be understood to be solely those of
the authors.

*Library of Congress Cataloging-in-Publication*

Names: Solís, Mireya, author.
Title: Dilemmas of a trading nation : Japan and the United States in
    the evolving Asia-Pacific order / Mireya Solis.
Description: 1st edition. | Washington, D.C. : Brookings Institution
    Press, 2017. | Series: Geopolitics in the 21st century
Identifiers: LCCN 2017010291 (print) | LCCN 2017020798 (ebook)
    | ISBN 9780815729204 | ISBN 9780815729198 (paperback : alk.
    paper) | ISBN 9780815729204 (ebook)
Subjects: LCSH: Japan—Commercial policy. | United States—
    Commercial policy. | Trans-Pacific Partnership Agreement (2016
    February 4) | BISAC: BUSINESS & ECONOMICS / International /
    Economics. | POLITICAL SCIENCE / Globalization. | POLITICAL
    SCIENCE / International Relations / Trade & Tariffs.
Classification: LCC HF3826.5 (ebook) | LCC HF3826.5 .S66 2019
    (print) | DDC 382/.30952—dc23
LC record available at https://lccn.loc.gov/2017010291

9  8  7  6  5  4  3  2  1

Typeset in Sabon and Scala Sans

Composition by Westchester Publishing Services

*For Natalia and Paola, always*

# Contents

# Abbreviations

| | |
|---|---|
| ACTA | Anti-Counterfeiting Trade Agreement |
| ACTPN | Advisory Committee on Trade Policy Negotiations |
| AFL-CIO | American Federation of Labor and Congress of Industrial Organizations |
| APEC | Asia-Pacific Economic Cooperation |
| ASEAN | Association of Southeast Asian Nations |
| BIT | bilateral investment treaty |
| BRIC | Brazil, Russia, India, and China |
| CEFP | Council on Economic and Fiscal Policy |
| CGE | computable general equilibrium |
| DPJ | Democratic Party of Japan |
| EFTA | European Free Trade Association |
| EU | European Union |
| FACA | Federal Advisory Committee Act |
| FDI | foreign direct investment |
| FOIA | Freedom of Information Act |
| FTA | free trade agreement |
| GATS | General Agreement on Trade in Services |
| GATT | General Agreement on Tariffs and Trade |

| | |
|---|---|
| GDP | gross domestic product |
| GVC | global value chain |
| ICSID | International Centre for Settlement of Investment Disputes |
| IMF | International Monetary Fund |
| IP | intellectual property |
| ISDS | investor-state dispute settlement |
| ITAC | Industry Trade Advisory Committee |
| ITC | International Trade Commission |
| JA | Japan Agriculture |
| JPI | Japan Post Insurance |
| KORUS FTA | U.S.-Korea Free Trade Agreement |
| LDP | Liberal Democratic Party |
| MAFF | Ministry of Agriculture, Forestry and Fisheries (Japan) |
| METI | Ministry of Economy, Trade and Industry (Japan) |
| MFN | most favored nation |
| MITI | Ministry of International Trade and Industry (Japan) |
| MNC | multinational corporations |
| MOF | Ministry of Finance (Japan) |
| MOFAT | Ministry of Foreign Affairs and Trade (South Korea) |
| MT | metric tons |
| M&A | mergers and acquisitions |
| NAFTA | North American Free Trade Agreement |
| NGO | nongovernmental organization |
| NPU | National Policy Unit |
| NTM | nontariff measure |
| OECD | Organisation for Economic Co-operation and Development |
| PARC | Policy Affairs Research Council |
| PHP | Preferential Handling Procedure |
| PITAC | Public Interest Trade Advisory Committee |

| | |
|---|---|
| RCEP | Regional Comprehensive Economic Partnership |
| RTAA | Reciprocal Trade Agreements Act |
| R&D | research and development |
| SMD | single member district |
| SME | small and medium-size enterprise |
| STR | Office of the Special Trade Representative |
| TAA | Trade Adjustment Assistance |
| TPA | trade promotion authority |
| TPP | Trans-Pacific Partnership |
| TTIP | Transatlantic Trade and Investment Partnership |
| UN | United Nations |
| USTR | Office of the United States Trade Representative |
| WIPO | World Intellectual Property Organization |
| WTO | World Trade Organization |

# Acknowledgments

THIS IS A BOOK shaped by professional and personal transitions, and as such, it reflects a much deeper process of learning beyond its subject matter. It marked my departure from academia—the only professional environment I had known, having gone straight from graduate school to become junior faculty and eventually a tenured professor, until I joined the policy world of a think tank.

This move was spurred by the intriguing possibilities of life as a public intellectual at the Brookings Institution, and the journey has not disappointed. It has compelled me to expand my range in U.S.-Japan relations to include the impact of this bilateral relationship throughout the Asia-Pacific, to partake in the intense public policy debates on the role that globalization plays in the future of nations in this region, and to consider how my scholarship can serve and engage the public. It has meant, more often than not, stepping out of my own comfort zone, because the quest to expand intellectual horizons begins and ends with a keen realization of one's own limitations. And it has offered valuable lessons. Never in my wildest dreams would I have imagined that after devoting a decade to the goal of achieving tenure, I would be willing to give it up a few years later (although not without some regret and trepidation) and remain full-time at Brookings.

Despite the change, my life remains one of scholarship, thanks to the commitment at Brookings to in-depth quality research. I was an unusual hire: a woman born and raised in Mexico put in charge of Japan studies at one of America's premier think tanks. I will be forever grateful to the Brookings leadership—President Strobe Talbott and Executive Vice President Martin Indyk—for placing their trust in me—and to Vice President of Foreign Policy Bruce Jones for continuing to extend that vote of confidence. And my deepest thanks to Richard Bush, director of the Center for East Asia Policy Studies (CEAP). Richard recruited me to Brookings, and at every turn, he has gone out of his way to ensure that I can succeed in my new endeavor. In the process, he has become a trusted friend, wise counsel, and a steadying presence.

My new professional chapter was enabled by the foresight and generosity of donors who fund Japan research at Brookings. Philip Knight gifted the endowment for a Chair in Japan Studies, and the Japan Foundation Center for Global Partnership (CGP) awarded a five-year grant to cover programmatic costs. In the best spirit of U.S.-Japan cooperation, the commitment from these donors enabled long-term research on Japan and a range of programs to foster U.S.-Japan policy dialogue and public outreach. My gratitude goes to Phil Knight and to the leadership of the Japan Foundation and CGP, as well as to their dedicated staffs in the Tokyo and New York offices, among them, Hiroyasu Ando, Junichi Chano, Osamu Honda, Ayumi Takita, and Carolyn Fleischer. Brookings is committed to quality, independence, and impact, and this book, and the support of these donors, reflects this commitment.

My path to policy-oriented research was paved by earlier transformative opportunities awarded through the collaboration of Japanese and American institutions: the Abe Fellowship (a collaboration between the Social Science Research Council and CGP) and the U.S.-Japan Network for the Future (a program of the Mansfield Foundation and CGP). I extend my appreciation to Mary McDonnell at SSRC and the past and current leadership at the Mansfield Foundation: Gordon Flake, Paige Cottingham-Streater, David Boling, Frank Jannuzi, and Ben Self. A note of admiration to my Harvard University mentors—Susan Pharr and Ezra Vogel—for their commitment to nurturing networks of rising Japan scholars.

In writing this book I have acquired many intellectual debts, too many to properly recount. Michael O'Hanlon, Richard Bush, and two anonymous reviewers read the entire book manuscript and provided valuable feedback. Saori Katada, David Dollar, and Susan Aaronson read standalone chapters and offered very helpful suggestions. I greatly benefited from the comments offered by my Foreign Policy colleagues during lunch roundtables as I presented work in progress, and I always enjoyed chatting with Ken Lieberthal about the ups and downs of the Trans-Pacific Partnership. As this book project took form and matured, I learned a lot about Japanese political economy and trade policy from several Japan hands and Japanese scholars. Among them are Saori Katada, Saadia Pekkanen, John Ravenhill, Kazuhito Yamashita, Yorizumi Watanabe, Takashi Terada, and especially my long-time mentor, Shujiro Urata. Any shortcomings in this book's analysis are, of course, my own responsibility.

My CEAP colleagues have always extended warm collegiality, and I am grateful to our staff for their good cheer and assistance. My deepest appreciation goes to Jennifer Mason for her invaluable contributions to all areas of my work. Jennifer brings excellent analytical and organizational skills, attention to detail, multitasking prowess, and good humor regardless of the challenge. Her superb research and copyediting assistance greatly improved the quality of the book.

My gratitude and affection goes to friends and family who offered unwavering support while the writing of this book coincided with a major personal transition. Mutsuko Yamaguchi first befriended me as I arrived as a graduate student in Tokyo and has remained one of my closest friends for two decades. Saori Katada, who is not only an ideal co-author, but also a dear friend, shared in the challenges of raising daughters. I am most fortunate because of my family. Joan and Ed Groobert have warmly welcomed me into their family—and in so doing they have become an anchor in my life. In my mother, Mireya, and sister, Luz, I always find a home, even if we live far away from each other and our shared time is limited. They are, literally, my roots.

I dedicate this book to my daughters, Natalia and Paola. They add meaning to who I am and provide purpose to what I do. Watching them grow has been my greatest joy.

## CHAPTER ONE

# *Introduction*

## A Trading Nation for the Twenty-First Century

THE RESEARCH FOR THIS BOOK was initially motivated by the critical choices that loom ahead for Japan in the twenty-first century. Can Japan deploy a proactive trade policy to tackle the structural reforms that have hindered its international competitiveness, find a path back to growth, and become a leading voice in drafting rules for the twenty-first century economy? If not, will the country remain shackled to its domestic political constraints, unable to use trade policy to leverage reforms needed to overcome decades of domestic stagnation? And if so, will the third largest economy remain a secondary player in the world of international trade negotiations?

At a time when Japan is concerned about being overshadowed by a rising China, and when its reliance on foreign markets as sources of growth will only increase (the domestic market is projected to shrink to reflect depopulation trends), getting trade policy right has never been more important. Granted, trade policy is not a magic bullet and will not do all the heavy lifting necessary to accomplish Japan's economic revitalization, but it is certainly an essential component of a strategy to advance productivity reforms and secure access to overseas markets.

This research was also animated by the prospect that the Trans-Pacific Partnership (or TPP, a twelve-nation trade negotiation pioneering the wave of mega trade agreements) could recast the role of trade in the U.S.-Japan alliance. In the past, trade had been a source of acrimony and friction in their bilateral relationship, but Japan's TPP entry suggested new horizons. Would the TPP finally allow the United States and

Japan to get past divisive market access issues and use trade policy as a vehicle for deeper economic integration and a joint endeavor in drafting next-generation rules on trade and investment?

At first glance, the substance of bilateral trade negotiations, even within the context of the TPP talks, seemed to have changed little. Disagreements over agricultural market access and the detrimental effects of nontariff barriers on important sectors such as automobiles continued to dominate the headlines. However, this superficial reading misses the significant changes of the last twenty-five years: the gradual but real erosion in the clout of the Japanese agricultural lobby and the changing industrial landscape as Japanese companies relocated production to the United States to avoid import friction, and foreign companies made inroads in Japan in areas such as banking and pharmaceuticals—notwithstanding low cumulative levels of inward foreign direct investment. Most significantly, in the TPP negotiations, the top Japanese leadership drew a direct connection between requests from foreign partners to eliminate access barriers and its number one priority: to revolutionize the "metabolism" of the Japanese economy through productivity-enhancing reforms. In the past, Japan had come reluctantly to the negotiating table to appease American demands for greater opening, but this time, sensing the perils of domestic stagnation and exclusion from the emerging mega trade agreements, Japan eagerly requested to join the negotiations. Moreover, Tokyo's growing appetite for participation in designing the rules of the road for the twenty-first century economy reinforced U.S. positions in the transpacific trade negotiations. The TPP project offered an entirely new proposition. Anchored in a shared vision of rulemaking, Japan and the United States could work together to close the significant governance gap resulting from negotiation paralysis experienced at the World Trade Organization (WTO).

Advanced as a joint project, the Trans-Pacific Partnership served well the foreign policy objectives of both countries and helped accentuate the broad alignment in core national interests. Central to Japan's international standing is the ability to arrest the narrative of economic decline. By entertaining greater liberalization of the domestic economy than ever, the TPP helped Japan address long-standing credibility problems related to its resolve to enact economic change. It boosted confidence that the Shinzo Abe government would deliver on needed structural reforms and, in so doing, would create the conditions for "Japan to be back." The Trans-Pacific Partnership trade deal, therefore, became inextricably linked to expectations of Japan's economic renewal and greater international leadership.

For the United States, the TPP promised to advance important foreign policy priorities: to execute the Obama administration's policy of Asian rebalance and to upgrade the international economic structure at a time of profound shifts due to the rise of emerging economies. Prior to Japan joining the TPP, this agreement did not augur major economic or political gains for the United States. Participating countries represented small markets or already had trade agreements in force with the United States, while the largest economies of Northeast Asia remained on the sidelines. Japan's entry into the TPP transformed the economic and geopolitical payoffs of this undertaking. By negotiating preferential access to the Japanese market—one of the largest economies in the world—for the first time, the United States doubled its expected economic benefits from the trade agreement. Moreover, Japan's entry put to rest the skepticism about creating an Asia-Pacific economic platform that did not include any of the major Asian economies. With Japan as a partner in the TPP negotiations, the United States gained traction in its campaign to upgrade international trading rules and anchor its place as a committed Pacific power in the world's most dynamic economic region, a region that is also experiencing a major power shift with China's rise.

The potential for proactive trade policy to help Japan address its economic challenges, redefine the U.S.-Japan economic agenda, and open new venues of bilateral cooperation to address multilateral governance challenges initially drove this research. But in the course of writing this book, the ground shifted. Profound questions related to the merits of globalization eroded support for economic liberalization in countries that have long been stalwarts of openness. The Brexit referendum vote—the decision of UK voters on June 23, 2016, to leave the European Union—is a stunning example, but certainly not the only one. Trade has been a hard sell in U.S. domestic politics since the negotiation of the North American Free Trade Agreement (NAFTA), when the consensus on free trade began to fracture, and labor and environmental groups increasingly challenged the benefits of these trade agreements. The rise of anti-trade populism on the right and the left of the political spectrum signaled an even deeper rift, one that cannot be wholly attributed to the magnifying effect of a full-blown presidential campaign in 2016.[1] Rather, the United States has veered toward what some aptly refer to as the politics of grievance: blaming trade for most of our economic hardships.[2] The political battle lines on trade policy have been redefined as the Republican Party officially nominated a presidential candidate, Donald Trump, who promised to withdraw from the TPP, renegotiate or terminate NAFTA, and impose punitive tariffs on the main trading partners of the United States to bring back manufacturing jobs. The deeper rifts on trade in the American body politic came into full view at a time when the TPP—the most ambitious trade initiative of a generation—awaited a vote from Congress to enter into force.

Therefore, along the way, this book became also about the critical choices faced by the United States, especially in the aftermath of the Trump administration's withdrawal from TPP: Will the United States abdicate leadership in sustaining open trade policies as it finds itself unable to create a consensus in favor of international economic engagement? How will it manage the economic and geopolitical fallout of losing preferential access to large markets in the most vibrant region in the world, making the trade agenda falter on other fronts as it loses negotiating credibility, planting doubts among friends and rivals about its ability to remain a committed Pacific power, and giving up on one instrument of international economic diplomacy that allowed it to be both proactive and inclusive (with the potential for China's future entry)? And more important, will it use this critical juncture to launch policies that address the growing income inequality that is eating up support for open economic policies?

Trade policy has catapulted to front and center in the national conversations taking place in each country about its desired future direction—economic renewal, relaunched social compact, and projected international influence. Trade liberalization has become a polarizing issue both because we expect it to do more (to offer off-budget sources of growth and impetus for structural reforms to kick-start slow-growing economies), and because we blame it for many of our tribulations (the rise of income inequality, or, in a more extreme rendition, the loss of sovereignty and the subversion of national identity). This book offers a new way to think about the domestic politics of trade, one that highlights the tensions that pervade national choices on trade policy.

## THE ARGUMENT

Trade policy has become incredibly complex with attempts to negotiate mega trade deals, a far more intrusive trade agenda that reaches into policy realms behind the border; profound changes in the nature of international production and trade flows with the rise of global value chains; a stagnant multilateral trade regime; and the increased questioning of the distributional consequences of globalization. Therefore, national choices on trade have also become more complicated, and we need an analytical framework that can capture the vexing challenges of articulating a trade strategy in a rapidly shifting landscape.

The workhorse model of the domestic politics of trade offers a predictable causal chain to explain liberalizing or protectionist outcomes:

$$\text{Preferences} \rightarrow \text{Coalitions} \rightarrow \text{Institutions} \rightarrow \text{Outcomes}$$

The first step is to determine the preferences of economic actors based on their international competitiveness. Efficient producers will favor market opening, as they can reap the benefits of increased access to foreign markets, whereas noncompetitive manufacturers will advocate protectionist policies to avoid the onslaught of inexpensive imports.[3] The next step is to establish the emergence of pro- and anti-trade coalitions that can make use of a wide range of advocacy tactics, from technical advice to political contributions, media campaigns, and judicial action, among others.[4] The success of these lobby groups will hinge largely on the institutional setup for trade decisionmaking (the third stage), as it will empower some interests over others.[5]

This book offers a different interpretation of the domestic dynamics of trade politics, one that does not see trade policy formulation moving in a straightforward progression depicted in conventional models. Instead, this study uses trade policy design as its focal point; identifies the essential goals of trade policy (competitiveness and leadership, social legitimacy, and political viability); and places the difficult trade-offs that emerge from attempting to reconcile these objectives at the crux of the analysis.

## The Goals of Trade Policy

Each goal is, of course, challenging in its own right, as this brief overview makes clear.

### COMPETITIVENESS AND LEADERSHIP

At the most fundamental level, trade is about enhancing economic competitiveness by harnessing the forces of specialization, efficiency, productivity, and innovation. The payoffs of trade agreements come not just from opening large markets abroad, but also from leveraging needed internal reforms. These gains—expanded reach in overseas markets and domestic transformation—will be realized only with ambition at the negotiation table; that is, by signing high-quality trade agreements. The quality of the liberalization effort can be gauged by the extent to which trade agreements open sizable foreign markets, achieve comprehensive tariff elimination, tackle nontariff barriers, and provide governance in new areas of the global economy. Trade agreements are not negotiated exclusively for the expected economic gains; they are also important tools of diplomacy. States can pursue a number of foreign policy objectives through trade deals, but only large powers will possess the requisite resources to advance "architectural trade agreements," to be understood as multilateral frameworks that codify rules of economic exchange to derive mutual gains. These mega trade deals can become bids for international leadership.

SOCIAL LEGITIMACY

Policymakers need to ensure society's support for open trade policies, but skepticism on the merits of trade liberalization has grown over time. Critics argue that trade agreements have produced massive job losses and exacerbated economic disparities, that they empower multinational corporations to erode regulatory sovereignty, and that secret negotiations alienate democratic oversight. Addressing these concerns must be a central task for policymakers to show that trade liberalization has not produced higher rates of unemployment, nor has it mortally wounded manufacturing or been a main contributor to income inequality; that the investor-state dispute settlement (ISDS) mechanism has not resulted in the onslaught of regulatory regimes; and that proper oversight over trade negotiators exists through legislatively approved procedures.

The critics are right on two fronts. The circle of consultation with different groups in society needs to expand in tandem with the greater domestic reach of trade negotiations, and the current policy framework has come woefully short in dealing with the adjustment costs for displaced workers. The key here is that we should care not just about what happens to workers affected by trade agreements but to all workers unable to navigate difficult economic transitions.

POLITICAL VIABILITY

At the end of the day, only trade agreements that make it to the finish line, that get ratified, matter in the realization of anticipated economic and geopolitical gains.[6] Negotiating an ambitious trade agreement with little chance of securing domestic approval is not sound policy. Hence, a dose of political pragmatism is necessary to secure the yes vote in ratification. This requires galvanizing the support of likely winners and neutralizing the opposition of potential losers. When opponents to a trade agreement operate as veto players in the political system (that is, they have the clout to derail the negotiations or deny approval of the final deal), it requires making accommodations for them: scaling-down liberalization commitments and/or extending side payments.

### The Dilemmas of Trade Governance

Delivering on each of these objectives is a tall order for policymakers, but the complexities of trade policy design are only fully appreciated by factoring in "interaction effects." In other words, there are unavoidable trade-offs when negotiating ambitious trade agreements that can both generate support from large groups in society and get clearance from veto players so as to be enacted. The simultaneous pursuit of core trade objectives creates two fundamental dilemmas: decisiveness versus inclusiveness and reform versus subsidization.[7]

#### DECISIVENESS VERSUS INCLUSIVENESS

This dilemma captures the tension between executive efficiency and responsiveness to civil society. Negotiation of ambitious trade agreements requires departure from the status quo, as far-reaching liberalization commitments will cut into the vested interests of powerful producers. But political systems with multiple veto players who agree on little (that is, where there is wide separation of power and purpose) are prone to gridlock and will be unable to launch significant trade initiatives.[8] Hence the shift to a proactive trade policy will be predicated on centralizing decisionmaking to avoid policy capture. However, excessive centralization of decisionmaking can undermine legitimacy if trade policy formulation becomes exclusionary. The risks are to encourage the formation of an unlikely coalition among excluded groups (vested economic interests fearing loss of economic rents and civil society groups mobilized by value-driven campaigns) and/or to provoke a significant amount of social contestation of trade liberalization efforts.

#### REFORM VERSUS SUBSIDIZATION

This dilemma captures the tension between politically expedient subsidization and desirable economic reforms. Because trade has distributional consequences, compensation to sectors disadvantaged by liberalization has long been a task of trade policy formulation. However, compensation can be given for different reasons. If used as a side payment, we should expect targeted benefits that aim to preserve the status quo, but if deployed to consolidate reforms, we should expect general safety nets and adjustment programs that favor exit from contracting sectors. The political viability of trade agreements may dictate targeted compensation, but political pragmatism could sidetrack economic reforms. The risks are that side payments to producer groups will prolong the status quo, negating the reform benefits of liberalization, and that targeted compensation programs may come at the expense of genuine adjustment for displaced workers, hollowing out support for free trade.[9]

Crafting trade policy is not for the fainthearted; it demands hard choices. Accomplishing a desirable goal means sacrificing other cherished objectives to some extent. Trade policy is comprised of myriad balancing acts to reconcile competing interests, and it is sorely contested because different groups in a society will have clashing preferences on the acceptable trade-offs. For Japan and the United States the Trans-Pacific Partnership trade negotiations represented a critical investment to advance national interests, deepen the alliance, and provide much-needed international governance at a time of stress in the international order. But the traction of the anti-trade message in U.S. politics (which culminated in the United States withdrawal from TPP) not only put those ambitious goals on hold, it underscored the centrality of a domestic policy framework to support the middle class as a precondition to sustain internationalism. If there is one message this book seeks to convey, it is that the future of a rules-based economic architecture hinges on the ability of these countries to spur on domestic renewal.

## THE PLAN

The first section of this book draws primarily (but not exclusively) from the U.S. experience, to flesh out the challenges of achieving the goals of trade policy and navigating uncomfortable trade-offs. The second section uses the trade dilemma framework to illuminate breakthroughs in Japan's trade policy and reform agenda as well as its die-hard habit of subsidizing inefficient sectors. Chapter 2 underscores the ambitions behind trade policy. On the economic front, it explores the track record of high-quality trade agreements in increasing trade flows and generating higher economic payoffs, and it discusses the potential of international commitments to leverage domestic reforms to increase productivity. On the foreign policy front, it provides an overview of the varied security externalities of trade agreements, but the thrust of the discussion is on the role of large powers in negotiating architectural trade agreements that display their global leadership ambitions.

The next three chapters address the legitimacy challenges of trade policy. Chapter 3 examines the critics' argument that trade policy militates against inclusive growth by undercutting employment and promoting income inequality. The chapter pays close attention to the problem of transitional unemployment (writ large as a result of broad economic change) and the need for a revamped policy framework to address this issue. Chapter 4 examines the argument that deep trade agreements compromise the ability of states to regulate in the public interest. It revisits long-standing debates on whether globalization has promoted a regulatory race to the bottom and whether the investor-state dispute mechanism has produced regulatory chill. The chapter notes that there is little public understanding of the reasons behind the migration of the trade agenda to regulatory matters and highlights the trend in trade agreements to adopt more explicit safeguards on prudential regulation. Chapter 5 addresses the democratic deficit debate in trade policy in the areas of transparency/oversight and consultation with stakeholders. It offers a comparison of the role of transparency in different venues of international negotiation (especially the WTO) to assess the critics' argument on exceptional levels of secrecy in the TPP. It provides an overview of the evolution of the trade advisory committee system in the United States to illustrate the challenges in expanding engagement with nongovernmental organizations (NGOs) and other civil society groups.

Chapter 6 discusses the role of political institutions in creating conditions for state decisiveness or indecisiveness, and applies these insights to trade policy formulation. Through an overview of different national cases, it discusses the balance of power between executives and legislatures and the role of bureaucratic politics in favoring (or not) narrow client interests. It notes different patterns of lobbying activity driven by anticipated losses or gains from trade initiatives and discusses the role of political compensation to mitigate opposition to trade liberalization. Chapter 7 builds on the insights from the previous chapters to elucidate the trade governance dilemmas that drive this book's analysis: decisiveness versus inclusiveness and reform versus subsidization. It offers broad strategies to tackle each dilemma: expanding the circle of consultation to improve trade policy representativeness and developing a pro-adjustment safety net to enable workers to navigate difficult economic transitions. The chapter underscores how U.S. solutions to trade governance dilemmas have become largely ineffective, and it explains the appeal of the trade backlash in the presidential election by looking at longer-term legitimacy challenges, in particular the debate on the distributional consequences of globalization. To sustain open economic engagement, the United States needs to strengthen and revamp its social compact. (In) action on this front will shape the choices of other trading nations like Japan.

The next three chapters in the book focus on Japan's struggles to use trade policy proactively in addressing its economic transformation challenges and securing preferential access to overseas markets; these loom large over its future economic prosperity. Chapter 8 discusses Japan's evolution from a passive rule-taker to a committed rulemaker in the world of international trade negotiations. It notes the modest achievements of Japan's early forays into preferential trade deals and discusses the TPP's transformational impact on Japan's trade strategy—enabling the country to participate in four concurrent mega trade negotiations. Chapter 9 zooms in on Japan's protracted and fitful search for executive leadership to undermine the influence of vested interests hindering liberalization efforts. It discusses the eroding but still significant clout of the agricultural lobby and the redefinition of "red lines" in Japan's trade policy. The chapter analyzes the emergence of prime ministerial leadership in the Shinzo Abe administration but notes that, despite higher levels of policy-making centralization, a pattern of "negotiated decisiveness" prevailed in bringing Japan into the TPP and reforming the agricultural cooperative system. Chapter 10 addresses Japan's economic reform imperative and discusses the areas where the TPP could create positive synergy to close internationalization gaps and promote productivity. It assesses the outcomes of the TPP negotiations for the Japanese economy and points to areas of future improvement to modernize Japanese agriculture.

The conclusion identifies defining dilemmas for Japan (the search for decisiveness, the quest for reform) and the United States (the reconstruction of a domestic consensus in favor of internationalism) as trading nations in the twenty-first century. It also offers suggestions to recalibrate national choices on trade that will require critical investments at home (on human capital) and abroad (on updated rules) to forge a new Asia-Pacific economic order.

## CHAPTER TWO

# *Competitiveness and Leadership*

THE QUEST FOR ECONOMIC competitiveness and international leadership is an essential driver of trade policy. With trade liberalization, countries aim to harness the forces of specialization, efficiency, productivity, and innovation to expand national economic welfare. They seek the benefits that come not only from opening large markets abroad but also from the synergy of leveraging international commitments to advance domestic reforms. Whether these economic payoffs are realized or not depends on the quality of the liberalization effort. High-yield trade agreements require ambition at the negotiation table: to open sizable foreign markets, achieve comprehensive tariff elimination, tackle nontariff barriers, and provide governance in new areas of the global economy. The track record is strong; deep trade agreements lead to larger increases in trade flows, promote greater economic interdependence, and generate higher income gains.

Economic objectives alone do not breathe life into trade policy. As a tool of diplomacy, trade agreements also have been used by states to advance important national security interests, from fortifying allies to improving trust among old foes. For leading economies, the supply of international governance is a hallmark of state leadership. The negotiation of an "architectural" trade agreement with updated or novel disciplines on trade and investment can help revive a liberal economic order at the time of a profound power shift in world politics and stagnation of the multilateral trading regime.

The Trans-Pacific Partnership embodies well the competitiveness and leadership ambitions of trade policy. If enacted, the trade agreement would deliver important economic benefits to participating economies; add much needed impetus to international trade flows at a time when they have slowed down significantly; allow reforming elites from diverse countries such as Japan or Vietnam to implement much-needed reforms; and encourage nonmembers to step up their level of ambition in trade policy. Geopolitically, the TPP represents the most effective strategy for the United States and Japan to engage in transformative leadership with the aim of setting forth new parameters in trade and investment rulemaking, buttressing the U.S. presence in Asia, and creating incentives for emerging economies to join the new trade architecture. It is a winning strategy, combining both competitive drive and inclusive pull.

This chapter starts by restating the case for international trade. It shows that despite the profound transformation of the world economy in the last several decades, a fundamental pattern remains: open economies outperform closed ones. It admonishes that the case for liberalization must rest not only on the economic gains to be had but also on the existence of support policies to facilitate the transition of affected workers and industries. Next, the chapter discusses the role of quality in liberalization efforts to explain the noticeable performance differential of trade agreements. The second half of the chapter addresses the twin goals of domestic transformation and international influence. It provides examples from across the Asia-Pacific realm of the role played by trade negotiations in spurring along domestic reform agendas and highlights the competition among different mega trade agreements to deliver competitive advantages to participating members.

## THE CASE FOR TRADE

Why trade? For political leaders, trade liberalization is politically costly and risky. It invites pushback from vested interests eager to protect the status quo and it risks the emergence of divisive politics if the distributional effects of market liberalization are left unabated. Yet, for centuries nations have opened up to trade in their quest for growth and prosperity. How then does trade make nations more competitive? What is the economic case for liberalizing markets that justifies the attendant political risks?

At the most fundamental level, international trade allows countries to reap the benefits of specialization and exchange. It enables economies to use resources most effectively by focusing production on areas where they enjoy comparative advantage and to overcome the limits of a single market to cater, instead, to global demand. Hence, firms can increase production to exploit the advantages of economies of scale and import inputs and equipment more inexpensively, while consumers can benefit from access to lower-priced products as well as a wider variety of goods.

But the benefits of trade go beyond the static efficiency advantages of specialization and exchange to encompass the dynamic gains of competition and innovation, as well. Increased exposure to international competition erodes the market power of oligopolies, dissipates opportunities for economic rents, and spurs along the reallocation of resources, not only toward the most productive sectors of an economy but also toward the most efficient firms within a sector. This "sift and sort" effect increases the average productivity of economic sectors.[1] Greater access to the global marketplace also creates opportunities to acquire new technology and foster innovation. For example, imports of advanced capital equipment and high-tech goods facilitate technological diffusion, and to the extent that liberalization encourages larger inflows of foreign direct investment (FDI), it opens other channels for the dissemination of knowledge through the transfer of managerial and product know-how.

The case for international trade is centuries old, but it is not outdated, despite the profound transformation of the world economy. The foundations of the argument for openness and commerce were laid out in the eighteenth and nineteenth centuries: Adam Smith on the folly of autarky; David Ricardo on the insight that opportunity costs belie the sources of comparative advantage; and Charles de Secondat Montesquieu on the role of commerce as a cure against "destructive prejudices."[2] Certainly the world economy of today bears little resemblance to the economy then. Smith and Ricardo formulated their theories presuming perfect competition and no capital or technology flows, but those assumptions no longer hold. Or consider the manifold transformations in the nature of international production and trade in the postwar era: the growing weight of developing economies; the internationalization of services; the emergence of intra-industry and intra-firm trade (as opposed to the classic pattern of inter-industry trade); the reorganization of productive activities around global supply chains with significant increases in foreign direct investment levels; the Internet communication revolution; and the onset of the digital economy.[3] However, the link between openness and competitiveness has remained unaltered through these tumultuous waves of change. This is the main insight of a 2015 World Economic Forum report: trade and investment integration plus an open society (tolerant and inclusive) are the key ingredients to sustained productivity (that is, the keys to competitiveness).[4]

The record on the merits of international trade is unequivocal: open economies outperform closed ones. Countries that decide to rely exclusively on internal demand impose their own ceiling on growth. Findings on the performance differential between outward or inward strategies are consistent across time and apply to economies at very different levels of development and with widely ranging characteristics. David Dollar and Aart Kraay, for example, contrast the post-1980s experience of globalizers and nonglobalizers in the developing world.[5] They found that countries with growing trade share over gross domestic product (GDP) and significant tariff reductions experienced accelerated growth rates and were able to reduce absolute poverty levels compared to the countries that did not choose trade openness. By focusing on the "Great Liberalization" accomplished by the Uruguay Round, Antoni Estevadeordal and Alan Taylor concluded that liberalizers grow faster (1 percent per year), especially if they slash tariffs on capital and intermediate goods, helping to lower the price of investment goods, which increases the share of investment over GDP and encourages larger inflows of capital.[6]

The experience of the overachievers in the world economy—the thirteen economies that registered 7 percent growth for a quarter century—again drives home the essential role of the global market. The most significant common denominator of economies achieving sustained high growth was strategic insertion in the world economy. A turn outward was essential to maximize their competitive advantages, whereas economies that turned inward (to tap into domestic demand and avoid the volatility of the world market) eventually saw the growth momentum fade.[7]

The growth benefits of trade liberalization are not exclusive to developing countries; they also extend to industrialized countries with more open trade and investment regimes. Jeffrey Frankel and David Romer, in a cross-sectional study of one hundred countries, found that the multiplier effect on income of an increase of 1 percent in the share of trade over GDP is 0.3 percent over twenty-five years. In the case of the United States this translated into a 15 percent income increase since the 1950s.[8]

Other economists concur that there have been substantial payoffs for the United States from greater integration with the world economy. Scott Bradford, Paul Grieco, and Gary Hufbauer gauge the combined benefits of globalization (trade and investment liberalization, technological improvements in transportation and communication, and rising income) to be on the order of $1 trillion per year for over half a century (1950–2003).[9]

But the case for trade must put the distributional costs of economic change front and center, acknowledging the fact that trade and technology shocks entail dislocation for workers with skill sets from the old economy. Although the overall economic benefits from trade liberalization are higher than the adjustment costs of market opening for affected workers and communities, recent research has shown that these transitional costs for affected groups are higher and more protracted than previously estimated. Policymakers ignore the costs of transition at their own peril, as they will generate even larger costs in the form of protectionism. The specious debate on trade policy during the 2016 American presidential race poignantly makes this point. The harm of reneging on existing trade agreements, failure to ratify negotiated trade deals, and/or the unilateral imposition of punitive tariffs will be much larger given the deeper integration of the world economy. The spread of global supply chains quite literally means that economies increasingly need to import to export, so raising national tariff barriers will be a self-imposed harm. Moreover, a protectionist turn will impose a heavy toll on consumers, especially those at the bottom of the income ladder. Trade has a pro-poor bias in every country. As Pablo Fajgelbaum and Amit Khandelwal show, a move toward autarky would erode the purchasing power of consumers in the top 90th percentile by 28 percent, but would have a much more devastating impact on the bottom 10th percentile: 62 percent.[10]

The case for trade must also be made realistically. The empirical evidence linking liberalization to growth is persuasive, but trade alone does not provide a sustained economic lift to an economy.[11] Openness is certainly a vital ingredient, but it is not the only one. A complementary domestic policy framework is essential and should comprise sound macroeconomic policies, rule of law, and protection of property rights, as well as safety nets, to manage the effects of globalization.[12] It will require bountiful investments in human capital, technology and science, physical infrastructure, and soft connectivity to promote the flow of ideas and knowledge.[13]

It is important to acknowledge that the quality of the liberalization effort matters a great deal to the economic payoffs from trade. Optimally, liberalization should be pursued through the WTO, as it stands to accord the greatest economic benefits because it pools together over 150 economies. However, the multilateral institution has been plagued by negotiation deadlock since its establishment in 1995 due to problems of institutional design.[14] This has created an incentive for policymakers to pursue the gains from trade through the preferential route: free trade agreements (FTAs) of varying quality.

## AMBITIOUS LIBERALIZATION AND THE RISE OF MEGA TRADE DEALS

Indeed not all trade agreements are created equal, and their level of ambition will determine the economic payoffs they can generate. Countries with an ambitious trade strategy will aim to negotiate significant tariff and nontariff elimination with major economic partners and/or with a group of countries, which, pooled together, represent a significant economic stake and offer the potential for widespread rule dissemination. In contrast, a low-ambition trade policy will settle for negotiations with minor economic counterparts, will set aside the most sensitive sectors and issues from liberalization commitments, and will generate idiosyncratic rules to each agreement not amenable to diffusion. Hence, it is possible to gauge the quality of the liberalization effort using at least three different indicators: (1) the share of trade covered through the FTA network, (2) the degree of tariff elimination, and (3) the scope and depth of rules that go beyond existing multilateral disciplines to address nontariff barriers (referred to as WTO-plus commitments).

The contrast between high-yield and low-yield trade strategies is evident in table 2-1. Some countries have proactively negotiated preferential market access with their main trading partners, while others have followed a much more cautious approach, negotiating mostly a string of small preferential trade agreements. For example, Mexico's existing FTA network already covers 82 percent of the country's trade, and the lion's share is captured by a single trade agreement (NAFTA: 66 percent). At the other end of the spectrum are countries like China and Japan, whose FTA networks (eleven and fourteen trade agreements in force, respectively) cover only 22 percent of their trade volume. The European

Union's (EU) record is not very impressive either, given that as of 2014 it had negotiated thirty trade agreements that represented only 29 percent of its external trade. These countries have invested a lot of resources to ink multiple trade deals, with only modest results as judged by the total FTA coverage of trade.

Another interesting finding from this table is that the transformational effect of ongoing mega trade negotiations varies substantially. Neither the TPP nor the Regional Comprehensive Economic Partnership (RCEP) would add significantly to the total FTA trade coverage of Mexico (TPP: 1.4 percent) and Singapore (TPP and RCEP: 0 percent), since they already have FTAs with most of the countries participating in these mega trade agreements. In contrast, other countries can use these large trade deals to leapfrog in the construction of an FTA network that covers most of their trade. The most outstanding example is Japan, which would add 62 percentage points to its trade coverage if these trade agreements were enacted. Other countries would also significantly increase their share of trade with preferential access to overseas markets: South Korea (43 percentage points), the EU (29), and the United States (25), for instance.

The economic value of mega trade deals, however, goes beyond the additional share of trade covered through each deal signed. To the extent that mega trade agreements offer improved market access over existing bilateral FTAs (by further slashing tariffs), incorporate a common set of trade and investment rules, and/or adopt a unified tariff schedule and cumulative rules of origin, they will offer fresh economic gains and cut the transaction costs of disparate tariff schedules, idiosyncratic rules, and barriers to the efficient use of supply chains. This in turn should boost FTA utilization ratios as companies are attracted by deeper market access preferences and streamlined administrative procedures.[15] Table 2-1 identifies the total share of trade covered by each mega trade deal to underscore the gains of improved and larger trade groupings, even for countries that already possess an extensive FTA network.

Beyond trade coverage, the level of ambition of an FTA is measured by tariff elimination targets. Setting aside sensitive sectors from pledges of market opening and/or adopting lengthy tariff reduction calendars are common sins of trade agreements. These exclusions and deferred liberalization commitments appease FTA opponents, but they also diminish the expected economic benefits for two main reasons. One reason is

Table 2-1. Potential of Mega Trade Agreements, Based on Volume of Trade in 2014

| | Current percent of trade share covered by FTA network | Number of FTAs | Ongoing major FTA negotiations (shares in %) | | | Potential trade share covered by expanded FTA network (%) |
|---|---|---|---|---|---|---|
| | (Based on FTAs in force as of July 2015) | | | | | |
| Mexico | 82.01 (NAFTA: 66.32) | 17 | *TPP* | | | 83.36 |
| | | | Additional coverage: 1.36 | | | |
| | | | Total share of trade: 69.76 | | | |
| Singapore | 70.52 | 14 | *TPP* | *RCEP* | *EU* | 81.37 |
| | | | Additional coverage: 0.00 | 0.00 | 9.88 | |
| | | | Total share of trade: 30.26 | 50.95 | 9.88 | |
| Malaysia | 62.77 | 7 | *TPP* | *RCEP* | *EU* | 82.43 |
| | | | Additional coverage: 8.94 | 0.00 | 9.94 | |
| | | | Total share of trade: 38.45 | 62.14 | 9.94 | |
| United States | 40.12 | 20 | *TPP* | *TTIP* | | 64.95 |
| | | | Additional coverage: 7.30 | 17.53 | | |
| | | | Total share of trade: 40.54 | 17.53 | | |

**South Korea** — 40.26 (KORUS: 10.57), 10

| | *China (signed)* | *RCEP* | *CJK* | |
|---|---|---|---|---|
| Additional coverage: | 21.43 | 29.56 | 29.26 | |
| Total share of trade: | 21.43 | 46.56 | 29.26 | 83.22 |

**European Union (Excludes intra-EU trade)** — 28.60, 30

| | *TTIP* | *Japan* | *MER-COSUR* | |
|---|---|---|---|---|
| Additional coverage: | 15.17 | 3.17 | 2.82 | |
| Total share of trade: | 15.17 | 3.17 | 2.82 | 58.10 |

**China** — 22.94, 11

| | *Korea (signed)* | *RCEP* | *CJK* | |
|---|---|---|---|---|
| Additional coverage: | 6.75 | 15.64 | 14.00 | |
| Total share of trade: | 6.75 | 30.11 | 14.00 | 45.91 |

**Japan** — 22.33, 14

| | *TPP* | *RCEP* | *CJK* | *EU* | |
|---|---|---|---|---|---|
| Additional coverage: | 15.18 | 26.44 | 26.10 | 9.92 | |
| Total share of trade: | 28.03 | 44.05 | 26.10 | 9.92 | 84.64 |

Source: Calculated from IMF Direction of Trade Statistics (accessed July 15, 2015).
Note: RCEP (Regional Comprehensive Economic Partnership) includes Australia, Brunei, Cambodia, China, India, Indonesia, Japan, Laos, Malaysia, Myanmar, New Zealand, the Philippines, Singapore, South Korea, Thailand, and Vietnam; TTIP (Transatlantic Trade and Investment Partnership) includes the United States and European Union; KORUS (U.S.-Korea Free Trade Agreement); CJK (China-Japan-South Korea Free Trade Agreement); and MERCOSUR (sub-regional block including Argentina, Brazil, Paraguay, Uruguay, and Venezuela).

that the opportunity to enhance the competitiveness of an economy along the lines of comparative advantage will be lost as pockets of entrenched protectionism remain. The other reason is that sectoral carveouts requested by one party will invite reciprocal demands from other parties to the negotiation and will end up lowering the overall level of tariff elimination in the trade agreement.

Tables 2-2 and 2-3 illustrate marked national differences in the level of ambition to slash tariffs in extant trade agreements. The WTO mandates that FTAs should substantially eliminate all barriers to trade, commonly operationalized at 90 percent tariff line elimination. Table 2-2 compares the track record of the United States and the three large Northeast Asian economies (South Korea, China, and Japan). It is clear that the United States and South Korea adopted ambitious commitments to eliminate almost all tariffs in ten years in several of their FTAs. For South Korea in particular this was a major accomplishment since many of its earlier FTAs were plagued by exclusions. In its agreement with the European Free Trade Association (EFTA), 65.8 percent of agricultural tariff lines were set aside.[16] While China's FTAs shown in the table meet the WTO standard, none of Japan's bilateral trade agreements do. Japan's trade policy has been hamstrung by the enduring power of the agricultural lobby, and only in the TPP negotiations was it finally able to break through this tariff elimination ceiling (see chapter 10).

Table 2-3 shows the tariff elimination percentages achieved by the Association of Southeast Asian Nations (ASEAN) member countries in their trade agreements with extra-regional partners (the so-called ASEAN+1 FTAs).[17] The table offers two interesting findings. First is the diversity of outcomes, not only in terms of the different tariff elimination results in the string of ASEAN+1 trade deals but also within ASEAN countries. In a single trade negotiation, some ASEAN nations (Singapore and, frequently, Brunei) aim for high levels of liberalization (97 percent or higher), whereas others fall below the 90 percent standard. Second, the surest predictor of the overall level of tariff elimination is the degree of ambition of the extra-regional partner. Australia and New Zealand offered full tariff elimination, and their ASEAN FTA scored the highest in tariff elimination (94.6 percent). Japan and India offered more modest liberalization commitments (86.3 percent and 74.3 percent, respectively), and their trade agreements with ASEAN recorded the lowest levels of overall liberalization.[18]

One last yardstick by which to measure the promise of trade agreements is their depth (that is, their scope in incorporating WTO-plus rules in areas such as investment and services liberalization).[19] Again, policymakers around the world have displayed sharply divergent levels of ambition in negotiating "thin" or "thick" trade agreements. On this score, the extent to which trade agreements go beyond obligations already acquired through WTO membership (deeper liberalization) and cover areas not yet incorporated in the multilateral regime (newer liberalization; for example, disciplines on state-owned enterprises) are important, as well as the extent to which they offer substantive and enforceable commitments (binding liberalization).

This last dimension can make a big difference on actual liberalization results and provides a reality check on how far governments are willing to go in opening markets. Andreas Dür, Leonardo Baccini, and Manfred Elsig underscore major differences between hortatory and actionable provisions in their analysis of over 500 FTAs. For example, while 70 percent of agreements include clauses on competition policy, only 2 percent mandate the creation of a common competition authority. And while more than half of trade agreements include provisions on intellectual property protection, the share of agreements with enforceable rules in this area is in the single digits.[20]

Temporal, regional, and national patterns are discernable in the negotiation of deep trade agreements. The NAFTA agreement was a precursor to the more far-reaching trade agreements, but comprehensive FTAs are mostly a twenty-first-century phenomenon. Consider, for example, the situation in East Asia. The majority (67 percent) of FTAs concluded in this region by 2000 only covered goods and services and incorporated no WTO-plus elements. By 2013, the situation had reversed, with "thin" agreements representing only 23 percent of concluded East Asian FTAs.[21] Regionally, Africa is characterized by lower ambition FTAs in the rules area.[22] And even though East Asia has gradually embraced deeper trade negotiations, marked national differences prevail. While Singapore, Japan, and South Korea exhibit a penchant for WTO-plus commitments, India and China more frequently negotiate shallower FTAs.[23] All in all, the two countries that rank the highest in the most comprehensive measurement of depth by Dür, Baccini, and Elsig are the United States and Japan.[24]

*Table 2-2.* Percentage of Tariff Elimination in Select FTAs: United States and Northeast Asia

| | U.S. | | | Korea | | | | | China | |
|---|---|---|---|---|---|---|---|---|---|---|
| Aus. | Peru | Korea | Chile | Sing. | EFTA | U.S. | EU | Switz. | Ice-land |
| | 99 | | 99 | | | | | | | |
| 97% | | 98 | | | | | 98 | 98.7 | | |
| High-ambition standard | | | | 96.3 | | | | | | |
| | | | | | | | | | | 95.8 |
| 90% | | | | | 91.6 | | | | 91.8 | |
| WTO standard | | | | | | 88.5[a] | | | | |

Sources: World Trade Organization, "Trade Policy Review: Republic of Korea, 2008," 2008; World Trade Organization, "Trade Policy Review: Republic of Korea, 2012," 2012; World Trade Organization, "Trade Policy Review: China, 2014," 2014; Ministry of Economy, Trade and Industry (METI), *White Paper on International Economy and Trade, 2012*; Shujiro Urata, "Regional Economic Integration in Asia-Pacific and Japan's Foreign Economic Policy," presentation (Brookings Institution, Washington, March 4, 2015).
a. Excludes some agricultural goods
Note: These are the percentage of tariff lines to be eliminated within ten years of the FTA's entry into force.

### Quality Translates into Outcomes

Higher-quality trade agreements (opening up larger foreign markets, aiming for comprehensive tariff elimination, and providing disciplines on trade and investment attuned to the realities of international production and exchange) deliver more economic benefits; econometric studies

| | | | | | | Japan | | | | |
|---|---|---|---|---|---|---|---|---|---|---|
| Sing. | Mex. | Malay. | Chile | Thai. | Indon. | Bru-nei | Phil. | Switz. | Viet-nam | Aus. |
| | | | | | | | | | | 89.0 |
| | | | | | | | 88.4 | | | |
| | | | 87.2 | | | | | | | |
| | 86 | 86.8 | 86.5 | | 86.6 | | | 85.6 | 86.5 | |
| 84.4 | | | | | | | 84.6 | | | |

projecting the gains from trade of different trade agreements attest to that.

In a 2012 study, Peter Petri, Michael Plummer, and Fan Zhai compared the economic impact of Asian and Asia-Pacific trade groupings by using precedent trade agreements to derive FTA templates on the likely reach and depth of the liberalization effort, and by disaggregating the dynamic effects of different productivity pathways from freer trade (enhancing the activities of established exporters, allowing new firms to enter the international marketplace, and investment liberalization). They projected substantial income gains from the TPP track ($295 billion per year by 2020) and from the Asian track ($500 billion). The larger absolute gains in the Asia-only scenario are due to the greater benefits of reducing higher average tariffs as well as the faster rates of growth in that region. But as these authors underscore, the level of ambition is

*Table 2-3.* Level of Ambition in Tariff Elimination: ASEAN+1 FTAs

| FTA | Tariff elimination ratio (%) | Lower-ambition countries (below 90%) | Higher-ambition countries (above 97%) |
|---|---|---|---|
| ASEAN-ANZ (Australia and New Zealand) | 94.6 | Cambodia, Myanmar | Singapore, Brunei, Thailand, Australia, New Zealand |
| ASEAN-China | 92.0 | Thailand, Indonesia, Philippines, Cambodia, Myanmar | Singapore, Brunei |
| ASEAN-Korea | 91.6 | Vietnam, Cambodia, Laos, Myanmar | Singapore, Brunei, Philippines |
| ASEAN-Japan | 89.2 | Indonesia, Vietnam, Cambodia, Laos, Myanmar, Japan | Singapore |
| ASEAN-India | 76.5 | Brunei, Malaysia, Thailand, Indonesia, Philippines, Cambodia, Vietnam, Laos, Myanmar, India | Singapore |

Source: Based on table 1 in Arata Kuno, "Constructing the Tariff Dataset for the ERIA FTA Database," in *Comprehensive Mapping of FTAs in ASEAN and East Asia*, edited by Chang Jae Lee and Misa Okabe, ERIA Research Project Report 2010–26 (Economic Research Institute for ASEAN and East Asia, March 2011).

critical to the payoffs from liberalization. An expansion of the TPP template to cover the entire Asia-Pacific Economic Cooperation (APEC) membership would generate double the income gains than the equivalent expansion of an Asian template, which makes more accommodations for excluded sectors and aims for shallower levels of economic integration.[25]

Since the conclusion of the TPP negotiations, a wave of econometric research has estimated the income gains from trade liberalization by factoring in the actual tariff elimination schedules and the commitments on nontariff barriers in the deal struck by the TPP parties in October 2015. A World Bank study projects that, on average, real GDP for member countries would be 1.1 percent higher by 2030, with countries like Vietnam and Malaysia registering the largest gains (10 percent and 8 percent, respectively), while other members were anticipated to achieve smaller but still significant gains (2.6 percent for Japan and 0.4 percent for the United States). As this study makes clear, one of the biggest expected benefits of the TPP is to increase trade volumes of participating economies by 11 percent. This would provide a powerful counter to current projections that the slowdown in international trade, if unabated, will shrink member countries' trade by 25 percent by 2030 compared to levels before the global financial crisis of 2008.[26]

The study by Peter A. Petri and Michael G. Plummer of projected TPP effects from 2016 shares many of the same assumptions of the World Bank study and reaches similar conclusions.[27] These authors forecast annual income gains of $465 billion for TPP countries by 2030 (1.1 percent of GDP), and gains of $131 billion for the United States alone (0.5 percent of GDP).[28] They estimate an increase of 11.5 percent in exports of TPP countries (9.1 percent for the United States), and an increase of 3.5 percent in inward FDI stocks and 2 percent in outward FDI stocks for TPP members by 2030. On the other hand, the International Trade Commission's (ITC) assessment of the TPP focuses exclusively on the impact on the U.S. economy and projects more modest gains. It puts the increase in real GDP for the United States at a smaller $42.7 billion by 2032 (0.15 percent of GDP), and expects only a 1 percent increase in exports, 1.1 percent increase in imports, and the creation of an additional 128,000 jobs.[29]

The differences in projected gains reflect the different assumptions of the econometric models employed. For instance, the World Bank and the Petri and Plummer studies incorporate the impact of nontariff barriers across the board. Taking into account that only a fraction of nontariff measures (NTM) operate as trade barriers to be subject to liberalization, they assume that the TPP would eliminate 56.3 percent of NTMs for goods and 37.5 percent of NTMs for services. One of their main findings is that behind-the-border liberalization generates the brunt of benefits compared to tariff elimination. The ITC study incorporates selected NTMs, but omits from the quantitative analysis many of the disciplines that are hard to quantify. It offers instead a qualitative assessment. Moreover, the ITC does not consider spillover effects to be enjoyed by non-TPP members from nondiscriminatory liberalization, nor does it factor in productivity differentials among firms, all mechanisms that expand the economic gains in the other econometric analyses of the TPP.[30]

Notwithstanding these different assumptions, all three leading econometric studies of the TPP's macroeconomic impact seek to answer a fundamental question: Are participating economies better off with the TPP compared to a baseline scenario of no trade deal? And the answer is, consistently, yes. Contrary to popular perception, the projections of gains from computable general equilibrium (CGE) models are not meant to be accurate predictions of how these economies will perform in the next fifteen or thirty years, given that these economies will be buffeted by many economic forces along the way. Rather, by keeping everything else constant, they identify how much the TPP will add to the national welfare of members, and they find that even for large, open economies (for example, the United States) with moderate reliance on trade as share of GDP, a single microeconomic tool (a trade deal among a dozen nations) can move the GDP needle and promote trade and investment activities.

The only econometric study that does not share this positive outlook on the TPP is by Jeronim Capaldo, Alex Izurieta, and Jomo Kwame Sundaram, who argue that the TPP would contract the incomes of both member countries (for example, −0.54 percent for the United States) and nonparticipating developing economies (−5.24 percent), and would bring major job losses on the order of 771,000 for TPP nations and upward of 5 million for nonmembers.[31] These authors are the only ones to use a United Nations (UN) Global Policy Model designed to gauge the macroeconomic effects of external shocks, and they argue that their demand-driven model is more useful because it relaxes the full employment assumption and captures income distribution effects.

There are major reservations regarding the fit and the assumptions of the model that raise questions about the validity of their results. First, the model cannot incorporate any changes in trade policy, such as tariff and nontariff elimination and, therefore, cannot really estimate the impact of a trade agreement on efficiency, specialization, and productivity.[32] Second, the authors assume that all international competition is zero-sum: firms enhance trade performance by firing workers, countries retain capital by squeezing labor's income share. The role of technology, value added production, differentiation of products in corporate strategy, and the host of factors that influence capital flows are outside this narrow conception of competition in the marketplace. So what the authors verify in their model is their pre-existing assumptions regarding the nature of economic adjustment (race to the bottom), but not the actual TPP effects.[33]

The debate on the fit of the assumptions or the accuracy of predictions will continue unabated, but in gauging the promise of deep integration agreements, the past performance of trade deals is also revealing. For example, comprehensive trade deals such as NAFTA and the European Single Market are estimated to have raised members' GDP by 1 to 2 percent and 2 to 3 percent, respectively.[34] There is strong evidence that deep integration agreements have a much larger impact on trade flows. Second-generation trade agreements among APEC members (signed after 2005 and containing many more WTO-plus commitments) are credited with significantly boosting exports, compared to older, shallower agreements.[35] In a robust econometric analysis of 536 trade agreements, Dür, Baccini, and Elsig confirm that the deeper the trade agreement, the more sizable the impact on trade flows. Just by looking at a subset of trade agreements from the last fifteen years, they find a 106 percent long-term increase of trade for dyad countries with comprehensive integration agreements.[36] The level of ambition in trade policy design, therefore, shapes economic payoffs from trade agreements.

## DOMESTIC ECONOMIC REFORM

Extensive liberalization commitments through the overhaul of tariff regimes and the reduction of nontariff barriers generate economic opportunities in two ways: they improve the terms of access and conditions of operation in foreign markets, and they enhance the competitiveness of the economy through efficiency-enhancing domestic market reforms. The removal of tariff and regulatory shelters for low-productivity sectors helps dissipate the economic rents secured by vested interests at the expense of economic growth. But the efficiency gains are not obtained exclusively through deregulation; they hinge as well on the supply of needed regulation (for example, regulations to avoid predatory behavior through competition policy or disciplines on state-owned enterprises, or to protect property rights, to name a few).

It is clear that a powerful motive for policymakers to engage in trade negotiations is to enact desirable economic reforms. Trade agreements can be effective levers of domestic reform in several ways. First, they can provide a greater degree of state insulation from the pressures of domestic interest groups by transferring the fate of an economic reform to the level of interstate negotiations. Indeed, observers of the European Union integration process have observed that in creating supranational institutions, European governments were not negotiating themselves away. Rather, they were intent on enhancing their autonomy through an additional layer of international regulation.[37] Second, trade negotiations provide a commitment device to lock in reforms. By elevating domestic reforms into international obligations through a trade agreement, policymakers can ensure their longevity. The new policy measures will no longer be easy prey to the whims of an incoming administration, as the cost of backtracking from international treaty commitments is much higher.[38] And third, because trade negotiations proceed on the basis of reciprocity, they help reformers shift the tide of domestic support for proposed economic reforms. A countervailing "coalition of exporters" endorsing the proposed trade agreement, to benefit from expanded market access abroad, will help in the fight against import-competing industries who oppose the trade negotiations.[39]

Examples of governments bent on economic reform relying on trade agreements to achieve their goals can be found across time and continents. Mexico offers a clear-cut example. When the limits of a growth model based on import substitution and oil exports became clear, Mexican technocratic elites promoted export manufacturing, both through unilateral liberalization and by joining the General Agreement on Tariffs and Trade (GATT) in the 1980s. However, the success of this new growth strategy was far from assured, and President Carlos Salinas proposed trade negotiations to the United States (what would become NAFTA, as Canada joined as well) to ensure the survival of the new policy regime. NAFTA made two essential contributions to the success of Mexico's economic reforms: (1) it tied the hands of incoming administrations to prevent rollback of the reforms (with a strong presidential system, sweeping policy changes at the whim of previous presidents had been recurrent), and (2) it obtained greater assurance regarding access to the U.S. market and flows of American investment into the Mexican economy, allowing the government to dole out side payments.[40]

Elsewhere in the continent, Peru's negotiation of a trade agreement with the United States in the mid-2000s offers another example. As Philip Levy notes, Peru's main motivation was not improved market access (since most of its exports already enjoyed duty-free status through preference programs). Its main objective was to institutionalize its prior liberalization measures via an FTA, to signal its commitment to broader governance reforms, and to encourage investment flows to improve economic performance.[41]

Across the Pacific, WTO accession played a key role in furthering Chinese market reforms. Before joining the multilateral trade regime in 2001, China had already executed significant changes to its trade policy regime (slashing tariffs, extending trade rights to allow more entities to engage in foreign trade, and adopting an exchange rate that did not penalize exports).[42] But it was the WTO-enabled reforms that would increase competition in the Chinese market (revamping inefficient banks and state-owned enterprises) and would allow China to emerge as an attractive site in the global supply chain. As Nicholas Lardy explains, in the view of the leadership, this was the set of reforms critical to overall economic performance and, therefore, to the regime's political legitimacy.[43]

North-South FTAs can become a vehicle for the adoption of deep economic reforms in the developing world, as Leonardo Baccini and Johannes Urpelainen demonstrate in their cross-country analysis, when three conditions are met: (1) a leader in the developing world is eager to implement economic reforms to boost economic growth, but (2) domestic opposition to change requires the internationalization of commitments via an FTA, and (3) the industrialized FTA counterpart embraces liberal reforms in its FTA negotiation template.[44] In this light, Japan is a puzzle. It is a large industrialized country committed to the negotiation of deep FTAs, but was, nevertheless, unable to codify significant reforms in its trade agreements with developing nations. In fact, Japan's unfinished process of economic reform thwarted its ability to leverage its WTO-plus agenda in trade negotiations with developing countries (commitments on investment, government procurement, and intellectual property are modest in its trade agreements with developing ASEAN nations). Its inability to offer significant market access in agriculture (or to increase the flow of foreign workers) prevented Japan from making headway in the adoption of WTO-plus rules with its developing country counterparts.[45] Only by joining the TPP was Japan able to close this credibility gap.[46] By acquiescing to more meaningful market access concessions (to advance its own domestic reforms), Japan was finally able to achieve its goal of disseminating deep integration agreements. But for Japan and the other TPP members, foreign policy considerations were also at stake in pursuing a mega trade deal.

## RULEMAKING AND INTERNATIONAL LEADERSHIP

The maximization of economic gains, the retooling of national economies to achieve competitiveness, and the leveraging of domestic economic reforms are not the only objectives motivating state leaders to negotiate trade agreements. Beyond these economic considerations, trade deals can serve broader national interests. As a tool of statecraft, trade policy can be deployed in pursuit of the fundamental aims of any state: power in addition to plenty.

### Commercial Treaties as Diplomacy

Commerce is one of the oldest instruments of interstate diplomacy and, over time, countries have used trade policy to advance important security interests. While the list is not exhaustive, some of the geopolitical objectives of trade diplomacy include the following:

**To recommit to allies and maximize the security externalities of joint gains from trade.** States will be more eager to sign trade deals among allies because the wealth generated by freer trade can enhance the security capabilities of alliance members.[47] Moreover, trade agreements can be pursued to "re-securitize" a partnership. In other words, they may be a deliberate attempt to set aside the economic irritants that have proven divisive among allies and to signal a renewed unity of purpose. For example, in addition to the pursuit of joint economic gains, the United States and South Korea engaged in trade talks with geopolitical objectives in mind, as both desired to consolidate Washington's strategic foothold in the region and were prepared to patch up differences over thorny economic issues (screen quotas to protect the domestic film industry, restrictions on beef imports).[48]

**To exclude security competitors from profitable markets to prevent their economic strengthening and subsequent gains in national power.** This is the flip side of the first strategy, and the pursuit of a hard balancing approach should result in separate spheres of economic integration. The best known case is the bifurcation of the world economy at the onset of the Cold War as the Eastern Communist bloc coalesced around the Council for Mutual Economic Assistance, and the Western bloc joined the

Bretton Woods institutions, which were multilateral in character but still far from achieving universal membership (for instance, twenty-nine countries signed the International Monetary Fund's [IMF] articles of agreement in 1945, and GATT had twenty-three members when it was created in 1947). In the current context, some have seen the TPP in this light, arguing it represents an American strategy to contain China.[49] However, the American TPP strategy vis-à-vis China has not been about exclusion but, instead, inducement. In other words, the goal has been to create incentives for China to reform its trading practices by adopting the more exacting disciplines of the TPP, leaving the possibility of future entry open.[50]

**To increase trust through webs of interdependence with former enemies or potential adversaries.** Deeper levels of economic interaction will raise the cost of conflict, and will create a cadre of stakeholders in each country with an interest in the continuation of stable political relations.[51] Through day-to-day business transactions, it will be possible to increase contact between societies and avoid the "demonization" of the enemy. The prime example of using functional integration to dispel the deep mistrust of longtime foes (Germany and France) is the European Economic Community.

**To cultivate economic dependence for the sake of political influence.** The goal is to cultivate asymmetric economic exchange to gain leverage over the smaller trading country. Albert Hirschman provides the classic analysis through his study of Nazi Germany's trading practices in Central and Eastern Europe during the 1930s. As a tool of national power, trade links were developed to create a significant adjustment burden to any stoppage of trade and to preclude trading alternatives by establishing, as much as possible, monopolistic or monopsonistic relations.[52]

**To engage in soft balancing by preventing a rival state from constructing an exclusive trade network.** This security rationale should yield a move–countermove dynamic in trade negotiations, as security competitors will closely match each other's FTA initiatives. Because official trade negotiations elevate the status of a bilateral relationship, a third-party competitor will seek to avoid the emergence of special relationships by negotiating a countervailing trade agreement that neutralizes such political gains. Moreover, no would-be regional hegemon will remain idle as its main rival negotiates a string of trade deals that shuts that country out of the preferential circle. Hence, the oft-noted "domino effect" in the FTA race can be attributed not only to economic but also political diversion. The end result of this political competition through trade policy should be the emergence of parallel and overlapping FTA networks. China and Japan's competitive courting of Southeast Asia illustrates this dynamic at work.[53] Japan negotiated its first preferential trade deal with Singapore in 2000 and this motivated China to launch ASEAN-wide trade negotiations a year later. Japan then felt compelled to announce a trade initiative with ASEAN as a whole in 2002 and proceeded, as well, to negotiate a string of bilateral trade deals in the region.

**To hedge against abandonment or domination by a leading power.** States can use trade agreements to deepen a bilateral bond or maintain the commitment to a region from a leading power. For instance, both Australia and South Korea were animated by a desire to boost their respective alliances with the United States through FTA negotiations.[54] And several Asian countries welcomed the TPP project as part of the Obama administration's policy of rebalancing toward Asia, seeking to enhance its status as a Pacific power. But smaller countries not only fear abandonment; in fact they may negotiate trade agreements with different lead countries to diversify economic relations and prevent the outright domination of a single power. Surveying the FTA strategies of ASEAN countries individually and collectively, Mike Mochizuki underscores their desire to avoid overdependence and mitigate major power rivalries by negotiating trade deals with the three lead powers (Japan, China, and the United States).[55]

*Architectural Trade Agreements: On the Supply of Governance*

For a few large economies, trade agreements offer a vehicle to play a different geopolitical game altogether: a bid for global leadership through the construction of an international trade architecture. International economic governance has long been sustained by state power and leadership. This is the main finding of Kevin O'Rourke's penetrating analysis of globalization waves in the last millennia, as "the pattern of trade could only be understood as being the outcome of some military or political equilibrium between contending powers."[56] While technological change has certainly been critical to the abatement of transportation costs in long-distance trade, O'Rourke admonishes that the ability of powerful states to deliver rule of law and security in vast expanses of land and sea enabled the flourishing of international trade in disparate eras such as the Pax Mongolica of the thirteenth century, the Pax Britannica (1815–1914) that emerged from the ashes of the Napoleonic Wars, and the Pax Americana in the aftermath of World War II.

State power is critical to the construction of open trade regimes in at least three dimensions: (1) powers of coercion: at home, the centralization of power in a national government capable of supplying rule of law, and abroad, the maintenance of unobstructed shipping lanes at sea and trading routes on land; (2) powers of persuasion: practicing the precepts of free trade and overseeing a dynamic economy that others wish to emulate; and (3) powers of inducement/enforcement: the carrots in a state's diplomatic arsenal to entice other countries to open their markets through membership in international institutions, and/or through reciprocal market access agreements; plus the sticks to ensure compliance with acquired obligations. Only a few leading powers will be able to muster the array of resources and capabilities required to construct an open trading system, which can range from maintaining open shipping lanes and operating as a locomotive of growth and market of last resort, to devising, through proactive diplomacy, an architecture that upholds the normative principle of open and fair economic exchange and the operational rules toward its realization.

The institutional configuration of trade architecture today is in flux and requires a recalibration of state strategies to display international leadership through institution building. The decay in the WTO negotiation process has brought about a tectonic change in international trade governance, one of fading multilateralism and the consolidation of plurilateralism and preferentialism as major elements of the new regime. Afflicted by design flaws, the WTO was unable to conclude the Doha Round, creating an incentive for clusters of countries to self-select into the negotiation of single-issue plurilateral agreements within the WTO, or to relocate the foci of negotiation outside the WTO through preferential trade agreements with member-only benefits.[57] The core principle of the multilateral regime—nondiscrimination—has been the main casualty in this process.

It is evident that the eclipse of the multilateral ideal has brought about an era of decentralized competition where rulemaking through mega trade deals is at the heart of bids for international leadership. FTAs offer leading powers an opportunity to cover the governance gap generated by WTO dysfunction through the supply of new rules on trade and investment better attuned to the realities of a world economy of crisscrossing supply chains. Moreover, state leaders can solidify their claim to international leadership by highlighting how trade agreements that tackle new forms of protectionism sustain the momentum for liberalization and preempt the systemic risk of economic predation, as beggar-thy-neighbor policies thrive when leading states abdicate their responsibilities. In so doing, they can also point out that, in contrast to the preferential trade agreements of the 1930s, deep FTAs offer a host of benefits to market participants irrespective of national origin—strengthened rule of law, regulatory transparency, competition policy, and so forth—that mitigate their discriminatory character.[58]

Finally, trade agreements provide state leaders a platform to underscore the advantages of their vision for trade governance and the broader economic architecture. For example, United States Trade Representative Michael Froman drew a distinction between the comprehensive TPP and "state capitalist, mercantilist models based on forced technology transfer, localization, state champions and generalized protectionism."[59] Others have underscored the Transatlantic Trade and Investment Partnership's (TTIP) potential to send a message that economic and political liberalism continue to be the most attractive principles to organize economy and society in the twenty-first century.[60]

Drawing a contrast between competing blueprints for trade governance, however, requires careful calibration to avoid a perception (which can turn into reality) of a zero-sum competition among clashing economic models.[61] Far from accepting the dictum that "geoeconomics uses the grammar of commerce, but is guided by the logic of conflict," mega trade deals are most effective as a tool of national power and influence in the current international system if and when they promote constructive competition and are guided by an inclusive vision.[62] The negotiation of ambitious trade deals can put competitive pressure on other ongoing trade negotiations to scale up their standards to remain attractive locales for trade and investment. Open platforms with explicit aspirations of enlargement that reward productivity-enhancing reforms in prospective member countries are the most effective strategy to disseminate standards and to ensure greater buy-in of the budding trade architecture.

In sum, policymakers can use trade agreements to promote international competitiveness, domestic economic transformation, and the construction of a rules-based economic architecture. But only ambitious trade agreements will deliver these substantive benefits, and this will require herculean efforts to cultivate public support for a much more intrusive trade agenda, and to navigate the treacherous domestic politics of both international negotiation and internal ratification.

## CHAPTER THREE

# *Legitimacy I:*
# *Shared Economic Prosperity*

THE DISTRIBUTIONAL CONSEQUENCES of market opening are at the core of the legitimacy debate on trade policy. For critics of trade agreements, the economic benefits of liberalization are not only modest but also skewed in favor of the few, while the dislocation costs for redundant workers and industries beleaguered by imports from low-wage economies are very high. Therefore, skeptics hold trade agreements responsible for undermining the cherished goal of inclusive prosperity by undercutting employment opportunities and exacerbating income inequality.

The empirical evidence provided throughout this chapter does not back such a thesis. Trade agreements have not escalated unemployment rates or hollowed out the industrial base, nor are they the main factor behind the marked increase in income inequality and the shrinking of the middle class. Trade liberalization, like all forms of economic change, creates and destroys jobs. Technological change, with its premium on higher skills, has exacerbated wage inequality across all sectors of the economy, both tradeable and nontradeable. And the difficulties of low value-added U.S. manufacturing in coping with import competition with China are not indicative of the positive impact that the Trans-Pacific Partnership trade agreement is estimated to have on U.S. employment and wages.

Beyond revisiting standard arguments on trade's employment effects, this chapter seeks to throw light on two important developments that should change our understanding of the jobs/wages debate on trade policy. First is the transformed composition of trade flows with developing countries due to the global supply chain revolution. Several of the top exporters to the United States in the developing world (for example, China and Mexico) are important cogs in production networks. They incorporate numerous components from other countries (many of them from high-wage economies) into their export products. As a result, we need not only a new way to measure international trade (identifying the value added in each location of the production chain) but also a new set of expectations regarding the impact of trade with the South on wages in the North. Second, time horizons should figure more prominently in assessing the costs of labor adjustment to trade and technological change. A fresh wave of research has shown that the much-flaunted flexibility of American labor markets is insufficient to produce genuine mobility: across regions, occupations, or skill brackets. Addressing the legitimacy challenge will require a concerted effort to tackle the problems of transitional unemployment or exit from the workforce.

The first section of this chapter provides an overview of the trade and jobs debate and discusses the implications of recent findings on the loss of U.S. manufacturing jobs to trade with China. The second section summarizes the expectations of conventional trade theory on wage inequality and discusses the transformation in the nature of North-South trade brought about by the spread of global supply chains. The third section fleshes out strategies to overcome the politics of grievance, tackling the root causes of income inequality and developing holistic safety nets that promote genuine adjustment.

## DOES TRADE GENERATE NET JOB LOSSES?

In the public's mind the foremost consideration in evaluating the pros and cons of trade agreements is jobs. Is international trade a venue for increased economic opportunity as new jobs are created by industries with improved access to overseas markets, or are those benefits dwarfed by the painful restructuring of industries shedding workers as they confront the onslaught of import competition? It is this "bread and butter" consideration of how trade policy affects workers' chances of being gainfully employed that, at the most basic level, turns the balance of domestic support or opposition for market liberalization.

Trade skeptics in the United States assert that the crop of trade agreements of the last twenty years following the North American Free Trade Agreement model have resulted in soaring trade deficits, sizable job losses, and the hollowing out of the manufacturing base. These critics identify two main mechanisms behind these adverse outcomes: trade deficits and offshoring by multinational corporations. In this line of argument, the overall creation of trade flows is irrelevant. What matters is whether imports exceed exports, as this eliminates jobs and does not have a positive economic impact on the domestic economy: "increased exports support U.S. jobs and increased imports costs U.S. jobs."[1] The investor protections awarded through free trade agreements (discussed in the next chapter) are said to distort the incentive structure, encouraging companies to relocate production to foreign countries, effectively exporting jobs and increasing the trade deficit through reverse imports.[2]

Through these twin effects, job losses from trade agreements are portrayed as sizable and well above the official statistic of 850,000 workers having received trade adjustment assistance (TAA) subsidies for job dislocation during the first ten years of NAFTA. Robert E. Scott estimates NAFTA's net job losses (factoring in job creation as well) to be in the neighborhood of one million jobs, and he puts the job losses from the trade deficit with South Korea after the implementation of the bilateral trade agreement at 40,000 jobs.[3] Of particular concern is the erosion of the manufacturing base attributed to trade agreements. Ben Beachy correlates the loss of close to five million jobs in manufacturing over the past twenty years not only to the launch of NAFTA but also to the establishment of the World Trade Organization, China's entry into the multilateral body in 2001, and the growing American trade deficit with China.[4]

The concern for trade critics is not only that workers leave manufacturing and take dead-end jobs in the service sector at a pay cut, but also that jobs in the service sector are increasingly vulnerable to offshoring. The service sector was traditionally deemed as nontradable and, thus, safe from foreign competition, but the growth of impersonal services means that many of these jobs can be relocated overseas and delivered remotely.[5]

Nevertheless, the empirical record does not support the notion that imports have aggravated unemployment levels in the United States. As Douglas Irwin notes, there is no correlation between a larger share of imports to GDP and higher rates of unemployment; rather, the opposite is true.[6] Because both import demand and job creation are affected by the business cycle, they move in tandem; when the American economy is

*Figure 3-1.* Reasons for Extended Mass Layoffs

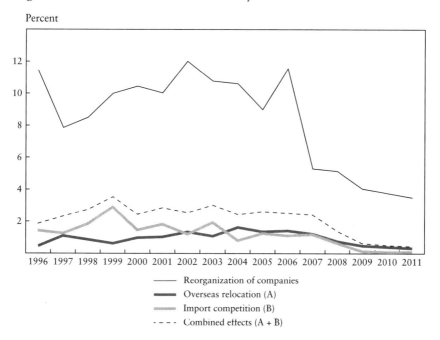

Percent

Source: Mass Layoff Statistics, Bureau of Labor Statistics (www.bls.gov/mls).

booming, imports and employment levels increase, and in times of recession both contract. Neither is trade the main culprit for large-scale job dismissals. As can be seen in figure 3-1, for the past twenty years, corporate reorganizations have been the main factor in mass layoffs, not trade globalization. In the years since the global financial crisis period, imports and overseas relocation have, in fact, played a minimal role in extended mass layoffs (1 percent of the total).

Moreover, the impact of job losses from trade agreements should be gauged by looking at the scale and normal activity of the U.S. labor market. While the job losses attributed to offshoring (or to NAFTA, in particular) might appear large in absolute terms, in fact, they represent just a fraction of the monthly churn in U.S. labor markets. One million jobs is less than the usual turnover in U.S. labor markets in a two-week period.[7] Nor does the reorientation of the American economy toward services foreordain an era of severe employment instability. As Bradford Jensen points out, the majority of service jobs in the United States are in the high-skill, high-wage bracket and are not susceptible to competition from service providers in the developing world, and there is no significant difference in employment growth between tradable and nontradable services.[8]

Although a favorite target, NAFTA is not the poster child to indict trade policy. Far from undermining the competitiveness of the American economy and hollowing out the employment base, NAFTA has delivered handsome economic payoffs for the United States. Intraregional trade flows showed dramatic growth (400 percent in the past two decades), and U.S. trade with Canada and Mexico is now equivalent to that with Japan, South Korea, and all the BRIC nations (Brazil, Russia, India, and China) combined.[9] It is the type of trade promoted by NAFTA that generates most economic benefits, as it is based on close integration with positive synergies. As the trade agreement encouraged the spread of regional supply chains, exports from Mexico and Canada to the United States have a high percentage of American input (40 percent and 25 percent, respectively).[10] Therefore, the export activities of NAFTA partners help boost U.S. production and employment. On the other hand, U.S. exports to Canada and Mexico sustain American jobs (eight million and six million respectively), with the added benefit that jobs in the export sector offer higher remuneration (on average 15 to 20 percent higher).[11] Nor is offshoring to Mexico (and other locations) a drain on economic activity in the United States. By controlling for macroeconomic conditions and industry or firm-specific factors, Theodore H. Moran and Lindsay Oldenski show that an increase in direct investment abroad by U.S. multinational corporations is positively correlated with investment, job creation, and research and development (R&D) activities in the U.S. economy.[12]

### Is China Destroying American Jobs?

The proposition that trade with a low-wage economy like China decimated the American manufacturing base is a focal point for the trade policy debate—one that permeates discussions on the merits of trade agreements like the TPP that include developing countries. The declining share of manufacturing to total employment in the economy, in fact, began decades ago and predates the emergence of China as an export powerhouse. During the 2000s, a steep contraction of manufacturing jobs (5.8 million) did coincide with rising trade exposure to China; however, the brunt of job losses was felt through the ravaging effects of the Great Recession at the end of the decade. Clearly, the structural changes in the composition of the American economy and powerful macroeconomic shocks are important to understanding the fate of U.S. manufacturing employment.

Even so, in an influential set of studies, David H. Autor, David Dorn, and Gordon H. Hanson found import competition from China played a significant role in the drop of American manufacturing employment.[13] They estimate that the China trade shock resulted in the loss of 985,000 manufacturing jobs during 1999 and 2011, equivalent to one sixth of the reduction in manufacturing employment during that period.[14]

These findings, however, should not be extrapolated to mean that the United States does not benefit from its economic relationship with China, that all American manufacturing has lost competitiveness and is contracting, or that retreating from international trade would yield more economic opportunity.[15] The China trade shock analysis does not provide an assessment of the overall gains from trade with China because it focuses only on import competition. It does not factor in the benefits of increased export opportunities (not only direct exports, but also spillover effects to upstream suppliers) and of decreased costs of living through lower priced imports. But in another study that just focuses on the job impact of expanding Chinese imports, Lorenzo Caliendo and his coauthors found that access to low-cost intermediate inputs from China increased employment in non-manufacturing sectors (retail, construction, services) to offset the job losses in manufacturing, yielding an increase in welfare in the short run of 0.2 percent, and in the long run of 6.7 percent.[16]

The attribution of manufacturing job losses to China should also be tempered by two important considerations pointed out by Philip Levy.[17] First, international trade is not just about two countries. If China had not taken off as a global factory, other developing countries would have played a larger role in labor-intensive assembly operations for export. Second, the counter-factual that more manufacturing jobs would have survived in the absence of rising trade exposure to China needs to consider the likely effects of automation. A poignant example is the announcement by Adidas to onshore the production of athletic shoes in Germany, but to rely entirely on robots in its new factory.[18]

Trade with China has not undermined American manufacturing as a whole, but did result in major competitive pressure in lower value-added production. These sectors (textiles, apparel, furniture) registered output contraction, but the rest of manufacturing activities did not. Theodore

Moran and Lindsay Oldenski remind us that the narrative of industrial decline has focused exclusively on manufacturing employment data, but it is important to take into account productivity rates (manufacturing has consistently been ahead of the rest of the economy since 1960) and the absolute increases in manufacturing capacity (with output levels above the 2007 peak in 2014).[19] These data points speak of underlying strengths in the American industrial base.

The American economy has already adjusted to the China trade shock, and reneging on the TPP will do nothing to bring those jobs back.[20] Moreover, the employment effects of the TPP are expected to be relatively modest. Using a number of scenarios, Robert Z. Lawrence and Tyler Moran estimate that, at most, the TPP would displace 169,000 workers per year in the first ten years (using the very expansive assumption in which every import displaces workers in affected industries and related suppliers). In their most conservative estimate (taking into account hiring freezes and voluntary resignations), the total job impact of the TPP at 228,000 jobs is less than the current weekly uptake on unemployment benefits.[21] Looking at net effects, the International Trade Commission estimates that the TPP would have a positive, albeit small, effect on U.S. employment (128,000 jobs created) and wages (a 0.19 percent increase in the wage rate) by 2032.[22] These results, showing a moderate adjustment burden and a long-term positive effect on jobs and wages, are not surprising given that the United States is already a very open economy (with a 2 percent average tariff) and has preexisting trade agreements with many of the TPP countries. The largest market to be opened by the TPP, Japan, is by no means a low-wage economy specializing in labor-intensive manufacturing.

The drop in U.S. manufacturing employment should not be the only indicator to gauge the strength of American productive capacity or the balance of benefits from the economic relationship with China, nor should it overshadow the sizable benefits of trade to the American economy and the potential of fresh liberalization gains through new trade initiatives. But it is fundamental in understanding the growing skepticism on the merits of international engagement through trade because it underscores the painful costs of adjustment to economic change, so policymakers seeking to shore up support for trade liberalization should first reckon that this frustration is grounded in a number of sobering facts: economic transitions are hard, the individual costs of job dislocation are steep, and policies to ease the pain of adjustment have not been effective enough.

### Time Horizons Matter: Doubling Down on the Problem of Transitional Unemployment

Job creation or destruction has driven the public debate on the merits of trade agreements but, ironically, economists consider this a moot question. In the long run, total employment is not determined by the degree of openness of an economy but by the size of the labor force, while the unemployment level at any particular time is influenced by a host of broader factors, such as monetary supply, technological change, shifts in consumer taste, and/or productivity growth.[23] Studies on labor market outcomes of trade liberalization that have a shorter time horizon find a larger role for trade in unemployment in import sensitive sectors, whereas analyses that focus on long-term effects of trade liberalization find that, with time, the economy adjusts back to full employment equilibrium.[24]

Nevertheless, for trade policymakers the admonition from mainstream economists that trade liberalization has little impact on long-term employment is unhelpful in shoring up public support for market opening. After all, as John Maynard Keynes famously remarked, "In the long run we are all dead." The public, and its elected representatives, care deeply about shorter-term job dislocations when they form their views on the merits of international trade. Nowhere is this truer than in public opinion trends for the United States. A Pew Research Survey in 2015 reports a consistent finding: a majority of Americans (68 percent) believe international trade is good, but only a minority believe it creates jobs (20 percent) and raises wages (17 percent).[25] And cross-national opinion polls reveal that Americans are more pessimistic on the impact of trade than many other publics. The global median on whether trade destroys jobs was 19 percent; in the United States it was 50 percent. The global median on whether trade lowers wages was 21 percent; in the United States it was 45 percent.[26] Moreover, the health of the economy influences public support for trade. A long-running Gallup poll shows that more Americans think foreign trade is an opportunity than a threat (58 percent to 34 percent) when the economy is on a recovery path and the unemployment rate is low (2016), compared to when recession hits and job losses are rampant (41 percent to 52 percent in 2008).[27] Furthermore, the demographic profile of respondents also matters; older, white, and less-educated respondents are far more critical of trade agreements.[28] The composite picture emerging from these different surveys is that workers who feel more vulnerable in their ability to keep their job or transition to a new one—because of age, lack of skills, or a negative economic climate—will be more critical of international trade.

Addressing the problem of transitional unemployment should be a high priority. A fresh wave of economic research on trade adjustment has shown that employment transitions are more prolonged and costly than previously expected, and if adjustment costs are left unmitigated, they could eat up a significant share of the gains from trade and erode support for further integration in the world economy. Carl Davidson and Steven J. Matusz broke new ground on this front by relaxing the workhorse assumption in the economics profession of full employment, by factoring in the impact of spells of unemployment and the costs for displaced workers of searching and training for new jobs. They note that even with long-term unemployment, the negative effects of trade on overall employment levels are small. The real issue is that the short-term adjustment costs for workers are larger than previously reckoned, and they eat up more of the long-term gains from liberalization, usually in the range of 30 to 80 percent.[29]

The experience of American local labor markets competing with Chinese imports has led us to reconsider our previous understanding of the speed and cost of the adjustment process for affected workers. For one, U.S. labor markets are more rigid, especially when it comes to geographical mobility. Even though the chances of finding new work improve by relocating from depressed areas to regions experiencing growth, this physical move does not happen often enough. Moreover, due to the difficulties of receiving training to acquire a thoroughly updated skill set, many of the unemployed find jobs in similar sectors with weak comparative advantage and, therefore, are more prone to future layoffs.[30] To these novel findings we must add the already established facts that laid-off workers frequently find jobs at a reduced salary, that many workers decide to exit the labor force altogether, and job dislocation impinges on lifelong earnings potential.

In making the case for trade it is certainly important to highlight that aggregate economic gains from heightened competitiveness and decreased cost of living far surpass the overall costs of transition for sectors losing out to international competition. But this is not sufficient to turn the tide of support for trade agreements. It is not enough to know that the winners have ample resources to compensate the losers. It is essential to know that they actually do compensate losers, and that we have policies to ensure that workers experiencing the brunt of the transition are not left behind. In fact, learning from the labor adjustment experience in sectors coping with intense import competition should be helpful in designing a more effective safety net to increase society's resilience in the midst of economic change (brought about by trade and/or technological or macroeconomic shocks), as discussed further in chapter 7.

## DOES TRADE DEPRESS WAGES AND FOSTER INCOME INEQUALITY?

The charge that trade policy erodes the social fabric by promoting economic inequality is making a serious dent in the legitimacy of trade negotiations. Undoubtedly, income disparities have grown over time in the industrialized world, producing a 10 percent increase in the Organisation for Economic Co-operation and Development's (OECD) average Gini coefficient in the two decades prior to the global financial crisis (to reach a level of 0.36).[31] Social polarization is evident in that the average income of top earners is now nine times larger than that of the bottom earners in developed nations.[32] And cross-national comparisons reveal a common pattern in Western advanced economies of concentration of income in the top 1 percent of the population, a hollowing out of middle classes with stagnant incomes, and reductions of the income share at the bottom of the distribution. Of particular concern has been the winnowing of the middle class in industrialized countries. For instance, many OECD nations have experienced job polarization, with growth of high- and low-paid jobs and a contraction of middle-paid jobs.[33] The hollowing out of the middle class in the United States has been striking. Looking at real income growth between 1979 and 2010 shows that the top quintile increased its market income by almost 80 percent, while the second and third quintile experienced meager (below 5 percent) and modest gains (above 10 percent), respectively.[34]

The facts on deepened inequality are incontrovertible and the malaise is widespread among many industrialized nations. Establishing the drivers behind the increasingly skewed income distribution is, however, a complex task. For starters, distinct types of inequality will be affected by different factors. In his famous treatise on inequality, Thomas Piketty attributes the rise of inequality to the essential workings of a capitalist economy generating higher rates of return to capital compared to the rate of national economic growth. Left to their own devices and without the ravaging effects of war, capitalist societies will become more unequal over time.[35] As Jason Furman notes, the three types of inequality identified by Piketty (labor income, capital income, and the share of income between labor and capital) are influenced by different factors. For instance, regarding wage inequality, the increased return on skills, lower levels of educational performance, and the erosion of unionization rates are important; whereas taxation policies and changing practices in corporate governance are obviously of great importance to the growth of wealth inequality.[36] So, an understanding of the varying sources of inequality will call for different policy responses.

Because growing economic and social polarization has coincided with an intensification of globalization, many have blamed international trade for the heightened level of inequality. The classic economics textbook explanation of how trade with lower-wage economies can negatively impact compensation for low-skilled workers is found in the Stolper-Samuelson theorem. In essence, it establishes a link between market opening, price of traded goods, and workers' wages. In advanced nations, expanded trade will increase the export of goods intensive in high-skilled labor, raising the wages of these workers. Because unskilled workers will experience the opposite effect as cheap imports from developing countries lower the cost of goods manufactured with low-skilled labor, the wage gap between skilled and unskilled workers should deepen and inequality levels should increase.

Determining the income distribution effects of trade acquired more urgency after the traditionally close correlation between worker compensation and productivity in the United States began to wane in the early 2000s, sparking a debate as to why wages were lagging.[37] By and large most studies on the distributional impact of trade have found only a modest contribution to income inequality. For example, after reviewing the extant literature, William Cline concluded that international trade was responsible for 6 percent of increased wage inequality.[38] In an influential 1995 paper, Paul Krugman found a smaller effect, with trade with developing countries responsible for 3 percent in the skilled–unskilled wage ratio.[39] Looking at the impact of outsourcing, Robert Feenstra and Hanson concluded that in the 1980s, offshoring increased real wages of skilled workers by 1 to 2 percent and high-tech capital raised them by 3 percent. On the other hand, they did not find any significant impact of offshoring on the wages of low-skilled workers.[40] This finding is important because it signifies that trade did not lower wages for unskilled labor, but educated workers reaped the gains from both globalization and technological change. Finally, in an exhaustive study of the impact of trade on the distribution of American wages, Lawrence concluded the impact was very small—lowering average wages of blue-collar workers by 1.4 percent in 2006.[41]

Why didn't the dire expectations on income redistribution from trade with low-wage economies materialize? Part of the answer can be found in changing production patterns that have weakened the link between imports and wages. Lawrence highlights two trends in particular: specialization—whereby industrialized countries focus on the manufacture of goods with high-skilled labor, so domestic wages are less sensitive to the import of goods with low-skill labor—and growing sophistication in the skill mix of products imported from developing countries.[42] The income distribution effect through the consumption channel is also significant. To the extent that trade liberalization eliminates regressive tariffs—high tariffs on items that represent a large share of consumption among the poor (such as food and clothing)—it will help raise living standards.[43] Finally, it is also important to ascertain the importance of other factors beyond trade in increasing wage disparities. Technological change has had a more pervasive effect across all sectors of the economy. The revolution in information and communications is the most powerful force behind the growing skill premium, resulting in growing demand for educated workers across the board, even in sectors little exposed to international trade.[44]

### Is a Globalizing South Responsible for a More Unequal North?

As mentioned in chapter 2, developing countries now play a much larger role in international trade and have availed themselves of participation in the world economy to lift millions of their citizens out of poverty. The question of whether a globalizing South is responsible for growing levels of income inequality in the North has, therefore, become more poignant. Influential economists like Krugman have revised their benign assessment of the distributional impact of trade with the South to argue that the rising share of imports in the United States from low-wage developing countries (for example, China and Mexico) has added more pressure on wages for unskilled workers.[45] With the advent of global supply chains, developing countries now operate in the low-skilled segments of high-tech industries (computers), so growing imports from the

South in these sectors put even greater pressure on wages of low-skilled workers in industrialized countries. In an effort to confirm Krugman's assessment, Josh Bivens replicated his original computable general equilibrium model, taking into account the growing share of developing country imports in U.S. trade, and found a much larger effect on the skilled–unskilled wage gap, on the order of 7 percent in 2006.[46] Other recent studies also attribute a larger influence of trade on U.S. wages. Avraham Ebenstein and others note that offshoring to high-income countries actually increases U.S. wages, while task relocation to developing countries has almost no impact on wages within manufacturing. However, the impact on U.S. wages is felt mostly by workers who perform routine tasks and leave manufacturing or change occupations. For these workers on the low-skill spectrum, downward pressure on their wages is on the 2 to 4 percent and 4 to 11 percent range, respectively.[47]

Nevertheless, studies on the redistribution effects of North-South trade that rely on developing country import share are bound to overestimate the wage impact on the industrialized country. In global supply chains, imports from developing countries incorporate multiple components manufactured by high-skilled workers in industrialized countries, and this mitigates their effect in depressing wages on low-skilled workers in the North. More fundamentally, it is important to recognize that the traditional model of trade, whereby nations would export and import final products, is outdated. In its stead, we find complex production networks, where lead firms have parceled out all stages of production (from R&D and component manufacture to assembly), with investments across national boundaries. Component trade has, in fact, eclipsed trade in final products. Trade in intermediate goods and services plus capital goods represents 70 percent of world trade.[48]

Consequently, it has become necessary to launch a new way to measure trade, one that does not focus on gross exports (which attribute the value of a product to the country exporting the final good) but, rather, traces the value added along all stages of the production network. The picture of world trade in value-added terms is strikingly different since it reveals that imports are a central ingredient of exports, and that export juggernauts such as China have, until recently, made more modest contributions to the value-added of the final goods they export, inasmuch as they operated as assembly lines for imported components. These points are clearly depicted in the following figures based on a new WTO/ OECD dataset measuring trade in value-added terms.

*Figure 3-2.* U.S. Bilateral Trade Balance, 2011

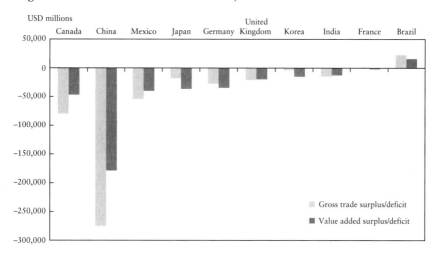

Source: OECD-WTO, "Trade in Value Added (TiVA)—October 2015," OECD. Stat database.

Figure 3-2 reveals that, in 2011, the U.S. trade deficit with China was one-third smaller, measured by value added when compared to the standard measure of gross exports and imports. Moreover, with respect to Mexico and Canada, the bilateral deficit is also much smaller because of the large number of U.S. components that are incorporated in imports from the two North American neighbors.

Rising imports in the electronics sector from developing countries have figured prominently in the U.S. debate about the impact of the South's globalization on wages. But again, a look at trade in value-added shows a picture different from the conventional wisdom. Figure 3-3 lists the largest exporters of electronics and optical equipment in 2011. The key point is the breakdown of the share of domestic and foreign content in these exports. As can be seen in the figure, top-performing developing countries register a high level of foreign content (which in conventional trade statistics would be wholly attributed to them): Malaysia, 66.4 percent; Thailand, 62.5 percent; Mexico, 58.3 percent; and China, 53.8 percent.[49] The globalization of the South, in this sector and others, is not a story of developing countries building whole products from scratch for export; rather, it is about their insertion into global value chains that pool the national competencies of many different countries. It follows that we need to recalibrate our understanding of the wage pressure generated by South-North trade.

*Figure 3-3.* Electrical and Optical Equipment Gross Export, 2011

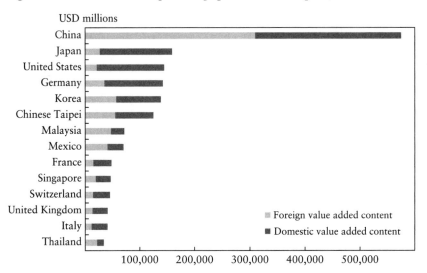

Source: OECD-WTO, "Trade in Value Added (TiVA)—October 2015," OECD. Stat database.

How much, then, has international trade affected income inequality? One useful way to answer this question is Lawrence Katz's suggestion that studies that rely on import share provide an upper bound estimate of trade's effects on wage inequality, while studies that trace the factor content of imports supply lower bound estimates. Combining both methodologies, the expected effect of trade on wage inequality ranges between 6 and 19 percent.[50] The body of academic work, therefore, supports the argument that trade has not been a major contributor to wage inequality.

Nevertheless, the negotiation of the Trans-Pacific Partnership, which groups together both industrialized and developing nations, fueled again the debate on the income distribution effects of trade. David Rosnick argued that if trade is historically responsible for 10 to 50 percent of the escalation in U.S. wage inequality, the expected increase of trade intensity (trade/GDP share) brought about by the TPP trade negotiations should depress median wages by 0.14 to 0.72 percent by the year 2025.[51] That the TPP would generate such direct impact on U.S. wages is surprising given that the only two low-wage economies with which the United States does not already have a trade agreement—Malaysia and Vietnam— represent only 5 percent of trade in goods among participating economies.[52]

In fact, Rosnick's upper-bound assumption (50 percent) of the impact of trade on wage inequality is much higher than most research findings on this topic. Even if we look only at the lower assumption (10 percent), Rosnick's estimates are bound to exaggerate the impact of the TPP on U.S. wages for two main reasons. First, traditional trade theory has long posited that it is imports from low-wage economies that can increase inequality, but Rosnick's estimate of trade intensity looks at the totality of trade with both high- and low-wage economies. Second, as discussed before, the import share from low-wage economies is no longer a reliable indicator since these imports may incorporate numerous components manufactured in high-wage economies.

Robert Lawrence and Tyler Moran use a very different methodology to ascertain the expected income distribution effects from the TPP. Their analysis unfolds in three steps: determining how value-added in TPP trade would alter factor incomes, ascertaining the distribution of factor income increases across household income brackets, and establishing how different income groups benefit from consumption of TPP goods and services. Their main findings are that by 2030 labor income (for both college- and noncollege-educated workers) would increase more than capital income, that the factor income increases would be distributed relatively evenly across income brackets, and that the TPP's positive— although modest—contribution to income distribution would come mostly from the consumption effect, as households in the lower rungs of income consume disproportionately more of the goods and services available at a lower cost through the TPP.[53]

## TACKLING THE LEGITIMACY CHALLENGE:
## OVERCOMING THE POLITICS OF GRIEVANCE

Mercantilist myths on trade policy are alive and well. The notions that the only effect of imports is to hurt domestic production and destroy jobs and that the incorporation of the developing world into the trading system has come at the expense of employment opportunities and fair wages in the industrialized world have gained new potency. The strengthening of these myths is particularly pernicious in a world economy transformed by global value chains as a new paradigm for international production and exchange among countries. These crisscrossing production networks have knitted economies more closely, creating opportunities for shared growth across borders, but have also increased the costs of an inward turn. Hence, it is important to take stock of several key facts: trade is not a zero-sum game; aggregate economic benefits—in terms of competitiveness and enhanced purchasing power—surpass adjustment costs for sectors impacted by trade competition; trade is not a major contributor to income inequality; and the ever-faster pace of technological change will continue to intensify the skill premium regardless of the fate of trade agreements.

Setting the record straight, as important as that is, is not sufficient to overcome the skepticism on trade's contribution to inclusive growth. Action is required to overcome under-investments that have eaten up support for trade liberalization. At the broadest level, we need a comprehensive and multifaceted policy commitment to tackle income inequality. Reassurances that trade is not the culprit for the hollowing out of the middle class will not be enough to generate support for existing and prospective trade agreements. Rather, securing the future of the middle class should be the foundation for sustained international economic engagement. Delivering on inclusive prosperity will be a complex and pressing task, as underscored by a report from the Center for American Progress highlighting five tracks: labor market policies (promoting wage growth, full-time jobs, and flexible working practices); education policies to increase skills across the economy through the promotion of early childhood education, apprenticeships, and reducing the cost of higher education; innovation policies that seek to maximize agglomeration economies through regional clusters; long-term investments in infrastructure and changes in corporate governance; and international cooperation to open overseas markets, promote financial stability, and avoid corporate tax avoidance.[54] Moreover, progressive taxation policies to distribute the burden of supplying public services (health and education) are critical to alleviate poverty and shore up middle-class incomes.[55]

In addition, we need to rethink and recommit to developing safety nets that allow impacted workers to adjust to broad economic change (not only trade liberalization). Doubling down on existing trade adjustment assistance programs is no longer viable as a political compact to gain acquiescence for trade liberalization (see chapter 6), and more important, it is not effective in enabling displaced workers to manage the risks of economic change.

## CHAPTER FOUR

# Legitimacy II: Sovereignty and the Regulatory State

A **POTENT NARRATIVE** undermining the legitimacy of trade policy equates market liberalization with the surrender of regulatory sovereignty. In this view, free trade agreements undermine the ability of states to uphold necessary regulations to protect consumer safety, preserve environmental standards, and enforce prudential market regulations through three main mechanisms. First, a "race to the bottom" dynamic is said to operate, whereby states that want to remain attractive sites for commerce and investment must lower their regulations, as multinational corporations (MNC) will flock to lax regulatory environments. Second, the scope of trade negotiations (with an intrusive agenda targeting behind-the-border measures) is deemed to undermine public interest regulations with the imperative of open markets trumping other cherished social objectives. Third, through the investor-state dispute settlement (ISDS) mechanism, MNCs are deemed capable of using the threat of expensive legal challenges to overhaul regulatory regimes that run counter to their corporate interests.

A review of the empirical record, however, shows that deep trade agreements have not undermined the ability of sovereign states to regulate in the public interest. Far from a race to the bottom, trade agreements like the TPP aim to export higher regulatory standards on labor and environment to raise the regulatory floor elsewhere. The reasons for the evolution of the trade agenda to encompass regulatory matters are still poorly understood: to combat new forms of protectionism beyond tariffs, and to leverage the growth opportunities of the global value chain

(GVC) by providing rules on trade and investment that facilitate the operation of fragmented production networks. While ISDS has become a controversial topic in ongoing mega trade agreement negotiations, the system has been in operation for decades and is prevalent in most bilateral investment treaties and modern FTAs. In its several decades of existence, it has not produced a rollback of prudential regulation. The system can definitively be improved by awarding more discretion to states to regulate in the public interest, establishing greater transparency in proceedings, and limiting investor rights to sue while applying penalties for frivolous suits. These are all changes that the TPP agreement would make operational.

The first section of this chapter examines the logic and empirical record of the race to the bottom hypothesis, and discusses an alternative effect of globalization: a regulatory race to the top. The second section highlights the forces behind the migration of the trade agenda to behind-the-border regulatory measures. It addresses the debates in industrialized nations about the curtailment of public regulations and in developing countries about the loss of policy space. The third section examines in greater detail the operation of ISDS and the claims of critics on its purported regulatory chill effects. The final section discusses strategies to provide more effective assurances on prudential regulation and the set of improvements that the Trans-Pacific Partnership aimed to make on this very important front.

## RACE TO THE BOTTOM: REAL OR IMAGINARY?

Detractors of globalization attribute the erosion of a state's regulatory powers to the twin forces of market opening and financial liberalization. With freer trade comes greater pressure from imports manufactured in countries that keep low labor and environmental standards. With greater capital mobility, MNCs can engage in regulatory arbitrage and select production locations where they will not be encumbered by onerous taxation and/or burdensome social and environmental regulations. Facing this competitive squeeze, governments will have no option but to abandon strong national regulatory standards, and public policies will converge toward minimal and ineffective environmental, consumer, and worker protections.[1]

The potential deleterious effects of government competition and capital mobility were, in fact, first identified at the domestic level in the operation of federal systems. The so-called Delaware effect captures the dynamics at work when state authorities outcompete one another in lowering (corporate chartering) disciplines. Globalization is said to have created the conditions for the same self-defeating regulatory competition to take place at the international level. Greater market integration among nations means that weak production standards can become a source of cost competitiveness; capital now flows freely as most countries have opened the capital account and abandoned their defensive posture toward foreign direct investment; and governments in the industrialized world are increasingly under siege as the integration of developing countries into the global economy has effectively lowered the regulatory floor.

The race to the bottom thesis, however, suffers from three main flaws: faulty assumptions, the existence of alternative dynamics, and the lack of empirical corroboration. As Daniel Drezner has observed, there are several problematic suppositions behind the race to the bottom thesis: business interests care only about low regulatory standards, environmental and labor regulations are the central determinants in location decisions for multinational corporations, and governments (even those operating in plural and democratic settings) are responsive to a single constituency in drafting regulatory policies—multinational business.[2] It is possible to counter these assumptions on a perennial corporate drive to lower regulatory standards by noting, as Drezner does, that the ability to comply with the exacting environmental and product standards of affluent markets is a source of competitive advantage for enterprises.

In fact, numerous statistical studies have shown that neither pollution havens nor lax labor standards drive the investment decisions of MNCs. Reviewing the scholarship on environmental standards and FDI, Arik Levinson concluded that "the literature as a whole presents fairly compelling evidence across a broad range of industries, time periods, and econometric specifications, that regulations do not matter to site choice."[3] The traditional large share of FDI flows among industrialized OECD nations also casts doubts on the argument that the exploitation of weak labor standards is a paramount consideration for global capital.[4] Finally, instead of governments capitulating to the demands of footloose corporations to dismantle regulatory regimes, the evidence shows that open economies tend to have higher levels of social regulation to hedge for the fluctuations of the world market.[5]

Globalization's impact on regulatory outcomes is more open-ended. An alternative form of policy convergence is, in fact, possible: a race to the top. At the federal level, a "California effect" is discernible when state regulators push for stricter environmental standards.[6] Similarly, international trade can further encourage the global dissemination of stricter regulatory standards because firms that seek to export to large affluent markets must comply with the stricter disciplines enforced in the export market. This, in turn, creates an incentive to advocate at home for the same level of regulation to achieve economies of scale and gain an edge over purely domestic firms. It is globalization, David Vogel admonishes, that opens the way for an alliance between Baptists (environmentalists) and bootleggers (corporations).[7]

The key question is this: Under what conditions will competition among regulatory authorities, fueled by market integration and capital mobility, generate an onslaught of regulatory protections or, instead, produce a race to lift standards worldwide? Which scenario is more likely? Regulatory regimes prone to beggar-thy-neighbor competitive dynamics exhibit certain characteristics. According to Miles Kahler, the cost of regulation is high and transparent, and there are low barriers to mobility.[8] Hence, in areas such as taxation and financial regulation, corporations have the incentive and the wherewithal to engage in regulatory arbitrage and governments in turn lower their standards to remain competitive. Yet even in these sectors no race to the bottom is discernible. "If a RTB [race to the bottom] had been completed, no tax havens, offshore banking, or Delaware effect would remain; the 'bottom' would have been reached."[9]

In turn, Vogel and Robert Kagan identify a different constellation of factors that enable a positive-sum regulatory race: (a) the nature of regulation: it is easier to adopt stricter rules for product standards that directly impinge on consumer and environmental safety than on production standards more removed from the glare of the public eye; (b) market size asymmetry: the larger the export market compared to the domestic market, the more likely it will encourage producers to adopt more stringent standards; (c) relative cost of switching to stringent regulatory standards compared to the gains from increased access in export markets; and (d) stringent regulations in main export markets.[10] Examples of a positive cross-national regulatory dynamic can be found in the dissemination of greener regulations across EU membership, in the adoption of an international dolphin protection treaty, and the negotiation of the Montreal Protocol to restrict the production of chlorofluorocarbons.[11] These examples highlight the role of international institutions and negotiations in scaling up regulatory standards worldwide.

The move toward regulatory stringency has not always been successful, though. For instance, Kate O'Neill documents the limited success of the Basel Convention to restrain the export of hazardous waste to developing countries.[12] And other issue areas speak to the resilience of national standards and the limits of policy convergence. The adoption of a sanitary and phytosanitary agreement in the WTO has made little impact on greater convergence toward international standards,[13] and despite the greater degree of market integration in the EU, no harmonization of core labor institutions (such as collective bargaining) has ensued.[14]

Most important for this discussion, the evidence of a race to the bottom is scant at best or nonexistent in most policy realms. Flags of convenience in the shipping industry are the best-known example of competition in laxity, as some states have carved a competitive niche by lowering standards in ship registration. Even here, a full-blown race to the bottom has not materialized, as industrialized countries have abstained from lowering their own shipping registration standards.[15] Overall, the evidence is quite robust that governments are not undercutting labor rights or promoting pollution havens to gain a competitive edge.[16] A more reliable predictor of the quality of labor standards implemented in export processing zones or the stringency of environmental protections are national labor standards and/or levels of development.[17] The real puzzle, as Kahler notes, is the enduring political appeal of the race to the bottom argument, given its weak theoretical underpinnings and lack of empirical corroboration.[18]

*The Deep Integration Agenda: Is Public Regulation Sacrificed to the Imperatives of Globalization?*

Even though governments are not lowering their standards in a self-destructive race to the bottom, it is undisputable that regulatory matters are now at the heart of the trade agenda. Indeed, the shift in the content of trade agreements to address behind-the-border issues is significant, widespread, and a rather recent phenomenon. The deep integration agenda at the center of preferential trade agreements revolves around two sets of issue areas. WTO-plus disciplines deepen the obligations already available at the multilateral level in areas such as services, intellectual property protection, sanitary standards, technical barriers to trade, government procurement, anti-dumping, and others. WTO-X commitments introduce rules in areas not yet covered by the WTO; for example, competition policy, foreign direct investment, environmental and labor standards, anti-corruption, and so on.[19]

The trade agenda has reached an unprecedented degree of complexity in a very short time. In the early 1990s, only four trade agreements covering services were notified to the WTO, but that number had risen to more than a hundred by 2014. Trade agreements entertaining a deep integration agenda were, in fact, a rarity in the twentieth century (10 percent of the total), but they represent a majority of all trade agreements (57 percent) signed since 2001.[20] Moreover, the regulatory agenda has not been adopted exclusively in market opening exercises among industrialized nations. On the contrary, a WTO study using a sample of ninety-six trade agreements found that trade agreements among developed and developing nations have, on average, a larger number of WTO-plus and WTO-X provisions than FTAs among industrialized nations.[21] Even South-South FTAs are very close to North-North FTAs in their coverage of WTO-plus and WTO-X areas (though on issues not covered by the WTO, fewer provisions are binding).

Why are national regulations at the center of trade negotiations in a way in which they never were before? A number of factors are at play. First, this reflects success in abating the most common form of traditional protectionism: tariffs. Average tariffs have gone down, from 20 to 30 percent in the pre-GATT era, to 4 percent in 2009.[22] This does not imply that sensitive sectors are no longer protected by steep tariff walls or that trade negotiators do not encounter fierce resistance when trying to negotiate them away. They certainly do. It does mean that, as average tariffs have been driven down through multilateral rounds of negotiations, preferential trade agreements, or unilateral bouts of liberalization, protectionism has morphed into new forms, that, for a lack of a better term, we call "nontariff measures." Following Bhagwati's "law of constant protection," we should expect policy substitution from tariffs to NTMs.[23]

The list of nontariff measures that governments can apply to restrict trade is extensive—from import quotas and special licensing obligations to "buy domestic" clauses, intensified used of trade remedies (such as anti-dumping and safeguards), and technical regulations on product standards. Since the global financial crisis, governments have resorted more actively to behind-the-border trade restrictive measures, with significant implications for the slowdown of international trade. A WTO report notes that between October 2015 and May 2016, G20 countries imposed twenty-one new trade-restrictive measures per month (the highest rate since the WTO launched this monitoring exercise in 2009). By far, anti-dumping was the instrument of choice (61 percent of all trade-restrictive measures).[24] The IMF concludes that the lack of liberalizing initiatives and the upsurge of protectionist measures are also significant factors behind the deceleration of trade (absent those trends, real trade in goods would have been 8 percent higher in 2015).[25] A study by the New Zealand Institute of Economic Research shows that within the Asia-Pacific region, there has been a 74 percent increase in the use of NTMs by APEC members since 2004 and that these measures raise trade costs three times more than tariffs.[26]

But there is another major reason why deep integration disciplines are at the core of trade negotiations. The rise of global supply chains has meant a rapid increase in foreign direct investment and a redefinition of the relationship between trade and investment. The stock of FDI to world GDP increased from 8 percent in 1990 to 29 percent in 2011, and the sectoral composition of FDI moved away from raw materials toward manufacturing and services (with 44 percent each of total FDI flows between 2008 and 2011).[27] In the past, trade and FDI could be seen as substitutes (with production abroad motivated by the desire to jump tariffs); in the global supply chain they are complementary. Companies disperse the production process in factories operating across borders and engage actively in export and import activities. This new reality is underscored by the fact that multinational corporations are responsible for 80 percent of goods and services trade.[28]

Supply chain trade implies much more than components crossing borders multiple times before they are assembled into a final product that is exported to a third market. It involves flows of capital, technology, services, and managerial know-how. Richard Baldwin has best articulated how the new realities of international production and trade are spurring the deep integration agenda in trade agreements; the trade-investment-services nexus in the supply chain requires a different type of bargain— "foreign factories for domestic reforms."[29] Iza Lejárraga concurs by noting that the driver of trade negotiations has shifted from concern over market access to ensuring market presence.[30]

Hence, FTAs are generating obligations in the areas that meet the institutional demands of supply chains: the liberalization of services that are critical to the efficient management of dispersed production chains (telecommunications, transportation, and so on); the protection of investments in foreign locations and intangible assets through intellectual property rights; the improvement of the business climate by streamlining customs; avoiding predatory market behavior through competition policy and disciplines on state-owned enterprises; anti-corruption provisions; and commitments to regulatory transparency to clarify the rules of the game.[31]

Global supply chains have put a premium on rules-heavy trade agreements, and to use Baldwin's terminology, there is a clear movement among "headquarter" economies (Germany, Japan, and the United States) to negotiate with "factory" economies commitments on deeper economic integration.[32] The degree of success has been mixed, however. Mapping the extent to which the network of deep trade agreements covers existing supply chains, Sébastien Miroudot, Dorothée Rouzet, and Francesca Spinelli found that Germany was well covered regarding its European supply chain, but it had yet to ink consequential trade agreements to cover its extra-European network trade. The United States has had success in the Western Hemisphere through NAFTA with Canada and Mexico and has made some inroads in Asia through the U.S.-Korea Free Trade Agreement (KORUS FTA), but it still does not have a deep FTA with its main Asian (China and Japan) or European counterparts (Germany and Great Britain) in network trade. For Japan, the situation was more dire, since it did not have a deep FTA with any of its main supply chain trade partners: China, the United States, and South Korea.[33] Seen in this light, the potential of the mega trade agreements becomes crystal clear: upgrading the governance arrangements that cover the global value chain.

If the deep integration agenda aims to combat new forms of protectionism and ensure the operation of global supply chains, why is it so divisive within and among countries? Several objections have been raised against making regulatory matters a core element of trade negotiations: disagreements on the discriminatory impact of nontariff measures; concern that market opening may trump domestic goals—such as ensuring consumer safety and environmental protection; and the worry that developing countries will lose access to important instruments of economic development.

The greater use of NTMs to keep a market closed has created a steeper challenge for trade liberalization. Tariffs are applied when products arrive at the border, are transparent, and their impact is easy to quantify. The new protectionism involves a host of regulatory measures applied inside the border, whose effect on trade flows is much harder to discern with any precision because they are opaque and, more important, because their discriminatory intent must be confirmed. The crux of the matter is that many public policies can be in place with the legitimate goal of safeguarding consumer, worker, or environmental protections. They can also be instituted for the mercantilistic purpose of creating an artificial advantage for domestic producers. Determining protectionist intent in regulatory policies that have an indirect effect on trade and/or are not very transparent is not an easy proposition. Moreover, NTMs may serve legitimate public policy purposes but be unnecessarily trade-restrictive. If that is the case, international negotiations may focus on adopting more trade-friendly regulations that do not compromise the domestic regulatory goal. The extent to which they are successful in that endeavor can and will be contested by opponents of the regulatory change.

While the concern of losing cherished social and economic protections drives the narrative of trade critics in the industrialized world, in developing countries the debate has centered on whether governments are surrendering, through international commitments, policy tools that industrialized nations availed themselves of in the past to climb the ladder of development. The key phrase here is "policy space"; in other words, the amount of latitude that the government preserves to intervene in the economy. Kenneth Shadlen, for example, argues that preferential trade agreements represent a different deal from the WTO; developing countries exchange greater market access for more restrictions on their industrial policy arsenals.[34] Examples of this include the stiffer tariff cuts that prevent them from sheltering infant industries or FDI provisions on rights of pre-establishment and national treatment, which eliminate their leverage to promote linkages to local industry or technological dissemination. Susan Sell notes that in the area of patents for pharmaceuticals, FTAs have eliminated many of the WTO flexibilities by prohibiting parallel importation of cheaper patented drugs, restricting compulsory licenses to override patent protection during health crises, and the de facto extension of patent protections by making trial data unavailable to generic manufacturers for a period of time (through data exclusivity provisions).[35] Another major concern raised by Kevin Gallagher is that U.S. trade agreements since 1994 have not contained a safeguard permitting temporary capital controls to prevent or mitigate financial crises.[36]

Undoubtedly, one of the strongest concerns about the development impact of deep integration agreements is that strengthened patent protections may deny access to lifesaving medicines through steep price increases in developing countries. Thomas Bollyky addresses this question in a study of fifteen countries with trade agreements with the United States containing WTO-plus intellectual property (IP) provisions for pharmaceuticals. He finds that these countries have not seen increases in average drug prices, larger shares of health expenditures over gross domestic product (GDP), or a shift away from generics, although a longer-term horizon may be needed to more fully assess the impact of trade rules.[37] Bollyky attributes the absence so far of a drug price spike or increases in medicine expenditure to the fact that only a subset of drugs are the object of heightened patent protection, and that many governments impose price controls to maintain lower costs.[38] On the controversial data protection rules on biologics adopted for the first time in the TPP, Lee Branstetter finds a balance between innovation and access.[39] Despite complaints by the business community that TPP rules fall short of the American standard, the arrival of generic drugs will be slower because biosimilars require additional clinical trials. On the other hand, access to essential medicines will not be compromised, as governments retain the discretion to override patent protection during health crises and negotiate price controls over patented drugs.[40]

The effects of trade agreements on the policy space of developing countries can run in both directions, either curtailing or enlarging autonomy. External commitments mean that some policy tools are off limits, but the codification of international rules can also prevent large countries from wielding their influence through market power.[41] Nor is policy autonomy, on its own, a panacea for growth, given the poor record of past industrial policies aiming to shelter infant industries through tariffs, subsidies, and performance requirements. International commitments can, in fact, give leverage to reforming elites to pursue their economic agenda. In an extensive cross-country analysis, Leonardo Baccini and Johannes Urpelainen demonstrate that political leaders in developing countries can avail themselves of deep FTAs to implement politically challenging reforms that boost their growth potential.[42]

The goal for developing countries in pursuing trade agreements is no longer primarily about securing greater access for traditional exports in overseas markets. Increasingly, it is about ensuring a strategic position in international production networks that dominate world production and exchange. The risk for developing countries in choosing to opt out of deep integration commitments is to be bypassed by global supply chains and to forego the accompanying benefits of economic growth and gains from trade.[43] The cost of marginalization may be high considering that developing countries that participate actively in global supply chains register GDP per capita growth rates 2 percent above the average.[44] Rather than opting out of service liberalization, IP commitments, or FDI promotion, the goal should be to make deep FTAs more favorable for developing countries. This requires the adoption of provisions for prudential financial management, balancing IP commitments to ensure affordable medicines, establishing reasonable implementation calendars, and capacity building assistance, in addition to tackling entrenched systems of agricultural subsidization in industrialized countries, to name some examples.[45]

As developing countries rethink the goals and tools of industrial policy in the era of global supply chains, the aims should include inclusion in global production networks and rising in the value-added chain. The tools to promote industrial capacity will be markedly different since the objective is no longer to create full-set manufacturing capabilities covering all stages of the production process—a shared goal in both import substitution and export promotion strategies—but to leverage the creation of cross-national productive links.[46] While entry into GVCs requires promotion of FDI, the focus should not be on whole sectors but on the production tasks to be undertaken through infusion of foreign capital. Also, upgrading GVC participation will necessitate the development of forward and backward linkages across the supply chain.[47]

In promoting entry and deepening of GVCs, some across-the-board measures are critical: supply of trade finance and infrastructural services, regulatory transparency, and investments in human capital and innovation.[48] But there is room for more micro targeted intervention; for instance, through sectoral technological investments and the development of higher value-added production niches.[49] None of this is to suggest that GVCs can solve all development challenges, but as Daria Taglioni and Deborah Winkler admonish, they can provide the policy space to undertake the much broader tasks of economic upgrading, social cohesion, and environmental sustainability.[50]

### *Does Investor-State Dispute Settlement Render the Regulatory State Powerless?*

Critics of trade agreements see a direct challenge to the regulatory sovereignty of states in the adoption of investor-state dispute settlement clauses, which allow foreign companies to sue host governments in arbitral tribunals in instances of uncompensated expropriation or unfair treatment. ISDS provisions first appeared in the 1960s in bilateral investment treaties (BIT) and have become a common feature in trade agreements as well. As of 2014, there were more than two thousand BITs, and the vast majority of them (93 percent) contain investment arbitration provisions.[51] The United States, for example, has ISDS provisions in its forty-one bilateral investment agreements in effect, and in most of its fourteen FTAs in force.[52]

Opponents of ISDS worry that in granting legal standing to multinational corporations (in contrast to the state-state enforcement mechanism of the WTO), governments will be unable to uphold public interest regulations, abdicating, as well, fundamental principles such as democratic accountability and equal treatment under the law. They note with great concern the sharp increase in ISDS cases since 2003; a total of 568 known cases as of early 2014, of which 115 took place in 2012 and 2013.[53] In its more benign version, the critique of investment arbitration considers it mostly unnecessary for a number of reasons: outright expropriation by developing country states has become a rare occurrence and MNCs can buy their own FDI insurance; it has little or no effect in promoting FDI flows to less developed countries; or because it is unwarranted among developed nations with advanced legal systems.[54]

But others see far more nefarious consequences to investment arbitration. These critics note that developing countries under economic stress are more likely to delegate dispute settlement to international arbitral tribunals instead of insisting that cases be heard in domestic courts and that they may not even be aware of all the concessions they are making since broad provisions on fair and equal treatment make it easy to subsequently challenge government actions.[55] Others warn that large MNCs can engage in "nationality shopping," choosing to incorporate in a specific location to take advantage of an existing BIT or FTA to challenge public regulations they consider disadvantageous.[56]

Critics assert that by demanding exorbitant claims, foreign investors can make state officials leery of implementing strict regulations to safeguard the public interest, de facto producing regulatory chill.[57] The arbitral tribunals are also criticized for producing inconsistent results, for the ad hoc selection of private arbitrators who may have conflicts of interests, and for the lack of transparency and an appeal process.[58] Finally, the ISDS is condemned for creating a system of unequal rights, given that only foreign investors can choose to lodge a legal complaint in international arbitral tribunals such as the World Bank's International

Centre for Settlement of Investment Disputes (ICSID), whereas domestic investors have recourse only to local courts. Recent decisions by developing and industrialized nations to either withdraw from the arbitral tribunal conventions (Ecuador and Bolivia), scrap existing investment and trade agreements with ISDS provisions (Venezuela, Indonesia, South Africa), abstain from including ISDS in future international agreements (Australia in 2011), or launch policy reviews on whether to include investment arbitration in the Transatlantic Trade and Investment Partnership (the EU) show the stress in the system of investor-state dispute settlement.

Undoubtedly, ISDS is suffering a serious legitimacy crisis as many publics and governments question its merits. However, many of the concerns raised by critics do not hold up to careful scrutiny of the data, and in some problem areas (especially transparency) the TPP would make further improvements. There is a substantial track record to evaluate the impact of ISDS on public interest regulation, given that the system has been in operation for decades and is prevalent in most BITs and deep FTAs. The original purpose of ISDS was to avoid the previous pattern of politicization of investment disputes, both through the interference of host states (by biasing local judicial processes) or home states through diplomatic espousal or in earlier times "gunboat diplomacy."[59]

Certainly the number of ISDS cases has grown in recent years, but as Roderick Abbot, Fredrik Erixon, and Martina Ferracane note, the increase is proportional to the growth in outward direct investment.[60] Therefore, it is not surprising that, as more companies invest abroad, more cases of investment arbitration have arisen. As Scott Miller points out, the vast majority (90 percent) of investment treaties have not generated legal investment disputes. Furthermore, a clear pattern exists showing that states that are most frequently sued by private corporations have weak legal institutions (Venezuela and Argentina), as can be seen from their ranking at the bottom of the World Economic Forum's Index on the Efficiency of Legal Framework in Challenging Regulations.[61] The data also shows that ISDS arbitration takes place in areas of heavy state involvement; 40 percent of known ISDS cases are in the primary sector (oil, mining) and electricity generation.[62] This should come as no surprise since these sectors are characterized by huge fixed investments, which create a "hostage effect" as host states can use the sizable sunk costs of these FDI projects to renegotiate terms of operation.[63]

Investment arbitration is not uncommon or unnecessary among industrialized nations with advanced legal systems. A case in point is the large number of intra-European ISDS cases (77 percent of all cases filed against a European state between 2003 and 2013 originated from a European investor).[64] More debate has surrounded the question of whether developing countries derive significant FDI promotion effects by signing BITs or FTAs with investor dispute mechanisms. In an extensive review of the literature, Abbott, Erixon, and Ferracane conclude that while some studies show a meager impact of BITs on FDI promotion, other studies show that BITs do encourage greater levels of foreign investment by providing a stable legal framework, greater regulatory transparency, and guaranteeing investor rights.[65] Moreover, the effect is larger when these agreements incorporate pre-investment rights. High-achieving developing countries will see larger benefits from ISDS as they become capital exporters. In the past, ISDS advantages were considered to be unidirectional (in favor of industrialized nations), but as emerging economies invest more actively abroad, they will also benefit from the prime objective of ISDS: investment protection.

The empirical record does not support one of the key arguments of ISDS opponents—that the deck is stacked in favor of large MNCs who win handily and extract enormous payments from governments, leaving them cash-strapped. Through a painstaking empirical analysis (building a dataset of 272 public awards as of 2012), Susan Franck demonstrates that both governments and investors win and lose, but that states win more often than investors (55 percent for states, 36 percent for investors). Franck also shows that there is a huge gap between mean award claims ($622 million) and mean damages awarded ($16.6 million), which means that investors only receive two cents on the dollar for their claims. Finally, success rates among different types of investors is highest for individuals (31 percent), not large MNCs.[66] Miller corroborates this finding by noting that two-thirds of American investors filing claims in ICSID are individuals and small- and medium-size enterprises.[67]

The erosion of domestic regulations to protect public health or the environment through legal harassment by MNCs is not borne out by the evidence either. Daniel Price notes that bilateral investment treaties have endorsed the right of states to regulate by explicitly stating that nondiscriminatory regulatory measures cannot be construed as cases of indirect expropriation, even if they harm the profitability of investors.[68] Christian Tietje and Freya Baetens point out that arbitral tribunals have by and large adopted a narrow interpretation of the fair and equal treatment clause, as illustrated from this ICSID ruling: "It is each State's undeniable right and privilege to exercise its sovereign legislative power. A State has the right to enact, modify, or cancel a law at its own discretion. As a matter of fact, any businessman or investor knows that laws will evolve over time. What is prohibited however is for a State to act unfairly, unreasonably or inequitably in the exercise of its legislative power."[69] And foreign investors do not enjoy special substantive rights compared to domestic investors. In the American case, Miller notes that protections granted to foreign investors are modeled on the takings clause of the U.S. Constitution.[70] BITs extend the same guarantees, that no person shall be deprived of property without due process and just compensation.

Foreign investors cannot use ISDS to change a host country's laws, nor is there empirical support for the regulatory chill thesis. The case used most frequently as an example of regulatory chill—Canada's decision to drop the ban on the gasoline additive MMT (methylcyclopentadienyl manganese tricarbonyl) after settling an investment dispute with Ethyl Corp—only ensued after the measure was successfully challenged domestically by several provinces.[71] Moreover, Jeremy Caddel and Nathan Jensen show that 90 percent of all concluded ICSID rulings challenged executive actions and not legislative bills, casting doubt on the argument that ISDS circumvents democratic policymaking.[72] This finding is corroborated by Tietje and Baetens's examination of all NAFTA investment arbitration cases, in that the legal challenges were mostly directed to administrative actions (that is, targeting specific contracts) and not to legislative acts.[73] The policy space of governments was not compromised, since the few cases that mounted a direct challenge to government regulation were unsuccessful.

Most important, states remain in the driver's seat in making changes to the ISDS regime to ensure their continued ability to regulate for the public welfare. A case in point is the evolution of the U.S. model BIT. Compared to earlier incarnations in the mid-1980s, the U.S. model BIT has, over time, shown greater concern for balancing investor rights with the ability of the state to regulate for the public interest. Consequently it has significantly narrowed the rights of investors (with fewer constraints on exempting sectors from national treatment and most-favored-nation status) and has reduced the scope of indirect expropriation.[74] Another trend in ISDS, exemplified by the 2008 China-New Zealand FTA, has been to introduce explicit safeguards to preserve the regulatory prerogatives of governments and to prevent investors from suing host states over public interest regulations.[75] Over time, the United States has also increased the level of transparency in the arbitration process, requiring open proceedings and publicly available documents.[76] However, the ICSID still does not mandate that parties disclose briefs of arbitration decisions, pointing to an important area that requires further improvement.[77]

ISDS, therefore, has not hollowed out public interest regulations. Even Australia, long a skeptic, included investment arbitration in its most recent trade agreements with South Korea and the TPP, indicating it no longer fears ISDS is incompatible with its regulatory sovereignty. But the system of investment arbitration has evolved over time, and further changes are both possible and desirable. Going forward, Tietje and Baetens suggest a number of institutional fixes to address concerns about the possible misuse of ISDS: rules on dismissal of frivolous cases or on denial of benefits to investors that do not have a genuine business presence (to prevent nationality shopping); further use of carve-outs for prudential or national security reasons; the inclusion of mandatory consultations prior to launching a legal challenge; and increased transparency through the publication of information about the dispute and the admission of amicus curiae briefs from civil society groups.[78]

### Tackling the Legitimacy Challenge to Trade Policy: Effective Assurances on Prudential Regulation

The legitimacy challenges to trade policy on the regulatory front will persist so long as there is insufficient understanding among the public as to why the trade agenda has migrated to behind-the-border measures. The onus is on policymakers to explain much more effectively how deep trade agreements aim to root out new forms of protectionism and leverage the benefits of a successful insertion in global value chains. The realities of domestic production and international exchange today are profoundly different, yet poorly understood. Manufacturing operations are fragmented geographically, yet synchronized through the operation of production networks; trade in components overshadows trade in final goods; and technology, services, and digital flows play a larger role in international economic transactions. The goals of deep integration agreements—to provide rules that enhance the operation of the global value chain—and their past performance in promoting trade flows and generating significant economic benefits deserve to be more widely understood.

Securing public support for trade policy will require tackling the widespread perception that trade agreements undermine the ability of states to regulate and result in the overhaul of cherished social protections and/or an abdication of development aspirations. As shown in this chapter, there is substantial empirical evidence to indicate that governments are not lowering labor and environmental standards to secure a competitive edge in a world economy of fluid capital flows, multinational corporations have not obliterated national regulatory regimes through arbitral tribunals, and deep FTAs offer a growth opportunity, since developing countries that partake in global supply chains record higher average rates of GDP growth.

It is important to understand that trade agreements are perfectible, and the quest for legitimacy demands effective assurances that prudential regulation will not be sacrificed to the imperatives of liberalization. On this front, two important changes in the TPP would help allay the concerns of skeptics that deep trade agreements cut into the ability of the state to regulate for the public interest.

Deviating from the practice in U.S. FTAs, the TPP would allow for temporary capital controls to address balance of payments crises or external financial difficulties. Article 29.3 of the TPP establishes that these measures must be temporary, nondiscriminatory, and consistent with the IMF's articles. It goes on to clarify that these controls can be applied by a party to protect legitimate public welfare objectives. In addition to this safeguard on financial prudential regulation, the TPP's ISDS provisions address critics' concerns on three fronts; they unequivocally endorse the rights of states to regulate for the public interest, limit further the rights of investors to sue for damages, and improve the operation of the arbitration process.

On the first front, Article 9.16 states that the TPP's investment obligations in no way prevent a party from adopting or enforcing a measure deemed appropriate to ensure that investment activity is "sensitive to environmental, health, or other regulatory objectives." It also gives TPP parties the ability to issue binding interpretations on any aspect of ISDS provisions, further bolstering their discretion to assert their right to regulate.

On the second front, the grounds for investors to sue are also restricted in the TPP agreement, by clarifying that frustrated investor expectations do not provide grounds for litigation, by defining fair and equitable treatment more narrowly, by placing the entire burden of proof on investors, and by restricting damages awarded to their capacity as investors, not their cross-border trade activities. The TPP ISDS provisions also introduce several changes to the arbitration process itself: an expedited mechanism for dismissal of frivolous claims with the option of imposing attorneys' fees, the future adoption by TPP parties of a code of conduct for arbitrators, rules to ensure transparency and public participation by requiring that all TPP members agree to public proceedings, dissemination of arbitral rulings, and the participation of civil society groups through amicus curiae briefings. And while the TPP reforms did not adopt an appeal process, the ability to challenge ISDS awards by domestic courts or international review panels remains.[79]

As this chapter has made clear, ensuring that liberalization efforts eliminate discriminatory measures but do not compromise public interest regulations is a central task in trade policy design. Different groups in society with dissimilar preferences on how to navigate vexing trade-offs will continue to question whether trade rules in deep trade agreements strike the right balance. Hence, ensuring responsiveness to demands and input from various stakeholders is a key element in the search for legitimacy of trade policy. This challenge is discussed in the next chapter.

## CHAPTER FIVE

# Legitimacy III: The Democratic Deficit Debate

PAST CHAPTERS HAVE FOCUSED on critiques about the substance of trade policy, examining whether it generates inclusive prosperity or undermines public interest regulations. For some critics, the most central problem is the process by which trade policy is formulated and international trade negotiations are carried out. These critics allege that trade policy undermines democratic procedures because trade negotiators are unaccountable to elected officials and oversight mechanisms have broken down; that there are meager opportunities for public input and consultation mechanisms are skewed in favor of corporate interests; and that complete secrecy surrounding trade negotiations is not only incongruent with the digital information revolution and the rise of social media but, more perniciously, it generates international commitments the public is unaware of.

The democratic deficit critique is not new. Because trade policymaking is characterized by delegation, executive authority, and technical expertise, concerns about insulation from public oversight and input are, in fact, long-standing.[1] However, the ever-expanding scope of trade negotiations into matters previously considered to be strictly the domain of domestic regulation has mobilized more groups in society demanding greater disclosure and participation in trade policy decisions.

The main argument advanced here is that the most important deficit to address in trade negotiations is one of representativeness, not transparency. Confidentiality at the negotiation stage is necessary to avoid a bargaining stalemate and the mobilization of interest groups determined

71

to sabotage the talks. But this veil of confidentiality at the negotiation stage does not result in secret trade agreements. In the case of the United States, the chains of oversight from Congress have not eroded, and trade promotion authority (TPA) has provided an effective mechanism to ensure the accountability of trade negotiators. Moreover, critics' claims of excessive levels of secrecy in the Trans-Pacific Partnership do not appear credible when a comparison is made to another major platform for trade rulemaking: the World Trade Organization. Without a doubt, the WTO has made excellent progress in boosting its external transparency, but NGOs are not privy to the interstate negotiation process. In the area where civil society groups have had the most substantive input, the dispute settlement mechanism—through the submission of amicus curiae briefs and disclosure of written submissions—U.S. FTAs, including the TPP, have been on par (or exceeded) WTO transparency standards.

On the other hand, expanding the reach of the consultation mechanism with stakeholders to match the much larger scope of trade negotiations remains a major challenge for most countries. Ensuring representativeness in domestic input provided to trade negotiators is essential to improve the substance of policy by allowing the reconciliation of competing interests. It is also a winning strategy to overcome legitimacy deficits by going to the core of some critics' concerns, that the diversity of stakeholders will be well represented and that there will be opportunities for timely input.

The first section of this chapter addresses one of the most potent narratives against trade agreements, that the information blackout during negotiations results in secret trade agreements. It explains why, even in democracies where there is a strong normative association between transparency and good governance, confidentiality at the negotiation stage is important to generate welfare-enhancing negotiation outcomes. The second section discusses the difficulties governments have had in developing truly multistakeholder consultation mechanisms and ensuring productive interaction between business and nonbusiness groups. While critics' arguments that the advisory system in the United States represents only one constituency (big business) are not accurate, there is, indeed, room for further inclusion of more diverse groups. The last section discusses strategies to implement sunshine policies that do not compromise the integrity of international trade negotiations.

## TRANSPARENCY AND OVERSIGHT

Transparency has emerged as a key issue in the public's evaluation of the legitimacy of trade policy. Critics of trade agreements advocate for greater—if not full—disclosure of trade negotiations based on both normative and instrumental grounds. Normatively, they point out that transparency has long been considered a hallmark of good governance. When the public is abreast of (trade) policy deliberations, it can keep public officials accountable, reduce instances of corruption or policy capture, and ensure that negotiated outcomes align with the public interest. Open decisionmaking processes, therefore, lead to greater levels of trust and acceptance of public policies. Instrumentally, they point out that transparency will lead to a more efficient negotiation process and will buttress the chances of ratification. David Levine warns that secrecy in international trade negotiations unnecessarily creates an adversarial relationship between the government and civil society.[2] NGOs will mobilize to counter provisions that they anticipate will be in the agreement, and will do so guided by Internet leaks that may be outdated or unreliable. In an era of instant communication, the hurdles to collective action are much lower, creating multiple, citizen-driven opposition campaigns. As a result, the government will face a steeper battle in winning public support for its trade initiatives and will spend time and resources fighting misinformation on the content of trade agreements.

The extreme level of secrecy in trade negotiations, and especially in the TPP, undermines the democratic process, according to critics.[3] This argument has several strands. The information blackout benefits the interests of a few corporate advisors and marginalizes congressional input into the trade agenda, thereby overriding the system of checks and balances.[4] Since the TPP delves into regulatory matters, it should abide by the same level of transparency as domestic bills on similar subjects taken up by Congress.[5] In the view of skeptics, only an open process that mirrors domestic legislative procedures (release of proposed text, public deliberations, and opportunities for public comment) should earn trade agreements like the TPP a positive ratification vote.[6]

Even by international standards, critics argue, the TPP comes short in disclosure and access compared to other international bodies that also engage in international rulemaking, such as the WTO and the World Intellectual Property Organization (WIPO). In these other international forums, they argue, all countries' negotiation proposals are publicly released in the course of the negotiations.[7] In particular, the WIPO's negotiation of the Marrakesh Treaty for the Visually Impaired is deemed as the standard to follow, with the publication of all negotiation documents, live webcast of negotiation sessions, and structured access to input from stakeholders.[8] Moreover, some of the United States's trade partners disseminate more information on trade negotiations. The EU has raised the bar on transparency by agreeing to disclose its negotiation proposals in the Transatlantic Trade and Investment Partnership talks.

This raises the question of how much transparency is required to make international negotiations legitimate. Some of the fixes suggested for U.S. trade policy would increase the level of transparency while still leaving other areas under the veil of confidentiality. For example, Susan Aaronson proposes applying differentiated disclosure standards: secrecy is justified in market access talks involving confidential business information, but transparency should prevail in regulatory matters such as food safety, labor, and environmental standards.[9] Other proposals would largely do away with confidentiality, for example, by demanding that the Office of the United States Trade Representative (USTR) disclose to the public all information given to cleared trade advisors.[10] Levine offers one of the most far-reaching proposals: to eliminate the exemption that trade negotiations have enjoyed from the Freedom of Information Act (FOIA).[11] Levine's reform would involve a public right of disclosure of information on foreign relations of the United States and a more limited right of disclosure on foreign government information (only if the foreign government explicitly consents to the disclosure). In his view, this would allow outside experts and the American public to access information on U.S. negotiation positions and tabled texts, bringing international lawmaking closer to domestic legislation practices.

There are, however, sound reasons to reject the notion that trade negotiations are excessively secretive or that they undermine sound democratic governance by overriding congressional prerogatives. In Richard Steinberg's view, trade negotiations are best described as "opaque," not secret.[12] Every member of Congress has access to the text, and no secret agreement will enter into force with provisions unknown to the public. Once trade negotiations are concluded, the agreement receives a full public airing, expert assessment of its impact will be available (for example, a report by the U.S. International Trade Commission), and Congress retains the prerogative to reject the agreement if it is found wanting. TPA, in fact, enhances transparency because it ensures that the executive branch will fully engage with Congress and will not have an incentive to work around Congress through executive agreements that do not have similar oversight and consultation requirements as pointed out by Oona Hathaway.[13]

Far from undermining the system of checks and balances, TPA provides an effective formula for Congress to define negotiation objectives, monitor the activities of trade negotiators, and decide on the ultimate fate of the agreement.[14] In approving TPA, Congress also has the ability to instill greater transparency in the trade negotiation process. For example, heeding concerns that access rules to the text for members of Congress were too cumbersome, the USTR announced in spring 2015 a number of eased procedures whereby members will no longer have to make an appointment to view the text, can come with one personal staff member, can see the text that discloses each country's negotiating positions, and will receive plain English summaries of the chapters.[15] A few months later, the USTR expanded access to cleared committee staffers, no longer requiring them to be accompanied by a Congress member.[16] Giving access to staff members with greater technical expertise may be more meaningful since, in the past, very few Congress members have actually requested access to the text (a total of forty in a three-year span).[17] In addition, the USTR has carried out more than 1,600 briefings with Congress members and their staff.[18] In the latest adoption of TPA, in June 2015, Congress established a new position of chief transparency officer within the USTR.

The parallels that critics make between domestic and international lawmaking are, in fact, misleading. Brian Schoenborn points out that international negotiations can neither be characterized as legislation (requiring fully open procedures) nor as contracts (operating under closed doors).[19] Because international negotiations have elements of both, confidentiality is required to preserve negotiation integrity, while TPA and the formal advisory system work to provide oversight and public input. Trade negotiators are dealing with a two-level game (with foreign counterparts and with domestic stakeholders), so while amendments make sense domestically, they would unravel international negotiations since there would be no certainty that negotiators could preserve the deal that was struck at the international table.[20] The interplay of international and domestic negotiations also affects transparency considerations. It is a common practice for countries to sign confidentiality agreements as they enter trade negotiations to facilitate the trust and bargaining over negotiation offers required to strike a deal. Many countries have also instituted national security exemptions to the public's right of access to government documents (as FOIA does) to avoid damage to foreign relations. So, while the principle of access to public information is essential to democratic governance, it has not been absolute.[21] It is important that the secrecy shield is temporary, as the trade agreement must be publicly released and fully vetted before any congressional vote, and all documents on the negotiation process are to be released four years after enactment or after the last round of negotiations.[22]

At the negotiation stage, transparency can increase the chances of stalemate by encouraging public posturing, rigidity, risk aversion, rejection of compromise solutions, and preventing the development of trust and candor among participants.[23] Disclosure of U.S. negotiating positions would reassure the domestic audience, but it would tie the hands of negotiators, preventing them from adjusting positions as the negotiations advanced.[24] Partial disclosure of just some areas of an agreement (regulatory matters) is difficult to realize. Rules on intellectual property protection, state-owned enterprises, and government procurement—to name a few areas—not only reflect a society's collective social values on public regulation but also have distributional consequences. Information disclosure would create an opportunity for disaffected sectors to mobilize, making it harder to reach an agreement. Moreover, the market access talks and negotiations on regulatory markets are deeply interlinked (with countries balancing concessions in one area with offsets in another), making it hard to apply different disclosure standards.

Despite the strongly held normative preference for transparency, Barbara Koremenos uses game-theoretic analysis to show how secret international negotiations can yield open covenants that improve social welfare.[25] The value of secrecy increases when the distributional consequences are severe and when the number of issues in the negotiation is large, conditions that trade agreements meet. Secrecy can produce better bargaining outcomes by shortening the length of negotiations; tamping down on the mobilization of interest groups willing to sabotage outcomes; allowing the executive branch to focus on social welfare gains and not distributive battles; and permitting the use of negotiation tactics such as bargaining chips—inflated initial demands to obtain concessions in other areas.

Comparisons to the transparency levels of rulemaking in other platforms do not support the argument of extreme levels of secrecy in the

TPP negotiations. As a norm-setting organization, the WIPO has recently focused on the negotiation of treaties dealing with very specific issues within the universe of the IP system: the Beijing Treaty on Audiovisual Performances (2012) and the Marrakesh Treaty for the Visually Impaired (2013).[26] The latter offers important limitations on copyright to make published works available to the visually or print disabled, but it gives leeway to member parties to implement commitments following their own legal systems and there is no dispute settlement procedure. Its narrow focus and the generation of soft law commitments underscore a very different negotiation dynamic from deep trade agreements, which have a much more complex negotiation agenda (not only the whole range of IP issues, but rules on a host of other regulatory matters in addition to market access commitments) as well as significant distributional effects and binding obligations that create a strong incentive for interest groups to mobilize and sabotage the talks. As noted, the nature of the negotiation affects the level of transparency and confidentiality required to strike a deal.

In comparing FTA negotiations to the WTO, it is important not to overstate the level of transparency that the multilateral body has accomplished to date, and to note the level of parity in public disclosure and access in its dispute settlement mechanism with that of U.S. FTAs. Without question, the WTO has made great strides in increasing external transparency and has launched a productive dialogue with NGOs to overcome a legitimacy deficit that erupted with street demonstrations during the 1999 Seattle ministerial meeting. The WTO's website offers a wealth of information, is committed to the publication of all official documents, and has embarked on trade education with a number of tutorials and online interactive tools. Regarding access and participation by NGOs, Maria Perez-Esteve offers a useful analysis of the areas where the WTO has expanded the access available to civil society groups, and areas that remain off-limits.[27] A continuous dialogue with NGOs has been created by awarding them accreditation to sit at the main plenary sessions of ministerial meetings, by the efforts of the secretariat to provide NGO briefings after council meetings and to organize open symposiums, and by hosting the WTO Public Forum, a conference where NGOs have agenda-setting power and decide which issues will be examined. But the decisionmaking activities of the WTO are out of bounds for civil society groups. Internal transparency in decisionmaking has followed from avoiding the exclusionary dynamics of the green room (in the past, only a subset of delegation heads would meet at the discretion of the secretary general to reach consensus on negotiation issues), but the WTO does not require governments to make their negotiation proposals open to the public (despite sporadic publication of proposals or consolidated texts). NGOs cannot attend WTO business meetings, nor is there a desire by many member governments to provide this access; they cite concerns that the NGOs may disproportionately advocate the interests of industrialized nations, lack the legitimacy of elected representatives, and could make the decisionmaking process too cumbersome.[28]

NGOs have made great strides in gaining access and participation in the WTO's dispute settlement mechanism, but Gabrielle Marceu and Mikella Hurley's report card shows that in three important areas—disclosure of written submissions by the parties, admission of amicus curiae briefings, and open hearings—U.S. FTAs are on par (and sometimes ahead) of the WTO transparency provisions.[29] In the WTO, publication of written submissions (after extracting sensitive proprietary information) is at the parties' discretion, but several countries (the United States, Canada, and the EU) have made this their standard practice. Access to this information is important for NGOs and outside parties interested in submitting amicus curiae briefings, which both the Appellate Panel and the North American Free Trade Agreement's Tribunal have ruled they may accept. And while open hearings at the WTO remain at the discretion of the parties and are not very common, they have been mandated for U.S. FTAs since 2002.[30] As noted in the previous chapter, transparency provisions in the TPP's investor-state dispute settlement mechanism would make these the default practices for the rest of the members.

By far, one of the most significant changes in transparency practices was the decision of the EU, in the fall of 2014, to release negotiation texts in TTIP talks, to limit the number of TTIP documents classified as restricted and to expand access to the text to all members of the European Parliament. These measures undoubtedly increased the flow of information to the public, but they did not represent full transparency or the eschewing of the principle of confidentiality in the consultation and negotiation processes. The EU identified several areas of nondisclosure (tariffs, services, investment, and procurement), where access requests can be denied if deemed harmful to the EU's foreign relations. The transparency guidelines also clarified that there would be no disclosure of U.S. proposals or common negotiation texts. Members of the European Parliament who gain access to the secure reading room must have the appropriate security clearances.[31] The full import of these transparency measures on negotiation dynamics cannot be assessed at this point. An early study of the first two years of negotiation suggests, though, that enhanced transparency may have come at a price by weakening the EU's bargaining position, especially since the United States has not released its own negotiation proposals.[32] Greater certainty exists on the fact that more transparency did not solve TTIP's legitimacy deficit. Opponents of the agreement had used the call for full transparency to gain traction in their anti-TTIP campaign, but were not mollified by greater disclosure, dismissing the changes as cosmetic.[33] Some evidence suggests that the public has not used the highly technical texts now available to form an opinion on the merits of the agreement. For example, Matthias Bauer's analysis of online German content shows that visits to the official negotiation texts are very modest (0.8 percent) compared to the number of signatories to anti-TTIP petitions in the same time period.[34]

## CONSULTATION AND REPRESENTATIVENESS

Trade policy is about balancing competing interests, and this is true for traditional bread-and-butter issues as well as for the newer regulatory agenda. It entails, for example, the pursuit of liberalization to promote efficiency and productivity without causing undue adjustment costs, or the desire to promote innovation through intellectual property rights while protecting access to ideas and technologies that enhance human welfare. Therefore, the strongest argument in favor of consultation with stakeholders is that it improves the substance of trade policy; representativeness can best ensure balance. Hence, to develop effective and balanced negotiation proposals, trade negotiators need to hear from stakeholders (that is, those affected by a proposed trade deal).

Trade consultation with society can produce other important benefits, as well: fostering a sense of ownership over new initiatives, eased implementation and sustainability of policies, greater legitimacy of the policymaking process, and accountability of public officials.[35] Out of a desire to generate society's buy-in of trade policy, several governments have launched consultation mechanisms, although frequently this has happened reactively. For instance, the need to shore up the legitimacy of an impending major trade negotiation with the United States acted as a catalyst for the adoption of advisory mechanisms in several Latin American countries.[36]

The benefits of consultation to improve the content of trade policy and boost legitimacy of trade negotiations are not in question. However, it has been difficult for many governments to navigate the actual operationalization of a consultation mechanism as they confront the issues of whom to consult with, how to ensure meaningful advice, and how to provide expanded input opportunities for larger groups of society without undermining the efficiency and confidentiality of the negotiation process.

There have been substantial changes in the way governments think about the contours of the circle of consultation. Long gone are the days when trade negotiators participated in multilateral rounds of negotiation largely insulated from domestic politics. This "club model" of multilateral trade cooperation was driven by a narrow set of technocratic elites with little input from outsider groups.[37] Demands, first from the business community and later from civil society groups, however, have put a growing premium on the development of more inclusionary processes. This has been reflected in the move toward incorporating advice from the private sector (dubbed an "adaptive club model") to secure technical expertise, and later on from civil society groups ("multistakeholder model") to generate greater acceptance of market opening policies.[38] This last transition has proven the hardest.

In many cases, a two-track deliberation process is at work, with closer coordination and information sharing with business and a consultative forum with NGOs that is kept more aloof from the actual process of negotiation. Government officials may find it easier to work with business groups who share the goals of trade liberalization and can provide valuable information on specific industries to serve as a baseline for trade negotiations, while at the same time they may be concerned that the incorporation of societal groups opposed to the trade agenda may highjack the consultation process.[39] As Michelle Limenta puts it, many governments remain skeptical of the merits of increasing the scope of consultation because NGOs are perceived as "antagonists rather than partners in the area of trade negotiations."[40]

Success in expanding the circle of consultation toward a more genuine multistakeholder approach can create its own problems. In 1998, Canada and the EU both launched concerted campaigns to intensify and broaden consultation mechanisms with NGOs, but as Brian Hocking documents, they had difficulty meeting the expectations of both civil society groups and business actors. For the former, questions about their lack of real influence on the substance of trade negotiations remained, while for the latter, their perception that commercial goals were watered down in the deliberations diminished their desire to participate.[41]

Developing a productive dialogue between business and nonbusiness actors is challenging, but so is the need to accommodate demands for greater public participation while preserving the confidentiality of domestic consultations to ensure the success of international negotiations. As Brian Schoenborn suggests, the advisory committee system can most effectively mitigate the public participation–government confidentiality conundrum since it "leads to increased impact and control by the general public, ultimately satisfying both the informational needs of government and the oversight requirements of a democracy."[42]

The United States has one of the oldest and most developed trade advisory systems in the world. First established in 1974, this consultative mechanism is composed today of twenty-eight committees with roughly seven hundred cleared advisors, and it is organized in a three-tiered structure. The first tier, providing advice on overall trade policy, is the President's Advisory Committee on Trade Policy Negotiations (ACTPN); the next tier of committees address crosscutting issues such as labor, environment, and intergovernmental coordination; and the third tier is composed of sixteen Industry Trade Advisory Committees (ITAC) providing technical advice. Even though by international standards the American trade advisory system is deemed one of the most participatory, in the United States it has become a lightning rod for those who oppose the direction of American trade policy.[43]

Some influential critics of the TPP, for example, have depicted the trade advisory committees as a corporate power grab, with a secretive group of business and lobbyist advisors whispering into the ears of trade negotiators and working to the detriment of public interest regulations.[44] Criticisms of the trade advisory system have centered on three main areas. First is the overrepresentation of business interests, with 85 percent of committee members coming from private industry or trade associations.[45] Second is the segregation of business advisors in the more active ITACs with token or no participation from nonbusiness groups in tier three committees. For example, reminiscent of the difficulties identified elsewhere in encouraging interaction between business and nonbusiness members, the chairs of the ITACs unanimously opposed the idea floated by the Obama administration of adding nonbusiness advisors to these committees. The chairs noted that the mandate of these committees is to provide technical advice representing the interests of economic sectors, whereas NGO members are focused on cross-cutting issues.[46] The third line of critique focuses on the confidentiality of the consultations, in particular the exemption of the trade advisory committees from the Federal Advisory Committee Act's (FACA) requirements on public meetings and publication of meeting documents.[47]

These criticisms notwithstanding, the charges of outright policy capture by an elite group of corporate interests are not credible. For one, there is greater overall representation of nonbusiness groups than some of these critics acknowledge. The leaders of four national unions sit on the ACTPN providing advice on the direction of trade policy, and there is a separate Labor Advisory Committee in the second tier. Not only is labor well represented, there are also advisors from environmental, consumer, and public interest groups, as well as academia (albeit in smaller numbers). Stephen Jacobi notes there is greater diversity within the business community, as many advisors come from small- and medium-size companies and not just large enterprises.[48] The pattern of segregation operates not only in the third tier industry committees. The Labor Advisory Committee is composed exclusively of union members. The only three committees in the whole system where there is greater mixing of different groups are the ACTPN, the Advisory Committee on Africa, and the Trade and Environment Policy Advisory Committee.[49]

All cleared advisors (regardless of background) have access to the same information, which until recently pertained only to draft U.S. proposals. Starting in July 2015, the Obama administration, for the first time and on an equal basis, made available negotiated text. The purpose of the measure was to allow the advisory committees to prepare their assessment reports for Congress.[50] Because cleared advisors have access to documents related to ongoing trade negotiations and provide advice based on that information, the meetings are not open to the public and advisors cannot disclose confidential information. However, the evaluation reports of completed trade deals that all advisory committees produce are publicly released. They, in fact, constitute an important source of expert judgment, which Congress factors in before deciding on ratification.

The trade advisory system is perfectible, with important improvements over time to ensure a more deliberative process and wider representation of interests. Following a 2002 Government Accountability Office report that pointed to shortcomings in these areas, the USTR adopted a number of reforms to enlist members from underrepresented sectors (services) and trade issues (for example, investment, food safety), and began listing the affiliation of committee members in the FACA database to increase transparency in the composition of the trade advisory system. Addressing concerns about responsiveness to input, the executive branch must now inform committees when there are "significant departures" from their advice. To improve interaction among different committee members, the USTR increased the number of liaison meetings, conducted plenaries of ITACs, and initiated a monthly conference call with the chairs of all committees.[51]

Still, the advisory system is in need of greater diversity of views and more meaningful mechanisms for further deliberation among different stakeholder groups. A particular challenge has been to increase members from civil society. The Obama administration tried to expand NGO participation in two main ways. One way was launching stakeholder meetings on location during negotiation meetings to give NGOs the opportunity to make presentations and interact with negotiators. The second initiative, the launch of a tier two Public Interest Trade Advisory Committee (PITAC), would have provided a far more substantive form of participation for public interest groups by giving them access to negotiation documents and establishing an ongoing dialogue with U.S. trade negotiators—if it had materialized. The initiative came in the later stages of the TPP negotiation process (February 2014), and with the explicit desire, as explained by U.S. Trade Representative Michael Froman, to add voices to the advisory system that would focus on issues such as public health, development, and consumer safety.[52]

However, critics remained unpersuaded. While many welcomed the addition of more cleared advisors from civil society, they complained that the segregation of business and nonbusiness interests would remain, and that the voice of civil society would be watered down because tier two committees do not meet as frequently as ITACs.[53] The refusal of NGOs to sign the confidentiality agreement that applies to all cleared advisors proved to be an insurmountable obstacle for the establishment of PITAC. The position of these NGOs was that they need to share all information for their organizations to develop their positions on ongoing trade negotiations.[54] Nevertheless, the confidentiality clause has not prevented cleared advisors from environmental and consumer groups and labor unions from engaging in public education on trade policy and/ or advocacy on specific trade initiatives, and they have done so without releasing confidential information. In this specific instance, however, concerns over transparency hindered efforts to bring more diversity to the consultation process.

## TACKLING THE LEGITIMACY CHALLENGE: SUNSHINE POLICIES AND NEGOTIATION INTEGRITY

In democratic societies with strong normative support for transparency as a foundation of public accountability, where a culture and practice of instant information disclosure has become entrenched with the digital communications revolution, and where more stakeholders have demanded participation opportunities, the traditional process of trade negotiations has been under attack. The most fundamental deficit, however, is one of representativeness, not of transparency. Confidential negotiations do not generate secret trade agreements. Concluded trade deals are published in their entirety and are examined and vetted by different groups and experts from civil society, public agencies, and the private sector. It is with a wealth of information that Congress decides on the ultimate fate of each trade agreement. On the other hand, making the consultation process more inclusionary, by incorporating stakeholders affected by the regulatory agenda of trade agreements, provides a more effective mechanism to address legitimate concerns: that trade rules provide a fair balance among competing objectives and that input can be provided in a timely manner to influence the course of the negotiations.

The transparency exemption at the bargaining stage serves a purpose: to avoid negotiation stalemate from rigid posturing and the inability to compromise, and to avoid the mobilization of interest groups trying to sabotage the talks. While the veil of confidentiality is necessary to protect the integrity of negotiations, sunshine should prevail in the other stages of the process (definition of trade policy objectives at the beginning, and assessment of benefits and costs of the concluded trade deal), and oversight from Congress and input from a balanced group of stakeholders should take place while negotiations are ongoing.

Clearly, a number of protransparency reforms could be adopted in the negotiation of free trade agreements that do not doom the negotiations to failure. There is much to be learned from the WTO's external transparency efforts, such as creating an ongoing dialogue with accredited

NGOs, giving them the power to set the agenda in addressing cutting-edge topics in public consultation forums, and demystifying international trade for the general public with its public education efforts. The benefit of such measures is that they create a permanent engagement loop with civil society groups and the general public. The process of national trade policy formulation could emulate some of these practices. As Susan Aaronson points out, trust can be built through responsiveness by establishing online interactive tools and by creating feedback loops with trade advisory committees.[55]

There is no question that confidentiality in trade negotiations has an added cost in the digital era, with the disruptive effect of leaks and the potential spread of misinformation. Too little transparency can compromise the legitimacy of trade policy, but too much can weaken bargaining leverage, putting cherished objectives out of reach without generating greater public buy-in of trade policy. The public's understanding of the need to carve out a transparency exemption at the negotiation stage cannot be built solely with assurances of a robust public debate after the negotiations are concluded and before Congress votes. Rather, it requires a more balanced set of voices providing input to trade negotiators at all stages of the process. Chapter 7 picks up on this challenge to improve trade policy representativeness.

## CHAPTER SIX

# Political Viability in the Quest for Ratification

A CENTRAL TASK IN trade policy formulation is to ensure the political viability at home of negotiated trade deals. Paving the way for a positive vote on ratification will require pragmatism to clear existing political hurdles and build a domestic coalition in support of the trade initiative. The battles to define the contours of trade agreements and their eventual enactment are shaped by the existing institutional framework. In particular, the degree of fragmentation or concentration of decision-making authority will determine the extent to which a government can display trade policy decisiveness. Political systems with multiple veto players pushing for the protection of their narrow interests will have great difficulty negotiating ambitious trade agreements that mark a significant departure from the existing status quo.

Because trade agreements have distributional consequences with winners and losers, the domestic politics of trade are largely shaped by the mobilization of opposing interest groups that rely on their existing resources (votes, political contributions) to influence policy outcomes. But the intensity of mobilization will be different, with prospective losers engaging in the most active campaigns. Therefore, policymakers must not only galvanize the support of likely winners, they must also neutralize the opposition of actors that expect to be disadvantaged by the liberalization effort. When opponents to a trade agreement operate as veto players in the political system because they have the clout to derail the negotiations or deny approval of the final deal, it becomes necessary to make accommodations for them, such as scaling-down liberalization commitments and/or extending side payments. Compensation, therefore, has always been a central element of trade policy design.

This chapter illuminates the domestic political dynamics influencing the ability to negotiate and enact ambitious trade agreements by drawing from different national experiences. But it pays close attention to the growing division of purpose among political actors in the United States, which has brought about greater indecisiveness, thus increasing the challenges in seeing major trade initiatives through to ratification. It discusses the mobilization of different interest groups opposing and supporting the TPP and analyzes the reasons the Trade Adjustment Assistance (TAA) program has ceased to be an effective political device to cultivate support for trade agreements in Congress. This chapter is composed of two main sections; the first examines the influence of the macro political structure on state decisiveness, while the second section looks at the different incentives for interest groups to enter the fray of political battles over trade and the growing ineffectiveness of TAA as a grand bargain in favor of liberalization.

## ON THE POWER OF INSTITUTIONS: DECISIVENESS VERSUS INDECISIVENESS

Political institutions shape policy choices, and the trade arena is no exception. At their core, institutions set the rules of the political game. They define the roles and level of influence of different government actors, the points of access or conditions for the marginalization of organized interests in society, the degree of responsiveness to broader societal interests beyond producer groups, and the process for both agenda setting and policy implementation. It is a country's institutional makeup that will determine its ability to embark on bold policy departures or to remain shackled to the status quo.[1] It will also impact a country's ability to generate welfare-enhancing policies or, instead, its proclivity for the dispensation of particularistic benefits to politically influential groups. Indeed, these are two powerful insights of institutionalist theory that directly connect macro political institutional design (the degree of separation of power and purpose) to the substance and quality of public policy.[2]

Political systems that fragment power among several actors will have a harder time adopting new policies. These actors operate as veto players with their consent required to approve new initiatives; hence, as their numbers grow with the dispersion of power, the harder it will be to gain the approval of all to change the status quo.[3] It is important to factor in not only the separation of power (determined by constitutional rules, which do or do not establish checks and balances) but also the separation of purpose among veto players (influenced by electoral outcomes), which reveals how far apart political actors are in their policy preferences and to what extent they aim for opposing goals.

Divided polities (with multiple quarreling political actors) will be prone to policy gridlock, whereas political systems with fewer veto players or greater confluence of preferences among them will display decisiveness in adopting new policies.[4] Moreover, greater levels of separation of power and purpose will conspire against the adoption of welfare-enhancing national policies. As Gary Cox and Matthew McCubbins posit, a larger number of veto players with narrow interests will be able to exact more side payments in the form of particularistic policies and targeted benefits as they bargain for their consent to any policy change.[5]

Operating within institutional constraints, trade policymakers aim for political efficacy: clearing political obstacles to the implementation of their policy initiatives. In the realm of trade negotiations, political efficacy means getting to yes on the ratification of a trade agreement, and it requires bringing on board all veto players by galvanizing the support of likely winners and neutralizing the opposition of potential losers—either overcoming their opposition or pragmatically carving out exceptions or extending side payments. This chapter fleshes out the impact of macro political design on the display of state decisiveness in trade negotiations and on the incidence of compensation politics.[6]

### Political Institutions and Trade Policy Decisiveness

Following the logic of veto player models, we should expect countries to display greater decisiveness in their trade policy (negotiating and ratifying trade agreements swiftly and deflecting pressures for protection or side payments from vested interests) when top-down executive leadership is present. Moreover, because different electoral constraints operate on the executive and legislative branches, the inter-branch balance of power will be of consequence to the substance of trade policy. A general observation in the U.S. trade policymaking literature is that legislators are more susceptible to the pressures from narrow constituency groups and will be inclined to support distributive policies, whereas the executive is more concerned with aggregate economic performance as it faces a national constituency.[7] And because the political executive is also likely to pursue trade negotiations as part of a foreign policy agenda, he or she may be more willing to block the efforts of domestic protectionist groups to secure the geopolitical payoffs of high-stakes trade negotiations.[8] Generally speaking, we should expect bolder initiatives when the executive has the upper hand in the domestic policy formulation process.

To make sense of the plethora of trade policymaking institutions around the world by placing them along a centralization–fragmentation continuum, the analysis that follows focuses on two key variables: the balance of power between the executive and legislative branches, and the number of bureaucracies involved (including whether or not there is an interagency coordination body or mechanism). The objective is to ascertain to what extent division of power (and purpose) is responsible for trade policy immobilism or decisiveness.

### Executives and Legislatures

Constitutional rules assigning primary responsibility for treaty negotiations (including trade agreements) and the procedures for their ratification set the parameters for executive–legislative relations. In countries with a legal tradition that awards the executive control over the negotiation of international trade treaties, the legislature has traditionally played only an ex-post voting role. In many Latin American presidential systems, the minor role of the legislature has been exacerbated by the lack of technical know-how and access to information about the substance of the negotiations.[9] In a survey of twelve Latin American countries, for example, only two legislatures were deemed to be actively involved in trade policy formulation—Chile and Mexico.[10] In some Southeast Asian nations, too, legislatures have been eclipsed by the executive branch in the negotiation of trade agreements. As two examples, consider the executive-led trade negotiations under Prime Minister Mahathir Mohamad in Malaysia (he quickly negotiated a trade agreement with Japan that entered into force thirty-one months after the launch of negotiations) and Prime Minister Thaksin Shinawatra of Thailand, who signed a string of trade agreements until his ouster from office in 2006.[11] South Korea was also able to swiftly launch trade negotiations with its major trading partners (United States, EU, and China) under the leadership of strong presidents, while the participation of the National Assembly was circumscribed to the final ratification vote.[12]

On the other hand, in some Westminster parliamentary systems, such as Canada, the prime minister not only has authority to initiate and negotiate trade deals, but also to ratify these international treaties — although the implementing bill must be voted upon in parliament.[13] The push to increase the role of parliaments in treaty making has been evident in some Westminster-style democracies. In Australia, the parliament's role had also been limited to voting on implementing legislation when it was required to give effect to trade agreements, but in the mid-1990s greater calls from opposition parties resulted in a number of institutional innovations: the requirement to table in parliament signed treaties at least fifteen days prior to their ratification and the creation of the Joint Standing Committee to assess signed treaties. Because these reforms did not give the parliament direct input in the drafting of negotiation objectives or an ability to interject opinions during the negotiations, they were deemed insufficient by many.[14]

By international standards, the American trade policymaking system—with a constitutional mandate for Congress to regulate foreign trade—is quite unique. For more than a century and a half, Congress set tariffs as part of its task of collecting duties, but in the aftermath of the infamous Smoot-Hawley trade bill (which drastically increased tariff levels), Congress moved in 1934 to delegate the authority to negotiate tariff reduction agreements to the executive through the Reciprocal Trade Agreements Act (RTAA). Why did Congress delegate this authority? To protect itself from producer interest pressure to impose high tariffs that could generate a protectionist logroll and to avoid blame for the economic and diplomatic fallout (as with the Smoot-Hawley bill). This insight from I. M. Destler's penetrating analysis accounts for how, with this delegation, Congress launched a new "bargaining tariff" dynamic, making the executive the chief trade negotiator and mobilizing a coalition of exporters supporting the opening of overseas markets.[15] Over time, as the scope of international trade negotiations changed with the reduction in tariff levels and the growing importance of nontariff barriers, the executive-legislative pact needed a major revamping. A new formula was found in 1974 with the launch of fast-track authority (known today as Trade Promotion Authority—TPA).

TPA is an inter-branch political compact designed to ensure that the division of powers (with the president responsible for international treaties while Congress has a constitutional mandate to regulate foreign trade) does not preclude the effectiveness of trade negotiations, which are treated as congressional-executive agreements. In essence, the president receives authority to negotiate complex trade deals and Congress agrees to a timely up or down vote without amendments on the implementing bill. In no way does TPA mean the abdication of congressional power over trade policy. Congress remains a formidable veto player because it lays out the negotiation objectives in trade policy and reserves the right to reject the finished trade deal if it comes short on its expectations.

Moreover, TPA creates a number of reporting and monitoring procedures to ensure that Congress is abreast of progress in trade negotiations (for example, the president must notify Congress ninety days before initiating negotiations and ninety days before signing a finished trade deal, and must generate a report on any modification to domestic law required in the trade agreement). In addition, the Office of the United States Trade Representative (USTR) must consult with the congressional committees with jurisdiction over trade policy throughout the negotiations, members of Congress may be appointed as trade advisors to specific negotiations, and all members of Congress have access to the negotiation text. Importantly, the delegation of trade negotiation authority has never been absolute or permanent: TPA must be renewed periodically, Congress can strip a trade agreement from the expedited voting procedures if it deems the executive has not met the reporting obligations or negotiation objectives, and Congress remains the final arbiter on the fate of a trade deal.

Moreover, U.S. legislators, like their counterparts elsewhere, can and have availed themselves of a number of strategies to ensure trade negotiators in the executive branch remain faithful to their preferences. Broadly speaking, these strategies are of two kinds: "police patrols," randomly monitoring a sample of bureaucratic policies, and "fire alarms," reacting to specific complaints from interest groups.[16] These monitoring strategies can be used at different stages of the negotiation process. Police patrol tactics include setting the trade policy objectives that will guide the negotiations; during the trade talks, they comprise the appointment of legislators to sit at the talks or lawmaker access to negotiation drafts. After the trade negotiations are concluded, these monitoring strategies comprise the arraignment of public hearings and/or the commission of impact assessments by neutral experts (for example, in the United States, the mandated report by the International Trade Commission). Fire alarm practices before the negotiation include FTA feasibility study groups or advisory committee systems, whereby interest groups can directly express their views regarding a proposed trade negotiation.[17] During the trade talks, they entail bureaucratic briefings to lawmakers and/or affected stakeholders.[18] Post-facto practices include reports from the trade advisory committees or the ability to use mock markup sessions to clarify aspects of the implement bill or press for compensatory benefits to disadvantaged sectors.[19] Unquestionably, the most potent legislative power in any country is to award or deny ratification of the trade agreement, for this ensures that trade negotiators will have to factor in legislative preferences from the onset of the negotiation process if they hope to build a winning coalition for the final vote.

In the U.S. Congress, the will to reauthorize TPA has eroded over time. In contrast to the successive bipartisan votes to delegate trade negotiation authority to the executive for most of the twentieth century (first through RTAA and, later, through the fast-track mechanism), the process of reauthorization became more contested. In the post-NAFTA era, support among congressional Democrats to renew trade promotion authority decreased markedly, and in subsequent votes only a fraction of Democratic lawmakers backed these bills. In 1998, the vote to reauthorize TPA failed, and in 2002, it was secured by a razor-thin margin (by one vote in the House of Representatives). After TPA expired in 2007, it was not possible to renew it until 2015, which happened, once again, with the slightest majority and after an unprecedented setback threatened the prospects of the TPA bill when Democrats voted down the accompanying TAA bill (discussed later in this chapter). The growing reluctance in Congress to reauthorize the delegation of trade negotiation authority is informed by the legitimacy deficits discussed in the previous chapters (on the distribution of the gains from trade, the representativeness of trade policy, and the significance of an expanding trade agenda for domestic regulations).[20] At the most fundamental level, a growing division of purpose among key veto players in the American political system has imposed a heavy toll on trade policy.

The symptoms of a divided polity are evident through expanding partisan divides, polarization among branches of government, and the erosion of intra-party cohesion. Republicans and Democrats have long sparred over the distribution of benefits and costs of trade liberalization, but also about the substance of rules in an expanding trade agenda. On May 10, 2007, a bipartisan compromise was worked out between President George W. Bush and the Democratic Congress, mandating enforceable labor and environmental standards (in addition to adherence to the

International Labor Organization's Declaration on Fundamental Principles of Rights at Work and seven multilateral environmental agreements) in U.S. trade agreements. The May 10 agreement also sought to strike a balance between intellectual property protection and access to medicines by endorsing patent protection through data exclusivity or patent linkage, while making accommodations for developing countries and reaffirming the right of countries to impose compulsory licensing during health crises.[21] Since then, this bipartisan understanding has eroded. Disagreements abound over whether recent trade agreements faithfully abide by the norms of the May 10 agreement, how to deepen and refine these standards in the current crop of trade deals, and how to balance the concerns of different stakeholders in drafting rules to cover cutting-edge trade issues in areas such as the digital economy and biologics.

The partisan divide on the merits and substance of trade policy has been magnified in recent years by the effects of deepened polarization in Washington politics. The lack of cooperation between Barack Obama's White House and the Republican Congress had a chilling effect on policymaking and resulted, at times, in serious crisis points, such as threats by congressional Republicans to not raise the debt ceiling and trigger a U.S. default in 2011, 2013 (with a government shutdown in October), and 2015.

At the same time, the loss of cohesion within the Republican Party in its support for free trade has been striking. It first became apparent when the Tea Party wing of the Republican Party rejected TPA renewal as an unconstitutional encroachment of presidential authority. But it reached new heights when Donald Trump captured the Republican Party nomination for president in July 2016 by mobilizing the party base with a hefty dose of protectionist rhetoric.

The fraying consensus on trade among political actors has led to proposals for easing the process to revoke fast track, and this issue figured prominently in congressional negotiations over the 2015 TPA bill.[22] The "procedural disapproval resolution" allows for stripping a trade agreement from the expedited voting procedures in cases where the negotiation objectives have not been met or the executive has not complied with notification/reporting requirements. Over time, there have been calls to amend the process by which a disapproval resolution can reach the floor for a vote. One such proposal would have effectively bypassed the Senate Finance and House Ways and Means Committees by permitting a sizable minority of members to directly sponsor a disapproval resolution.[23] This proposal was not adopted, but it would have had profound consequences. Because TPA reassures foreign counterparts that deals reached in the negotiations will not unravel at the ratification stage with a flurry of amendments, doubts on the durability of the TPA compact among branches of government would undermine U.S. bargaining power. De facto, the United States would see its number of veto players increase markedly (as different groupings in Congress could torpedo a trade deal), and in such a scenario trade policy would become more indecisive.

The renewed 2015 TPA bill did introduce an additional procedure to strip fast track from a trade agreement known as the "consultation and compliance resolution," which for the first time allows each house to move independently in this process. However, because the majority leaders in the House and Senate, respectively, retain the power to bring it, or not, to a floor vote, the new procedure has not effectively increased the number of congressional veto players.[24] Nevertheless, the growing calls to expedite the disapproval procedures attest to the waning will in Congress to delegate trade negotiation authority.

What ails American trade policy is not the separation of powers per se (as the TPA inter-branch compact has in the past allowed for the appropriate functioning of checks and balances without hindering the trade negotiation credibility of the United States). Rather, it is the separation of purpose that brought to the surface the potential dysfunctions of a fragmented decisionmaking system.

### Bureaucratic Politics

Bureaucratic politics also affect the degree of trade policy centralization. The problem of bureaucratic coordination is inherent to policy areas, like trade, where ministries have overlapping mandates, but it has only intensified with the transformed nature of trade negotiations. The expanding focus on behind-the-border issues has meant that bureaucracies that were in the past considered purely domestic now have a stake in international trade negotiations. As bureaucracies enter the fray of trade policy design and implementation, they are also trying to advance organizational interests, such as the maximization of budgetary allocations, the expansion of turf, the safeguard of autonomy, and the protection of interest groups under their supervision.[25] The bargaining advantages of each bureaucratic player will derive from its formal authority control over resources, policy expertise, manipulation of issue linkages, and alliances with other actors. This tug of war among bureaucratic agencies is best captured by Graham Allison and Philip Zelikow: "The context of shared power but separate judgments about important choices means that politics is the mechanism of choice."[26]

Bureaucratic competition is shaped by institutional rules that define the number of bureaucracies with veto power over trade negotiations and the mechanisms to reconcile bureaucratic differences.[27] These rules can be implicit or explicit, and will differ based on the number of bureaucracies that define the trade agenda and the existence of mechanisms to solve interagency disagreements. Japan and the United States illustrate these differences. Bureaucratic interaction in Japanese trade policy was traditionally guided by the informal norm of unanimity, the *yonshō taisei* system (four ministry structure), and weak coordinating powers vested in the Ministry of Foreign Affairs.[28] These operating procedures made it difficult to override the opposition of recalcitrant ministries seeking to protect narrow interests, so Japanese trade policy was characterized by time-consuming inter-bureaucratic negotiations and modest departures from the status quo (the changes to the negotiation setup that allowed for Japan's participation in the TPP are discussed in chapter 9).[29]

On the other hand, in the United States bureaucratic rules on trade policymaking are formalized and work to establish mechanisms to facilitate interagency coordination. By approving the 1962 Trade Act, Congress formally created the Office of the Special Trade Representative (STR) to act as an honest broker among domestic and international interests in commercial policy. As Destler explains, Congress pushed for the creation of the STR because it was dissatisfied with the performance of the State Department as chief trade negotiator, since it deemed the State Department prioritized foreign policy over domestic interests.[30] The idea was to go beyond the line agencies to strike a better balance between domestic and international interests and to facilitate a broader consensus among the disparate bureaucratic positions.[31] With congressional approval of the 1974 Trade Act, the Special Trade Representative was awarded a cabinet position, and reforms in 1980 better demarcated its functions of developing, coordinating, and negotiating trade policy, as well as renamed it the Office of the United States Trade Representative.[32]

In the United States, the one-step removal of trade negotiation from the line ministries, with the USTR leading interagency negotiations and acting as chief trade negotiator, facilitates speedier domestic and international negotiations and creates fewer obstacles to policy change compared to Japan. But the USTR does not monopolize responsibility over all areas of trade negotiations. Agricultural trade policy and unfair trading remedies (for example, antidumping) remain outside the area of jurisdiction for the USTR, with the Departments of Agriculture and Commerce, respectively, in charge. Periodically, there have been calls to modify this institutional setup. The latest was a proposal in early 2012 to subsume the USTR and several other agencies (the Export-Import Bank, Overseas Private Investment Corporation, Small Business Administration, and so on) under the Commerce Department. However, concerns over the impact that stripping the USTR of its cabinet-level position and its proximity to the president would have on the U.S. ability to strike deals abroad and coordinate domestic interests prevented this proposal from moving forward.[33]

On the other hand, South Korea illustrates how a major realignment in bureaucratic structure can have a significant impact on the conduct of trade policy. Like Japan, South Korea's bureaucracy had been characterized by fragmentation with specific ministries objecting to trade initiatives that could hamper the interests of economic interests under their jurisdiction. The reforms instituted by President Kim Dae-jung in 1998—assigning trade negotiation capabilities to the newly minted Ministry of Foreign Affairs and Trade with a cabinet-level Office of the Minister of Trade—greatly concentrated policy planning and trade negotiations in a powerful bureaucratic agent. The creation three years later of a coordinating mechanism (the Ministerial Meeting on External Economic Affairs) made it possible for the first time to effectively override the opposition of line ministries that had operated as powerful veto players.[34] With strong backing from the president and the newly centralized bureaucratic lineup, South Korea launched a proactive trade policy, inking agreements with the European Union and the United States with robust liberalization targets.[35] Nevertheless, incoming President Park Geun-hye decided in 2013 to devolve trade negotiation authority to the Ministry of Trade, Industry and Energy (which enjoys less autonomy from domestic interest pressures). In its new FTA roadmap, the ministry attached top priority to bilateral trade talks with China and the Regional Comprehensive Economic Partnership (RCEP). In the trade agreement concluded with China in 2015, South Korea displayed a lower level of ambition, since the deal offered modest initial liberalization and both sides agreed to multiple tariff elimination exclusions.[36] RCEP negotiations have been slow moving and the deal is expected to result in lower tariff reductions and slimmer rules. Therefore, in the past few years there has been a marked shift in the level of trade negotiation ambition displayed by South Korea.

The takeaways from this brief overview of bureaucratic politics in trade policymaking are straightforward. Policymaking systems with high fragmentation disperse the trade negotiation mandate over several government agencies, do not establish hierarchical patterns of authority among them, and lack formalized mechanisms to reconcile divergent positions of government agencies.[37] Highly fragmented systems generate policy inmobilism as contested trade policies pit one bureaucratic agency against another in the pursuit of parochial organization interests. To the extent that line agencies control the definition of trade policy positions, it will be harder to break strongholds of protection as bureaucrats will look after the interests of their clients—either to appease the demands of politicians or because of the power derived from presiding over a system of protection (monitoring quotas, disbursing subsidies, and so on). While direct intervention from the political executive can, in principle, break this bureaucratic logjam, such ad hoc intervention will depend on the importance of the trade agenda for the incumbent leader.

In contrast, cohesive decisionmaking should result from the concentration of negotiation authority in a single ministry, the creation of a specialized trade negotiation agency above the line ministries, and/or the establishment of formalized coordination mechanisms to hammer out a unified set of negotiation objectives to diminish the influence of pork barrel politicians and clientelized line agencies. Gains in negotiation efficiency in top-down decisionmaking may, however, come at the expense of a wider representation of interests, as discussed in the next chapter.

## THE POLITICS OF COMPENSATION

Trade liberalization has distributional consequences, prompting actors to mobilize to shape policy outcomes. Resource capability is certainly important to the success of lobbying efforts, but so is the intensity of preferences, with losers from market opening or from exclusion from preferential trade agreements displaying greater lobbying zeal. The clash of organized interests revolves around not only the scope and pace of liberalization but also around compensatory measures that may—or may not—promote genuine social adjustment to economic change.

*Interest Group Politics: Losers Lobby Harder*

The differential impact of trade liberalization on various sectors of an economy accounts for the mobilization of organized interest groups to support or oppose market opening measures. The trade policy preferences of these sectors are largely determined by their position in the international division of labor. Internationally competitive sectors will press for trade agreements to increase export and investment opportunities in foreign markets, to level the playing field vis-à-vis competitors in third markets by neutralizing the advantages of their pre-existing FTAs, and to enhance domestic competitiveness with access to cheaper inputs and technology. On the other hand, import-competing sectors will aim to block the elimination of trade barriers, as they fear the loss of market share to foreign producers, factory closings, and worker layoffs. Therefore, a clash of organized interests is a perennial dynamic in trade politics.

Interest groups have a keen interest in shaping policy outcomes and have availed themselves of a wide repertoire of advocacy strategies to gain influence: lobbying, political contributions, offering or withdrawing campaign support during elections, judicial action, public testimony, and/or participation in deliberative councils on trade negotiations.[38] In fact, the vast academic literature on this topic has yielded important insights on the sources of lobbying effectiveness, the impact of political contributions, and the intensity of mobilization campaigns in trade policy.

With regard to lobbying effectiveness, three main factors are of central importance: internal cohesion, technical sophistication, and electoral mobilization clout. Influential producer associations are able to aggregate the different demands from their members and offer coherent positions, whereas interest groups that are internally divided will be hard-pressed to articulate unified demands to government officials. This pattern is well established in studies that look at foreign economic policy lobbying success both in Latin America and Asia.[39] Given the growing complexity of the trade agenda, the influence of interest groups has increasingly hinged on their technical sophistication. Behind-the-border regulatory matters and complex rules of origin have put a premium on government officials to understand in great detail the operation of specific industries, and interest groups that want to have a say in trade policy must command the ever-growing set of technical issues involved.[40] This has led, as Cornelia Woll and Alvaro Artigas point out, to the emergence of "regulatory lobbying," whereby government officials trade access to policymaking for highly technical market advice.[41]

To the extent that politicians benefit from or fear the ire of interest groups at election time, they will be more sensitive to their demands. Union mobilization to prevent the renewal of TPA in 2015 illustrates these dynamics. On one hand, unity among unions in denouncing TPA has grown. The letter sent on March 2, 2015, by sixty-four member unions of the American Federation of Labor and Congress of Industrial Organizations (AFL-CIO) to urge Congress members to vote down the bill included unions that supported past trade agreements (for example, the United Automobile Workers and the U.S.-Korea FTA).[42] But the union movement also stepped up its efforts to impose an electoral cost on Democratic lawmakers who parted ways on this priority issue. The AFL-CIO executive council moved for the first time to suspend all political contributions until after the TPA vote, promised to withhold help with electoral mobilization (door knocks, phone banks, and so on) at the time of the polls, and, according to some reports, approached undecided House Democrats to warn of potential primary threats funded by the union if they supported TPA.[43]

In assessing the influence of organized interests in public policy formulation, no other issue attracts more attention than the power of money. And trade policy is no exception. One of the most compelling analyses on this issue is Robert Baldwin and Christopher Magee's investigation on the role of political contributions in three signal trade votes in the U.S. Congress: NAFTA, the Uruguay Round, and most-favored-nation status for China.[44] Their key finding is that campaign contributions give access to lawmakers but do not buy votes. These authors demonstrate empirically that an increase in political contributions from business and labor increases the chances of a positive or negative trade vote (respectively), but that lawmakers' votes were also influenced by their ideological preferences, the economic makeup of their constituency, and the state of the economy (export versus import competing employment, unionization rates, worker skills, unemployment rates).

The TPP is the most important trade initiative after the major trade votes of the 1990s, so it should come as no surprise that lobbying for and against this initiative has been intense. According to the Center for Responsive Politics, lobbying filing reports referencing the TPP by all groups peaked in 2014 (1,317 reports) and were still high in 2015 (763 reports), definitely a far cry from the initial level of reports in the early stages of the negotiation (sixty reports in 2009).[45] The amount of political contributions dedicated to their TPP lobbying is not available from this dataset, but the financial clout of the U.S. Chamber of Commerce (the strongest advocate for TPA and the TPP) is well established. It has consistently had the largest lobbying budget of any organization ($124 million in 2014 for its advocacy on all issues) and hefty allocations for outside spending, mostly supporting Republican candidates ($33.4 million in 2014).[46]

In understanding the political viability of trade agreements, one last important dynamic of interest group politics must be factored in: losers lobby harder. Why? This insight was first derived from psychological studies of decisionmaking, which showed that people follow a more cautious approach when presented with the possibility of securing gains but are prepared to take bolder action to prevent losses. Known as prospect theory, this insight has been used to explain international economic cooperation and multilateral trade negotiations.[47] Loss avoidance is, in fact, a key motivating factor of the FTA race that has yielded a spike in the number of trade agreements notified to the World Trade Organization (WTO). The key insight of Richard Baldwin's "domino effect" theory is that, motivated by the prospect of trade and investment diversion of existing preferential trade agreements, outside parties will respond by negotiating their own countervailing FTAs.[48] Chapter 8 shows how this dynamic is alive and well in the era of mega trade agreements as the expansion of a major trade negotiation (Japan joining the TPP) helped overcome obstacles that had hindered the launch of other trade groupings (RCEP, the Japan-EU FTA, and the China-Japan-South Korea FTA).

Within countries, the most intense lobbying battle can be expected between two types of prospective losers: those who will lose if a trade negotiation is launched (because of import competition) and those who will be harmed if it is not (because of trade and investment diversion). If opponents to the trade agreement enjoy sufficient clout to block its eventual ratification, political pragmatism dictates accommodations (in the form of exclusions from tariff elimination, prolonged liberalization calendars, and special safeguards to prevent market disruption from imports) and/or side payments to compensate for concessions on the liberalization front. Hence, the political aims of compensation are clear, but as discussed next, its ability to generate genuine adjustment will be critical to its long-term political effectiveness.

### The Political Effectiveness of Compensation

The notion that offering compensation to losers is essential to liberalization is as old as the debate on free trade itself. Indeed, a noted philosopher, John Stuart Mill, articulated the principle of compensation as necessary to win over the trade battle of the day, the end to the Corn Laws. The case for compensation rests on three grounds: fairness (to make those disadvantaged by trade liberalization whole), efficiency (to solve the market failures in the trade adjustment process), and political efficacy (securing the consent of all veto players opposed to trade liberalization). Criticisms of each of these rationales have long been heard: that trade-impacted workers do not deserve special treatment, that unemployment benefits will discourage people from looking for work, and that compensation is ineffective in making trade initiatives politically viable.

These criticisms notwithstanding, we know from cross-national and cross-temporal studies that safety nets enable liberalization. This is the key finding of Thomas Brambor and Johannes Lindvall's ambitious study covering thirty-two countries over a span of 140 years (from the 1870s to the present).[49] They find that state capacity is central to bringing about liberalization: fiscal capacity to forego tariffs as a major revenue source for government activities, and social capacity to offer unemployment insurance. This second insight demonstrates that states that lack credibility in offering a basic fallback option for displaced workers have been frustrated in their attempts to lower tariffs.

Rather than debating whether or not to extend compensation to losers from liberalization, the central issue is how to do it in a manner that achieves its two central goals: to accomplish genuine economic and social adjustment and to create the political conditions to sustain free trade. Absent the first, the second objective will not materialize. These are the powerful lessons to be gleaned from the evolution of the Trade Adjustment Assistance program in the United States. The TAA was born as a quid pro quo deal with labor to preempt mobilization against trade liberalization. However, over time, the limits of a trade-specific adjustment program to deal with the broader challenges of economic transition for the American workforce, especially at a time of growing income inequality, have become clearer (see chapter 7). This, in turn, has strained the ability of TAA to operate as an effective grand bargain in favor of liberalization. In fact, in the latest congressional reauthorization vote, it became an instrument to torpedo the TPA bill. We seem to have come full circle.

The political need to offer compensation to obtain acquiescence for trade liberalization gave birth to TAA. Unions were early advocates of assistance for trade-impacted workers. The president of United Steelworkers introduced this notion in the Randall Commission, which was chartered by President Dwight Eisenhower in 1953 to draft recommendations on foreign economic policy. During the rest of the decade, the AFL-CIO continued to press for its adoption, insisting that adjustment assistance was a prerequisite to support trade liberalization authority.[50] Launched in 1962, as the United States prepared to participate in the Kennedy Round, the TAA program offered workers extended unemployment benefits and retraining and relocation assistance; for firms, it made available technical assistance, tax breaks, loans, and loan guarantees. Soon after its launch, organized labor became disenchanted with the new worker assistance program. The original TAA set strict eligibility criteria requiring petitioners to demonstrate that tariff cuts were producing material injury. Since this was a very high bar, the program remained inactive during its first few years with no certifications. To rebuild labor support for the trade agenda, the Trade Act of 1974 substantially loosened TAA's certification guidelines in that it was necessary only to show that imports had contributed to a decline of employment or sales.[51]

However, from that moment forward the link between TAA and union support for trade liberalization began to fade, reaching a low point by the early 1970s (where it has remained) and leading to the oft-used characterization of TAA as "burial insurance."[52] Hence, a new pattern emerged whereby unions supported TAA but sought to disconnect it from reauthorization of trade promotion authority or ratification of trade agreements. Most recently, AFL-CIO President Richard Trumka articulated this view: "The Trade Adjustment Assistance program has a history of success helping U.S. workers get back on their feet when their jobs are offshored. And we owe it to them to prevent TAA from being linked to the undemocratic Fast Track process, which paves the way for fewer jobs and lower wages."[53]

For a long time, unions have tried to sever the tie between TAA and trade liberalization, but this was not the dynamic of congressional votes, where the fates of TAA and TPA were joined at the hip. Examples of this abound. For instance, NAFTA generated strong resistance from organized workers who feared the loss of employment opportunities due to lower wages in Mexico. To ensure ratification of this free trade agreement, the U.S. government, for the first time, included an FTA-specific TAA program in the NAFTA implementing bill. Reauthorization of the TAA program was similarly considered crucial for the George W. Bush administration to obtain trade promotion authority in 2002, and more recently Democrats insisted on the reauthorization of an expanded TAA program to pass the three FTAs with Korea, Panama, and Colombia in 2011.[54] As Congress prepared to vote on renewing trade promotion authority in 2015—essential to the eventual passage of the TPP—an accompanying TAA bill was also at hand. In fact, the 2015 version of TAA was more generous than its previous 2014 version in very significant ways: it extended coverage to services industry workers and to workers impacted by trade from all sources (not only that originating from FTA partners), and it provided a sizable increase in funding for training from $220 million per year to $450 million.[55]

Why has TAA been so integral to the congressional politics of trade, considering it has not guaranteed labor's endorsement of trade agreements for a long time? Electoral politics provide the best answer; voters care deeply about job losses attributed to foreign trade, and TAA is an effective political device to hedge against electoral punishment. Relying on survey analysis in the United States, Yotam Margalit found that U.S. voters are particularly sensitive to job losses created by foreign competition and that incumbents are better able to escape electoral punishment in districts where more workers have received certification for trade-related assistance.[56] There is, in fact, a strong political rationale for offering assistance specifically for trade-displacement, as those who expect to lose from liberalization have an intense preference for targeted relief but not as much for general unemployment schemes.[57] Moreover, TAA has been essential to building a bipartisan coalition in support of trade. Given the strong ties of the Democratic Party to organized labor, the promise of some form of assistance for displaced workers was essential for any Democrat in Congress to consider voting positively on TPA renewal or ratification of specific trade agreements, so for a long time the bulk of support of TPA bills came from the Republican side of the aisle and support for the TAA bills from the Democratic side. Approving one measure was contingent on passing the other.

This predictable pattern was upended when the majority of House Democrats, with the backing of their union supporters, voted against TAA on June 12, 2015, to prevent approval of TPA and, thus, stall the Obama administration's trade agenda. In fact, in that vote, a much larger number of Republicans (eighty-six) voted in favor of TAA than Democrats (forty). This vote flipped the traditional partisan divide on TAA and introduced a novel element, with House Democrats prepared to scuttle a worker training program they had supported for fifty years to prevent the approval of TPA. Indeed, while the House narrowly approved the TPA bill that same day (with the support of twenty-eight Democrats), it could not be enacted, as both bills were part of a combined package. The eventual approval of TPA and TAA was only possible through the coordinated efforts of the Obama White House, a fraction of the Democratic members of Congress, and the Republican congressional leadership. It required a number of coordinated moves: votes in both houses on a stand-alone TPA bill, overcoming a potential Senate filibuster, and approving TAA by attaching it to a separate Trade Preferences Act. It represented a high mark in cooperation among political actors who had long sparred over many issues but shared a common purpose in rescuing the trade agenda, and it underscores why the disagreements between the White House and the Republican leadership, over several provisions of the final TPP agreement, exerted a powerful shadow on the prospects of TPP ratification during the remainder of the Obama administration.[58]

The discussion above underscores how strained the political compact between TAA and TPA is. President Obama had to delink these two bills to pave the way for Democrats to support TAA. In "freeing the hostage" (signaling his willingness to sign a stand-alone TPA bill), President Obama eliminated the rationale for House Democrats to vote down TAA to block trade negotiations.[59] The wisdom of House Democrats in voting down a bill that provides important benefits to workers in import-competing sectors aside, the dwindling political effectiveness of TAA is unquestionable. Key challenges loom ahead in recasting a more effective safety net that can sustain open trade policies; a topic that is addressed in the next chapter.

## CHAPTER SEVEN

# Dilemmas of Trade Governance

## Navigating Vexing Trade-Offs

THE PREVIOUS CHAPTERS laid out the essential goals of trade policy: to maximize economic competitiveness and secure international leadership; to gain public support for the trade agenda by addressing concerns over income inequality, job displacement, the protection of public interest regulations, and adequate oversight over trade negotiators; and to align domestic politics to ensure the ratification of trade agreements. Each goal (competitiveness, legitimacy, political viability) is desirable and challenging in its own right, but the simultaneous pursuit of these objectives creates uncomfortable trade-offs, as achieving one goal may require sacrifices elsewhere.

Policymakers confront at least two fundamental dilemmas as they chart their trade policy strategy. First, the centralization of trade policymaking helps override the hold of vested interests on trade policy but insulates government officials from bottom-up demands from civil society, so that efficiency gains of expedited decisionmaking and greater market opening may come at the expense of social support and legitimacy of trade policy. Second, side payments to losers from trade liberalization can help gain their approval of market opening initiatives, but the steady flow of subsidies may hinder the revamping of inefficient sectors and political compensation can come at the expense of developing genuine safety nets for trade adjustment. Therefore, the political pragmatism of co-opting powerful vested groups and awarding targeted side payments may compromise economic reforms and support for economic internationalism.

This chapter draws from varied national experiences to illuminate the trade governance dilemmas at work, and offers concrete strategies to navigate these exacting trade-offs. The first section, on the decisiveness versus inclusiveness dilemma, underscores the importance of increasing trade policy representativeness. Expanding the circle of consultation to include a more diverse set of stakeholders responds to legitimate demands for public input without compromising the degree of centralization required to avoid policy capture by vested interests. The second section, addressing the subsidization versus reform dilemma, highlights the importance of developing a pro-adjustment general safety net with skill acquisition and upgrading at its core. Investments in human capital are essential to avoid increased inequality and a turn inward. The third section of this chapter summarizes the lessons learned in the previous chapters from the experience of the United States. It underscores the relevance of the trade governance dilemmas to understand the critical choices the United States confronts today if it is to renew the internationalism that has undergirded its postwar leadership role. The path the United States chooses, and any future correction course, will loom large in how Japan navigates its own trade policy dilemmas.

## DILEMMA 1: DECISIVENESS VERSUS INCLUSIVENESS

Centralized political systems are more capable of enacting new policies, quite simply because there are fewer actors that can stop the process by exercising a veto. Moreover, top-down executive decisionmaking facilitates the execution of economic reforms by overriding vested interests and preventing the emergence or continuation of iron triangles (the collusion of politicians, bureaucrats, and economic groups) that favor a status quo of inflated profits and/or protection.[1] But what is gained in policy efficiency (both ambition and speed) may be lost in terms of inclusion of other institutional actors or other groups in society, with a consequent erosion of public trust and acceptance of the reforms. The lack of input from affected stakeholders may negatively impact the quality of proposed policies, undermining their positive impact as well, and the lack of access itself may generate opposition to the newly charted policy course and invite unlikely alliances among groups that have no shared stakes in the negotiations other than the grievance of exclusion. Striking the right balance between decisiveness and inclusion is not easy; every decision to expand the decisionmaking circle must be weighed against the possibility of reform foes gaining access to undermine the process from within.

The tension between decisiveness and inclusion is particularly acute in trade policy. As mentioned in chapter 4, the evolution of the trade agenda toward regulatory matters drastically increased the number of groups in society with a stake in trade negotiations. Moreover, the information and communications revolution has increased demands for information disclosure, and social media has helped connect many groups that in the past would have had few opportunities for interaction. These trends have presented governments with the steep challenge of increasing transparency without eroding the confidentiality of trade negotiations and expanding the circle of stakeholder consultation without compromising the ability to generate a cohesive trade policy. As many governments are perceived to come up short in improving transparency and consultation, bold executive actions in negotiating major trade agreements have frequently produced backlash from actors that resent their exclusion, be they interest groups, public advocacy organizations, and/or legislators.

Chapter 6 discussed the evolving balance of power between the legislative and executive branches of government, which has also shifted with the transformation of the trade agenda. Legislators not only respond to the traditional import-competing/export-oriented constituency demands, but must also react to the host of groups affected by regulatory changes. Legislatures in many different countries have been dissatisfied with their post-facto powers of ratification of completed trade agreements, and have advocated for greater input earlier in the negotiations and/or tighter monitoring of trade negotiators. Disagreements with the executive branch over the extent to which legislative preferences have been incorporated in a trade deal can lead to ratification crises and/or amendments to specific chapters to secure legislative approval.[2] As a rule of thumb, top-down action by the executive will raise the temperature of the legislative vote on trade agreement approval.

Access (or lack thereof) has been critical to the response of civil society to trade negotiations. Societal actors interested in influencing the trade agenda have bifurcated into insider and outsider groups. The former, while challenging some aspects of the government strategy, still seek to influence policy from within established mechanisms for deliberation. The latter reject proposed trade initiatives more forcefully and eschew consultation with public officials in favor of media campaigns or direct protest.[3] Therefore, while both groups use a mix of strategies, there is a clear predisposition in the choice of advocacy tools. Groups that can trade resources (such as votes, campaign funds, knowledge) to secure access rely on strategies that maximize benefits from proximity to policymakers: briefings, participation in advisory councils, and expert testimony, for example. On the other hand, groups without direct access will primarily use outside lobbying strategies such as online petitions, press releases, traditional and social media campaigns, sit-ins, and demonstrations.[4] Some of these public interest advocacy groups have little interest in acquiring insider status; their high level of public activity is critical to their survival by maintaining the loyalty of their diffuse membership and increasing the number of their supporters.[5]

When is outside lobbying effective? Essentially when it increases the visibility of a policy issue, turns around public opinion, and triggers a mobilization cascade from other NGOs, thereby persuading policymakers it would be politically costly to disregard the souring public sentiment.[6] Chances of success are higher when public campaigns center on issues that generate strong emotion, can identify direct causes, and offer quick remedies.[7] These are the factors that Andreas Dür and Gemma Mateo identified in the successful campaign of European citizen groups to derail the Anti-Counterfeiting Trade Agreement (ACTA).[8] Prior to their mobilization, ACTA had not been in the public eye, nor had the European Parliament displayed a critical disposition toward the agreement. But a successful outside lobbying strategy collecting millions of signatures, bringing large demonstrations to several European cities, and enlisting the support of multiple NGOs eventually turned the tide in the European Parliament, which decisively struck down the agreement.[9]

In East Asia, top-down decisions on major trade policy departures have generated significant pushback from legislatures and civil society with complaints over nontransparent deliberations and little inclusion of stakeholders. Eric Batalla details how Malaysia and Thailand were able to negotiate trade agreements with Japan more expeditiously, given the higher degree of centralization in the executive (no ratification by the legislature was required), compared to the slower pace of negotiations of the Philippines, where Senate concurrence for international treaties is mandatory for enactment.[10] The Malaysian cabinet was adamant about excluding government procurement (to continue special treatment of ethnic Malays), but agreed to significant tariff elimination in autos to lure Japanese investment and move forward with major reform of the automobile sector (adopting a revamped National Automotive Policy). Prime Minister Thaksin Shinawatra of Thailand unleashed a whirlwind of trade diplomacy and singlehandedly decided to exclude rice in the negotiations with Japan to expedite the talks. But swift executive action in both countries triggered major opposition campaigns to trade agreements, which crystallized during subsequent negotiations with the United States and brought those negotiations to naught. In the case of the Philippines, the ratification process added significant delays to the enactment of the trade agreement with Japan. The Senate denounced the meager disclosure of information during the negotiations, it clashed with (and prevailed over) the presidency over its authority to ratify the agreement, and it requested additional notes of assurance from Japan (for example, on rules on toxic waste) before it voted positively.[11]

South Korea provides one of the clearest examples of the dynamic interaction between state decisiveness and social contestation.[12] As noted in chapter 6, the centralization of trade negotiation authority in the executive branch (Ministry of Foreign Affairs and Trade—MOFAT) enabled the launch of a high-yield trade strategy, with South Korea negotiating trade agreements with large economic partners (the EU and the United States) and making unprecedented liberalization commitments. However, the top-down process of trade policy formulation triggered serious domestic opposition from excluded groups. Although the government established a consultation mechanism with nongovernmental sources after it encountered serious opposition to the enactment of the Korea-Chile FTA, it mostly incorporated input from business interests, not the losers of trade liberalization (farmers and unions) and NGOs. These groups opposed the trade liberalization campaign and mobilized against their exclusion from the consultation process. The anti-FTA movement evolved into an eclectic mix of student activists, unions, farmers, opposition party politicians, and citizen groups. The Korean Alliance Against KORUS FTA (the U.S.-Korea Free Trade Agreement familiarly known as KORUS or KORUS FTA) alone gathered 300 member organizations, and the level of protest activity was very high, with large worker strikes (gathering 74,000 and 100,000 protestors).[13] Social dissent reached its heyday in the summer of 2008 with widespread candlelight vigils to protest President Lee Myung-bak's decision to end restrictions on American beef imports to facilitate the ratification of the KORUS FTA.[14] These vigils were spurred by a new wave of netizens (predominantly women and students) expanding the reach of traditional NGO activism, and they eventually compelled President Lee to revert back to restrictions on beef imports of older cattle.[15]

The demonstrations in the streets denouncing a democratic deficit in Korean trade policy occurred in tandem with attempts in the National Assembly to expand the role of the legislature in trade policy, making it compulsory for the executive to disclose information on FTAs to legislators and ensuring that the National Assembly would be involved in the negotiation much earlier, not just at the ratification stage.[16] In their quest to curb executive power over trade policy, Korean legislators resorted to judicial measures, filing a complaint in September 2006 in the Constitutional Court that the administration had infringed on the prerogatives of the legislature.[17] And legislators also attempted to enact greater oversight, submitting different versions of a Trade Procedures Act over the years. These attempted reforms aimed to give the National Assembly greater clout over the direction of trade negotiations by requiring legislative approval over the appointment of the chief trade negotiator (then the director of the Trade Negotiation Headquarters in MOFAT) and the selection of half of the participants on the Private Advisory Committee, in addition to full disclosure of FTA policies from the executive to the legislative before, during, and after the negotiations. Korea's trade negotiators (then housed in MOFAT) fought back, arguing that these reporting obligations would hamper the executive's ability to negotiate trade agreements.[18]

The profound disagreement over the proper balance of executive–legislative powers on trade policy formulation translated into recurrent ratification crises in Korean FTA policy. Due to the determined opposition of Korean legislators, it took four attempts for the National Assembly to finally vote on the FTA with Chile, and later on, the main opposition party boycotted the ratification vote on the trade agreement with the European Union.[19] The most volatile ratification crisis centered on the KORUS FTA, and the actions of both the ruling and opposition parties inflicted a serious blow to the confidence of the democratic process in Korea. In a surprise move, the ruling party called for a closed plenary session to vote on the KORUS FTA with only a handful of opposition party members present. To delay the vote, a lawmaker from the opposition Democratic Labor Party detonated a tear gas canister in the chamber, creating a chaotic situation.[20]

Eventually, the trade agreement passed, but the deep sense of political crisis from this episode led, finally, to the approval of the Trade Procedures Act in 2012. As discussed by Younsik Kim, the gist of the reforms was increased public input and a strengthened role for the National Assembly.[21] The Trade Procedures Act mandated MOFAT to establish a Trade Advisory Committee to receive expert advice from specialists, and also created a new FTA Domestic Measures Committee to disseminate information, gather public views on trade agreements, and assist in the legislative process. The Trade Procedures Act also made significant changes to transform the reactive role of the National Assembly (with legislators kept out of the information loop and playing a role at the end of the process through the ratification vote). The new system gives power to the National Assembly to request the executive to start trade negotiations, and it mandates the establishment of a monitoring committee to scrutinize ongoing FTA talks.

These examples of trade politics dynamics in nations across the Pacific display the competing pressures to centralize decisionmaking to avoid policy capture and to open access windows to remain responsive to society's concerns with the pace and direction of liberalization. These tensions create the first dilemma of trade governance:

> Centralization of trade policymaking facilitates the negotiation of more ambitious trade agreements by breaking the stronghold of protectionist interests. However, it can also undermine legitimacy if trade policy formulation becomes exclusionary. The risks are to encourage the formation of an unlikely coalition among excluded groups (vested economic interests fearing loss of economic privileges and civil society groups mobilized by value-driven campaigns) and/or to provoke a significant amount of social contestation of trade liberalization efforts.

### Tackling the Trade Governance Dilemma: Increasing the Representativeness of Trade Policy

Social backlash and ratification crises can undermine the original goals of launching an ambitious trade strategy if they erode support for the trade agenda and/or doom the prospects of enacting trade agreements. Therefore, moves to centralize trade policymaking to avoid policy capture from vested interest groups should be concurrent with efforts to strengthen legislative oversight during negotiations and establish an inclusionary consultation process with civil society. Better governance ensues from decisive welfare-enhancing reforms, democratic account-ability, and public participation. National systems for trade policy for-mulation must strive to deliver on all three fronts, notwithstanding the challenges identified.

Trade advisory mechanisms offer an effective vehicle to reconcile a purposive trade strategy with public demands for participation. Expand-ing the loop of consultation is not akin to expanding the decisionmaking circle. The former implies more diverse advice, the second a larger num-ber of vetoes. The former fosters deliberation on balancing competing interests and generates social trust; the latter risks policy paralysis by adding actors with the power to block trade initiatives. Nevertheless, as noted in chapter 5, many governments have established consultation mech-anisms in a reactive way, pressed by the need to overcome a legitimacy deficit, and have made limited progress in expanding the range of views represented or in encouraging dialogue among diverse constituencies.

The slow move toward a multistakeholder consultation system is not due to government hesitation alone. The evolution of the American trade advisory system shows both reluctance from business groups to work in mixed committees and the refusal of NGOs to agree to confidentiality clauses that protect the integrity of trade negotiations. The American trade advisory system has been reformed in the past, and it should be reformed again. For example, expanding and energizing tier two com-mittees should be a priority. This is not a call to revive the Public Inter-est Trade Advisory Committee; lumping all public interest organizations in a separate committee is not conducive to the examination of cross-cutting issues from across the range of stakeholder interests. Rather, it would mean elevating some of the Industry Trade Advisory Commit-tees, which have much wider implications beyond specific economic sec-tors, to tier two committees with mixed membership. The committees on intellectual property and digital economy clearly fit this description. And far from being "slow-action" committees with infrequent meetings, there should be an expanded effort to generate an ongoing, robust dialogue, since these committees would be best geared to address the man-ifold dimensions of the regulatory agenda in trade negotiations. Mecha-nisms to encourage interaction among advisory committees across the three tiers, such as liaison meetings or plenaries, should also be devised. These reforms could create feedback loops among committees, diversify membership, and maintain the role of ITACs in providing technical ad-vice. Another useful suggestion comes from the U.S. Government Accountability Office; it proposes that the Office of the United States Trade Representative discuss in its annual report how the particular membership of each committee achieves a fair representation of interests.[22]

The goal should be to upgrade the internal consultation mechanism with stakeholders to reflect the transformed agenda of deep trade negotiations. Solving this governance dilemma calls for increasing the representativeness of trade policy formulation.

## DILEMMA 2: SUBSIDIZATION VERSUS REFORM

Compensation to losers from liberalization has long figured prominently in debates over trade policy formulation. This is not surprising given that policymakers are trying to achieve a number of important goals through compensatory policies: facilitate economic and social adjustment, cultivate public support for trade, and reward political allies. But the fact that different rationales are at play in trade compensation is important. Depending on which motive has a stronger pull—economic reform or political appeasement—the substance of the compensation package will vary, with significant implications for the impact of trade agreements and the subsequent political battles over further market opening.

Whether the prime driver of compensatory policies is subsidization for political aims or adjustment assistance to enable economic reforms will be reflected in two main ways. At the macro level, it will affect patterns of government spending (that is, the choice between funding a general safety net or targeting succor to select, politically powerful, sectors). At the micro level, it will influence the design of the compensation program to make assistance contingent on reform implementation or to extend subsidies without conditionality. In other words, depending on their content, compensatory policies can be a boon or a bust for economic reform through trade agreements.

Why are economy-wide safety nets that cushion the blow of globalization preferable to narrowly targeted benefits for just a few sectors or workers in the economy? The key difference is that general safety nets aim to assist, not block, adjustment by providing assistance to workers and companies to exit contracting sectors, whereas the purpose of sector programs is often to extend subsidies to preserve dying sectors. In other words, their intended effect is to blunt economic change.[23] Horizontal policies that aim to solve market failure in the adjustment process have in fact proven to yield more benefits than sectoral programs that aim to address firm failure.[24]

This consensus on the advantages of general safety nets over targeted subsidies notwithstanding, there is strong evidence that governments frequently opt for directed compensatory programs because they can derive the political benefits of shielding powerful political actors from the brunt of adjustment. The political pull is strong; affected constituencies will demand policies to preserve the status quo, while politicians can claim credit for delivering specific benefits to their support groups.

The choice for targeted support has important consequences. When fiscal resources are finite, monies devoted to particular sectors can come at the expense of spending on general safety nets. This is the pattern that Stephanie Rickard documented by looking at government spending patterns of forty-four developing countries from 1981 to 1997.[25] In essence, powerful interests acquiesce to trade liberalization by staking a "new claim on governments' fiscal resources."[26] This amounted to the perpetuation of rents through other means.

Beyond the balance of government spending toward general or targeted compensatory programs, the design itself of compensation programs will determine whether they will encourage or discourage the process of economic reform. Pro-adjustment compensation policies should be transitory (not create a claim on permanent rent flows), transparent (to avoid diversion to other purposes), commensurate with the adjustment cost (to avoid an excessive fiscal burden), and should not blunt market signals (to avoid stalling the prospects of reform implementation).[27] Regarding displaced workers, governments can facilitate labor market adjustment by complementing unemployment insurance with active labor market policies that encourage workers to upgrade skills and/or move to expanding sectors of the economy. In particular, the aim should be to encourage labor mobility and incentivize reemployment with measures such as wage insurance (temporarily covering income losses from new jobs with lower wages) and portable pension plans.[28] On the other hand, to the extent that compensation programs offer open-ended commitments to the subsidization of inefficient firms/industries, contemplate exclusively passive labor market policies that discourage reemployment, overcompensate in direct relation to the political clout of the recipient, and fail to condition assistance to positive adjustment, they will thwart the goal of reform implementation.

In sum, the adjustment impact of compensation policies is not a given. It depends on their design. A look at the experience of two countries with trade-specific adjustment programs, the United States and South Korea, illustrates the challenges of devising targeted compensatory packages that deliver genuine market reform and social adjustment.[29] The heart of the American Trade Adjustment Assistance (TAA) program has been adjustment assistance for workers, with much smaller programs for firms and farmers.[30] In addition to extended unemployment insurance, TAA benefits have expanded over time to include training subsidies, relocation and job search allowances, a health insurance tax credit, and wage insurance for older workers (to compensate temporarily for reduced wages in a new job). The trend has been to emphasize active versus passive labor adjustment measures by making unemployment benefits contingent on training, with growing emphasis on job search and reemployment subsidies.

Despite these gradual improvements, the limitations of TAA in facilitating worker adjustment are clear. In its earlier iterations, the program did not have a built-in mechanism to assess its efficacy, although the Labor Department has since identified three key long-term goals to measure success: reemployment, retention, and wage level.[31] Most studies concur that TAA has helped workers find new employment, but at a much lower wage.[32] Between 2009 and 2014, 70 percent of TAA petitions were accepted to cover 780,000 workers; the average rate at which these participants found employment during this period was 68 percent, and 90 percent of them had retained the new job six months after the initial hire.[33] However, these new jobs have frequently come with deep wage cuts. For example, Kara Reynolds and John Palatucci found that workers enrolled in TAA reported a 30 percent wage reduction in their new jobs.[34] Hence, income erosion is the most trenchant critique of adjustment assistance for workers. Moreover, a comprehensive assessment of implementation outcomes of the 2002 TAA Reform Act failed to find significant economic payoffs to certified workers enrolled in TAA compared to noncertified workers.[35] In other words, the program was not deemed cost effective since it did not provide a leg up to participants to rebound from dislocation compared to the rest of the workforce. Despite the training and employment search benefits, TAA certified workers received lower wages upon reemployment compared to non-TAA participants, and this gap was not fully closed after the four-year observation period. As these authors point out, one of the reasons for this unimpressive outcome was that half of TAA participants did not enroll in training since they requested waivers while still receiving extended unemployment benefits.[36]

Other problems in the TAA program have also hindered its ability to smooth the transition for displaced workers. One is that the certification process itself is time-consuming and creates uncertainty about whether the program's benefits will be available to applicants. Another is the inconsistency in eligibility criteria and benefits across the different TAA bills approved over the years: whether or not coverage extends to service workers, whether coverage extends to workers impacted by all trade or only trade originating from FTA partners, and whether or not an important set of reemployment services, such as case management and vocational orientation, is funded. Another limitation is that the benefits awarded to workers to promote geographical mobility are woefully insufficient (a $1,250 relocation allotment). The ability to leave depressed communities is critical to future prospects as TAA participants who moved to states with stronger economies reported higher employment rates.[37] Finally, one of the TAA benefits that clearly incentivizes employment (wage insurance upon reemployment to alleviate income erosion) is only extended to a subset of eligible workers (those in the older cohorts).

Given these shortcomings, TAA has been justified not as a cost-effective mechanism to promote genuine worker adjustment but in terms of its powers of persuasion: "if TAA made even a relatively modest contribution to the ease of enacting free trade policies, the program's benefits would outweigh its costs."[38] However, as discussed in chapter 6, the political effectiveness of TAA has significantly eroded over time. Recent research on the marginal role of TAA in facilitating adjustment in regional labor markets impacted by import competition with China provides clues as to why this is the case. David Autor, David Dorn, and Gordon Hanson estimate that benefits transfers for impacted workers offset only a small portion ($58) of the annual wage loss per adult ($549), and that the least consequential were TAA benefits ($3.65).[39] Because TAA compensation has not delivered effective adjustment, it has lost ground in cultivating support for free trade.

A similar concern with mitigating opposition to trade liberalization prompted South Korea to institute an FTA compensation program for farmers (and later, firms and workers). From the launch of its first FTA with Chile in 1999 to the signing of its most ambitious trade negotiation with the United States in 2007, the South Korean government resorted to side payments to farmers to avoid a ratification crisis. In its earlier versions, the farmer compensation programs did not seek to promote agricultural modernization and overcompensated for damages expected from trade liberalization, and the eligibility criteria were loose enough that producers not impacted by FTAs also could seek benefits. For example, the Chile FTA compensation fund provided direct payments for price drops and buyout funds for retiring farmers but no competitiveness enhancement measures. Moreover, even though import competition adjustment was estimated at 5.6 billion won, the compensation program ran at 1.2 trillion won as repeated attempts to bring the FTA to a successful ratification vote came to naught and compensation demands escalated. Payments for farm closures were poorly targeted; the largest beneficiaries were the producers of peaches (who received 88 percent of the total) even though there were no peaches imported from Chile.[40] Farmers were also known to game the system by temporarily closing their orchards to receive subsidies, only to reopen them later.

Significant development took place when the KORUS FTA compensation package earmarked 7 trillion won (out of 20.4 trillion won total) to competitiveness improvement programs (for example, promoting crop diversification), although the largest share was dedicated to income stabilization efforts (12.2 trillion won).[41] Despite this improvement, South Korean agricultural competitiveness continues to be impaired by the small scale of production and the ageing of farmers. Between 1990 and 2012, the average farm size grew from 1.19 to only 1.50 hectares, and the average age of farmers continues to increase.[42] To promote genuine agricultural modernization, the Organisation for Economic Co-operation and Development (OECD) recommends South Korea move away from the traditional reliance on price and product supports and promote long-term competitiveness through measures that have been underfunded, such as agricultural research and innovation.[43]

The bulk of South Korea's trade compensation programs have targeted farmers, but the government opened a new program to provide adjustment assistance to firms and workers when it negotiated the trade deal with the United States. South Korea's TAA program is, however, the mirror image of its American counterpart. The majority of funds (92 percent) go to firms, not workers. Benefits to trade-impacted firms include discounted loans as well as consulting services, but funds for the latter purpose represent only a fraction of spending: 2 percent of the 9.6 billion won allocated to thirty-nine certified firms by 2013.[44] The contribution of this program to positive adjustment is questionable. In a survey of Korean firms, Inkyo Cheong and Jungran Cho found that firms not damaged by FTAs had often obtained support, that no firm received consulting services to retool their production strategies, and that many firms did not know that improving performance was a prerequisite and would not have applied to the TAA program if they were expected to change their business strategy.[45] On worker adjustment, there are no expanded unemployment benefits, but certified workers qualify for financial assistance for retraining, relocation, and reemployment. However, the financial amounts channeled to workers have been very modest.[46] More generally, South Korea still ranks below the OECD average in terms of spending on active labor market policies.

The inherent tensions in the design of trade compensation policies are captured well in the national experiences reviewed here. On the one hand, political pragmatism dictates the use of compensation as a side payment to win the acquiescence of opponents of liberalization, who will seek targeted benefits that prolong the status quo. On the other hand, the reform agenda mandates designing compensation programs that aim to bolster, not retard, economy-wide upgrading along the lines of comparative advantage. These cross-purposes create a second trade governance dilemma on the tension between politically expedient subsidization and desirable economic reforms:

> Side payments may ease the resistance from disadvantaged sectors to liberalization, allowing the government to participate successfully in trade negotiations. But politically motivated compensation may sidetrack economic reforms and empower vested interests to demand further subsidization. The twin risks are that side payments to producer groups will prolong the status quo, negating the reform benefits of liberalization, and that targeted compensation programs will come at the expense of genuine adjustment for displaced workers hollowing out support for free trade.

### *Tackling the Trade Governance Dilemma: Pro-Adjustment Safety Nets to Manage Economic Transition*

Intensified anti-globalization backlash and the growing appeal of inward-looking economic policies underscore that inclusive growth is a prerequisite to sustain open-economy policies in democratic polities. This realization calls for major reconsideration about how to address the uneven reach of economic opportunity and the hollowing out of the middle class in many industrialized nations. In the American case, it certainly means that doubling down on the current approach of incremental changes to TAA will accomplish little. Rather, the United States should launch a pro-adjustment safety net to address the risks of economic transition for all workers. A general safety net will eliminate the difficulties and uncertainty of certifying workers as impacted by trade and will avoid endorsing the view that the "harms" of trade liberalization require special compensation.[47] More important, a universal safety net has a much better chance to deliver effective adjustment assistance to displaced workers.

Job dislocation from economic change—the result of numerous forces such as technological waves, trade liberalization, or macroeconomic downturns—imposes a heavy toll on affected workers. The challenge for laid-off workers in finding new employment at a comparable wage is steep, and it may compromise their lifelong earnings potential. Some of the costs emerge from the loss of seniority and occupation-specific human capital investments. A skill mismatch may also prevent the redundant workers from transitioning to new economic sectors with growth potential. Job competition among redundant workers will be particularly steep during recessions, triggering high unemployment rates, mass layoffs in a specific industry, and situations where limited geographical mobility hinders relocation from depressed communities with dire employment prospects.

Hence, a pro-adjustment safety net must set as its mission the protection of people and incomes, not the preservation of specific jobs.[48] Attempting to block economic change will deny growth opportunities to all, but a safety net that allows displaced workers to bounce back from economic hardship is essential to economic vitality and social stability. Moreover, this safety net must be informed by the fact that labor flexibility (ease of firing and hiring workers) is not sufficient to generate smooth adjustment. Rather, policies that target labor mobility are required, and this mobility must be broadly understood to enable workers to relocate geographically, to enter new occupations and fields, and to move up in the skill ladder.

Therefore, the revamped safety net must embrace and invest in active labor market policies that seek to increase the employability of workers and match job-seekers with employers through training, job-search assistance, direct job creation, and employment incentives (for instance, making wage insurance available to all workers and loosening the eligibility criteria for the Earned Income Tax Credit for lower-income workers). Critical to these efforts must be skill acquisition and upgrading. In fact, skills figure prominently in the answers to some fundamental questions: Who is out of the workforce? Why is wage inequality rising?

A study by the Council of Economic Advisors recently documented the worrying decrease in U.S. labor force participation of prime-age (ages twenty-five to fifty-four) male workers from 98 percent in 1954 to 88 percent in 2015.[49] The withdrawal from work has not been even among groups of different educational attainment. In 1964 there were minor differences in the rate of labor force participation for prime-age workers regardless of the educational background (all in the 96 to 98 percent range). By 2015 a radically different picture emerged, with the level of worker skills playing a significant role in the rate of workforce participation: 93 percent for prime-age males with a bachelor's degree or higher, 87 percent for those with some college experience, and 83 percent for workers with a high school diploma or below. The gap in salary remuneration also greatly expanded in these years. In 1975, the wage of a high school graduate was equivalent to 80 percent of the wage for workers with higher educational attainment; today it is only 60 percent.[50] These data points speak to the rising problems of skill mismatch and labor market rigidities (with close to 5.9 million unfilled job openings in the United States in July 2016) and growing wage inequality.[51] They corroborate a larger finding for the group of OECD countries as a whole: educational attainment largely influences likelihood of employment, and economies that are unable to fill the growing demand for high-level skills experience higher wage inequality—with the United States registering the second highest level of wage disparity after South Korea.[52]

Active labor market policies have a proven record in ameliorating the problems of wage erosion and unemployment in OECD nations. Several studies corroborate that training has helped increase the lifelong earning potential for workers, that increased spending in active labor market policies reduces the unemployment rate, and that these labor market programs help sustain free trade policies in the industrialized world—with training, job search assistance, and start-up incentives as some of the most influential tools.[53]

Given the growing gaps in labor force participation and the disparities in wage income and the prospects of turning inward and giving up on the benefits of trade, American underinvestment in active labor market policies is striking and in need of correction. The United States dedicates a mere 0.1 percent of its GDP to active labor market policies,

*Figure 7-1.* Active Labor Market Programs in OECD Countries, 2013

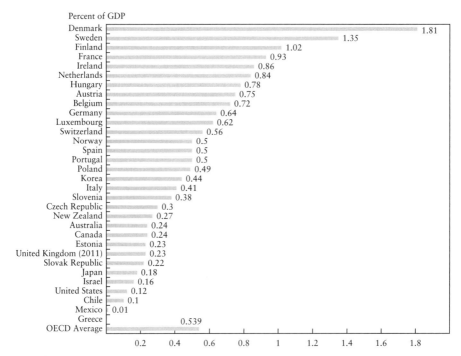

Source: OECD, "Labor Market Programmes: Expenditures and Participants," OECD Labor and Market Statistics Database.

Note: Recent data is not available for Greece, and data for the United Kingdom is from 2011. The OECD average does not include Greece or the United Kingdom.

coming ahead of only Chile and Mexico in the OECD ranking, and well below the OECD average of 0.54 percent (see figure 7-1).

A sustained effort to invest in skills, worker employability, and labor mobility will require a major overhaul of current worker assistance programs. The shortcomings of TAA were explored earlier, and as Robert Maxim points out, recent reforms through the adoption of the Workforce Innovation and Opportunity Act (2014) have not corrected the underlying problems of "eliminating the inequities between TAA and other programs, providing enough funding to guarantee adequate assistance for every worker, or insulating financing from the politics of the congressional appropriations process."[54]

Extending the reach of wage insurance and scaling-up funding for active labor market policies will certainly increase federal expenditures.

Rather than seeing these appropriations as mere outlays, they should be considered critical investments.[55] From this discussion, it should be clear that one of the most effective ways for the United States to tackle the eroding support for international economic engagement is through investments in human capital. The costs of doubling down on the existing worker assistance approach (which fails to enhance needed labor mobility to navigate economic transitions) go beyond passing up on key initiatives (such as the Trans-Pacific Partnership) to reap trade liberalization gains and shore up U.S. international leadership. The risks are increasingly profound: heightened tensions in the social fabric and ever more divisive politics.

## RENEWING INTERNATIONALISM

The unprecedented trade backlash in the 2016 presidential election was years in the making. American trade policy has suffered an expanding legitimacy problem fueled by the three central concerns identified in this book: distributional consequences of liberalization and deeper integration in the world economy; growing reach of trade commitments on the domestic regulatory agenda; and a representativeness deficit in the trade policymaking process necessary to balance competing goals in drafting trade and investment rules.

The trade policy legitimacy challenge has been compounded by a broader process of political, economic, and social fragmentation in the United States. The polarization of the American political system came into full view in the aftermath of the global financial crisis with gridlock in Washington between the Obama White House and the Republican Congress and with growing economic grievances from the continued rise of income inequality, the squeezing of the middle class, and the curtailment of social mobility. The depth of this problem is revealed in a sobering analysis by a group led by Stanford economist Raj Chetty, which found that absolute mobility in the United States has fallen sharply. While 90 percent of children born in 1940 earned more than their parents, only 50 percent of children born in 1980 did. As these authors aptly point out, the American dream is fading due to growing inequality.[56]

With hindsight, it is possible to see that the Obama administration pursued the most ambitious trade strategy in a generation—with mega trade agreements across the Pacific and the Atlantic, and plurilaterals to liberalize services and environmental goods—in the midst of this sharpening domestic cleavage. It did so while relying on traditional solutions to the trade governance dilemmas that had long ceased to be effective. The merits of the behind-the-border trade agenda are still poorly understood: to abate new forms of protectionism and leverage the growth opportunities of global value chains. The trade consultation process, while the most developed by international standards, has come up short in terms of representativeness. The task still remains to expand the circle of consultation with civil society groups and to promote mixed committees with input from diverse stakeholders on how to balance competing goals in trade rules. The challenge of allaying public concerns about the impact of the deep trade agenda on domestic prudential regulations remains steep.

The debate on the distributional consequences of globalization gained most traction in American trade politics. The pushback against trade agreements can be traced back to NAFTA, but the record shows that during the first years of its implementation, the unemployment rate went down and the United States added—not subtracted—manufacturing jobs. Import competition with China during the 2000s had a much larger impact (up to one-fifth of the manufacturing jobs lost during that decade), but technology, with the spread of automation and the growing skill premium, played a much larger role in the loss of manual jobs and the increase in wage inequality. It is the other side of the China trade shock that yields the most profound lessons; displaced workers faced a much more difficult and prolonged transition than we had previously reckoned, with long spells of unemployment, wage losses, and the lack of opportunities in depressed communities. The American solution to the problem of adjustment, a targeted compensation program exclusively for trade-impacted workers, was woefully inadequate by design and execution to address the needs of all workers to gain skills and mobility to cope with the faster pace of economic change.

The ineffectiveness of TAA to generate support for trade initiatives was all too evident in the battle to renew trade promotion authority in 2015. In a first, House Democrats moved to vote down the trade adjustment assistance bill, to torpedo trade promotion authority and doom the chances of TPP ratification. The only way to rescue each bill was to delink them, exposing a political compact that was now completely hollow. The division of powers in the American system of checks and balances had not prevented the United States from displaying leadership in international trade in the postwar era—with TPA providing a working formula. However, as the division of purpose among political actors deepened, indecisiveness set in, with prolonged battles to ratify trade agreements and the uphill quest to renew trade promotion authority.

As the TPP agreement awaited congressional approval, a perfect storm set in with the corrosive effects of growing income inequality, the prolonged adjustment costs to dislocated workers, and the onset of the presidential election season. The largest free trade agreement negotiated to date by the United States—one geared to export American rules and standards to level the playing field, shape the future of Asia's economy, and yield positive effects on U.S. employment and wages—became a political orphan during the 2016 presidential election. All main contenders were on the record opposing the trade agreement.

The American election went to the candidate with the harshest views on trade, which closely reflected the preferences of his base. A Pew opinion poll conducted in spring 2016 showed that 67 percent of Trump supporters saw free trade agreements as a bad thing, while the overall average for Republicans with critical views was 53 percent. Democrats, as a whole, were more supportive of free trade agreements as a good thing for the American economy (56 percent), and the supporters of Hillary Clinton and Bernie Sanders had more favorable attitudes toward trade agreements (58 percent and 55 percent with positive views, respectively) than their candidates.[57] Both parties displayed a disconnect between base and leadership. Mainstream Republican leaders with strong backing from the business community have supported trade liberalization, but Republican voters are far more skeptical. Democrat leaders have been critical of trade agreements, especially during elections, as they rely on the organizational power of unions, but Democrat voters have more favorable views.

The appeal of trade-bashing during the presidential election cannot be attributed to a decisive turn in public opinion against trade agreements in general, or the TPP in particular. The Pew surveys show that the level of positive/negative views on trade agreements in 2016 (51/39) was not far from 2009 levels (52/34), although support was down from its peak in 2015 (58/33) as the campaign entered full swing.[58] A Chicago Council 2016 survey found that 60 percent of respondents had favorable views on the TPP.[59] However, as mentioned in chapter 3, the American public has been skeptical about the benefits of trade agreements for jobs and wages, and this skepticism has been more acute in the rustbelt states, which have experienced economic decline due to international competition and structural change in the economy. Cullen Hendrix provides important insights as to why this geographical concentration had important electoral implications. In essence, support for trade agreements was lowest in battleground states, which concentrate a large portion of electoral college votes, despite population decline in many of them.[60] Other data support the notion that a huge economic divide influenced voting patterns. Marc Muro and Sifan Liu show that the counties that elected Trump represent only 36 percent of the American economic base (measured by total output), whereas Clinton prevailed in a much smaller number of counties that, nevertheless, represent 64 percent of the American economy.[61]

Like other populist movements, Trumpism is not fueled exclusively by economic deprivation, but also by cultural grievance. As explained by Ronald F. Inglehart and Pippa Norris, cultural wars can be a powerful driver of populism as a once-predominant sector in society reacts to the loss of a traditional way of life and opposes rapid cultural change. Rejection of immigration and multiculturalism are potent motivators in the selection of anti-establishment leaders.[62] Fitting this pattern, the anti-immigration sentiment has been much stronger among Trump core supporters. For instance, the Chicago Council survey shows that 80 percent of Trump supporters see immigration as a critical threat, whereas the average for other Republicans, Democrats, and Independents is 43 percent. This survey is also useful in highlighting that support for Donald Trump is not fueled only by social frustration stemming from economic dispossession. Demographically, Trump supporters tend to be older white men, and half of them do not have a college degree. Nevertheless, in terms of household income, 34 percent of Trump supporters in this survey earn less than $40,000 per year, 54 percent are in the $40,000 to $125,000 annual income bracket, and 13 percent have higher earnings.[63]

Parsing out the complex forces behind the election of Donald Trump is beyond the scope of this study, but the electoral outcome will have profound implications for U.S. trade policy, as the Trump administration has followed through with withdrawal from the TPP, announced renegotiation of existing trade agreements, and shown a shift toward bilateral deals. The other members of the TPP have experienced the full pendulum swing from U.S. indecisiveness in securing TPA and enacting the TPP, to a sharp U-turn in U.S. trade philosophy and negotiation strategy. As pointed out in chapter 6, neither extreme of immobilism or irresoluteness

*Figure 7-2.* Rising Trade Dependence, Eroding Safety Net

U.S. trade and government expenditure (% share of GDP)

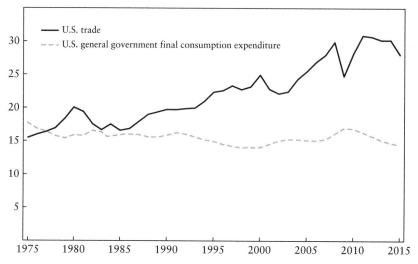

Source: World Bank, World Development Indicators database.

is beneficial to American credibility, and as stated before, the centralization in trade policy decisionmaking accounts for a major policy departure. The areas where President Trump has hinted at swift change are areas of wide executive discretion, where his actions are not encumbered by other veto players: refusing to sign a negotiated trade agreement, giving notice of exit from NAFTA, and imposing temporary punitive tariffs invoking emergency conditions under U.S. trade law.[64]

However, a very different type of U-turn is, in fact, needed: one that provides a different solution to the trade governance dilemma by moving from targeted trade adjustment assistance to an encompassing pro-adjustment safety net. The United States is a laggard when it comes to investments on human capital and on social programs that enable workers to weather transitions brought about by globalization and automation. For example, Cullen Hendrix shows that the United States is in a league of its own in terms of the low level of public expenditures as a share of GDP, even when compared to other countries that have similar exposure to foreign trade (Australia and Japan).[65]

Figure 7-2 extends that analysis by looking at trends over time, and shows that as the United States defined itself more as a trading nation (with the rising importance of trade to economic activity), the social safety net lagged behind. Even though the share of foreign trade to GDP doubled in the last forty years (from 15 percent to 30 percent), public expenditures as a share of GDP were lower in 2015 than in 1975.

We have to relearn, and with great urgency, an old insight: liberalization *sans* a safety net is neither socially nor politically sustainable. Whether the United States engages or not in a correction course in this critical area will have profound implications for other trading nations, like Japan, as they chart their course in navigating the vexing trade governance dilemmas.

## CHAPTER EIGHT

# The Transformation of Japan as a Trading Nation

THE REMAINING CHAPTERS of this book focus on Japan's path in the search for prosperity and leadership in the evolving Asia-Pacific order. The aim is to both describe and explain Japan's choices regarding the core dilemmas of trade governance fleshed out in the first half of the book. To that end, this chapter discusses the remarkable transformation of Japanese trade policy at the onset of the twenty-first century. In the past fifteen years, Japan has traversed the road from dedicated multilateralist and passive rule-taker to become an active preferential trader and proponent of new disciplines on trade and investment. As a "nation built on trade," unfettered access to overseas markets has long been a lifeline for the Japanese economy, but for most of the postwar period this had largely meant exclusive support for the multilateral system.[1] A core tenet of Japanese postwar trade policy was the explicit rejection of member-only trade agreements, which deviated from the GATT and the WTO's central tenet of nondiscrimination. However, in the 2000s Japan began to ink a string of mostly bilateral preferential trade agreements and to insist on an ambitious WTO-plus agenda to disseminate new trade rules. While this marked a major departure from Japan's traditional approach, a decade of FTA negotiations, in fact, yielded only modest results.

This chapter aims to provide answers to three central questions: What brought about the onset of Japan's FTA strategy? Why were initial outcomes limited? What explains the second transformation in Japan's trade policy, as a country now capable of embarking on four concurrent mega trade negotiations and meriting its designation as a "pivotal state"?[2] The first section of this chapter addresses the first two questions. It underscores the complex array of factors that compelled Japan to abandon decades of an "only multilateralism policy": the stagnation of WTO negotiations, the pinch of trade diversion from proliferating FTAs, the need to retool the supply chain in East Asia, and the desire to partake in international rulemaking. It shows how, prior to its accession to the TPP negotiations, Japan was unable to meet its original ambitions due to its own domestic constraints (the veto of the agricultural lobby). The next section describes the central role TPP membership played in propelling forward Japan's trade strategy by closing this credibility gap. By signaling that it was ready to undertake far more significant market opening with entry into the TPP, Japan was able to leverage the launch of long-sought mega trade negotiations: a trilateral trade agreement in Northeast Asia, a sixteen-nation East Asian trading group, and a Japan-EU FTA.[3]

## DEPARTING FROM A PASSIVE TRADE POLICY

Japanese trade officials broke the long-standing taboo over negotiating preferential trade agreements in the late 1990s. Central to their decision was the structural reorientation of the international trading system as hope for the newly minted WTO began to peter out and a proliferation of preferential trade deals ensued. The failure to launch a new multilateral round at Seattle in 1999 and the perennial stall of the Doha Round, launched in 2001, raised doubts about the ability of the WTO to move the liberalization agenda forward. The uncertain prospects of the multilateral system prompted many governments to negotiate free trade agreements as an insurance mechanism, compelling many East Asian nations to play catch-up in joining the FTA bandwagon.

For Japan in particular, NAFTA represented a wake-up call on the potential perils of remaining on the sidelines in a trading world increasingly defined by preferential trade deals. NAFTA's provisions to phase out tariff advantages enjoyed by third parties participating in its export platform program (*maquiladoras*) and to significantly tighten rules of origin in the auto industry presented a serious challenge to the successful operation of Japanese companies in the region. Concern about the discriminatory effects of preferential trade deals, underscored by changes under NAFTA, brought about the first serious discussion in business and government circles about launching an FTA strategy.[4] The Japanese business community advocated FTA negotiations not only to escape the pinch of trade and investment diversion but also to streamline and upgrade their production networks in East Asia. Japanese multinational corporations were interested in revamping production facilities to forestall the advances of rival MNCs in Southeast Asian countries, which, in the aftermath of the Asian financial crisis, had courted foreign direct investment and export production more aggressively to increase foreign exchange earnings.[5]

Trade bureaucrats championed the shift toward a multilayered trade strategy with an FTA track to accomplish the cherished goal of domestic structural reform and to acquire a larger voice in international trade rulemaking. Given that participants in trade agreements must substantially liberalize all trade to be WTO-consistent, champions of reform in Japan underscored the potential of using trade agreements to gradually erode the clout of vested interests opposing market opening.[6] Elite trade bureaucrats were also aiming for a proactive role in the international trade regime. One of the drafters of the 1998 Ministry of Economy, Trade and Industry (METI) report first endorsing the negotiation of preferential trade agreements, noted that the countries that lagged in joining the FTA trend were also the countries that remained passive in negotiations at Geneva.[7] The aim was to use trade agreements to revitalize Japan's trade posture so it could play a more influential role in rulemaking.

A range of objectives motivated the launch of preferential trade negotiations: to neutralize the deleterious effects of trade and investment diversion; to reposition its regional supply networks to better compete with new arrivals in the region; to lift the domestic political constraints on trade policy by eroding the power of liberalization foes; and to partake in the international effort to craft and disseminate new rules as the WTO process stalled. Despite the multiplicity of motivations and high hopes, Japanese FTA policy accomplished modest results in its first decade.

Table 8-1 presents in chronological order the evolution of Japan's FTA negotiations. Though the business community advocated negotiations with Mexico first, to counter NAFTA's effects, and the trade ministry selected South Korea as its top candidate (due to the size of trade flows, potential effects of eliminating trade barriers, and the symbolism of negotiating the first FTA with an Asian nation), Singapore became Japan's first FTA partner. Japan chose to launch its new policy by nego-

*Table 8-1.* Japan's FTAs: From Defensive to Proactive

| FTA partner | Negotiations initiated | Agreement status | In Japan's top 10 agricultural import sources in 2014 (rank) |
|---|---|---|---|
| Singapore | January 2001 | In force, November 2002 | No |
| Mexico | November 2002 | In force, March 2005 | No |
| Malaysia | January 2004 | In force, July 2006 | No |
| Thailand | February 2004 | In force, November 2007 | Yes (5) |
| Philippines | February 2004 | In force, December 2008 | No |
| ASEAN | April 2005 | In force, December 2008 | Thailand (5); Indonesia (10) |
| Indonesia | July 2005 | In force, July 2008 | Yes (10) |
| Chile | February 2006 | In force, September 2007 | No |
| Brunei | June 2006 | In force, July 2008 | No |
| Vietnam | January 2007 | In force, October 2009 | No |
| India | January 2007 | In force, August 2011 | No |
| Australia | April 2007 | In force, January 2015 | Yes (3) |
| Switzerland | May 2007 | In force, September 2009 | No |
| Peru | May 2009 | In force, March 2012 | No |
| Mongolia | June 2012 | In force, June 2016 | No |
| Canada | November 2012 | Under negotiation | Yes (4) |
| Colombia | December 2012 | Under negotiation | No |

Defensive

Table 8-1. (*continued*)

| FTA partner | Negotiations initiated | Agreement status | In Japan's top 10 agricultural import sources in 2014 (rank) |
|---|---|---|---|
| China-Japan-Korea | March 2013 | Under negotiation | China (2) |
| EU | April 2013 | Under negotiation | Netherlands (7); France (8) |
| RCEP | May 2013 | Under negotiation | China (2); Australia (3); Thailand (5); New Zealand (9); Indonesia (10) |
| TPP | July 2013 | Agreement reached October 2015 | United States (1); Australia (3); Canada (4); New Zealand (9) |

*Proactive*

Source: Ministry of Foreign Affairs, Japan, "Free Trade Agreement (FTA) and Economic Partnership Agreement (EPA)" (www.mofa.go.jp/policy/economy/fta/); Ministry of Agriculture, Forestry and Fisheries, *"Norinsuisanbutsu yushutsunyu gaikyo*: 2014 *nen kakuteiatai"* [Outlook of agriculture, forestry and fishery imports and exports: 2014 definitive values], March 26, 2015 (www.maff.go.jp/j/tokei/kouhyou/kokusai/pdf/yusyutu _gaikyo_14.pdf).

tiating with a duty-free economy where Japanese companies faced no major access barriers, for the all-important political reason that Singapore is not an agricultural exporter. From its birth, agriculture has been the Achilles' heel of Japanese FTA policy, imposing sizable constraints on strategy and outcomes.

The core of Japanese protectionism has centered on a few sensitive agricultural commodities (rice, wheat, sugar, dairy, beef, and pork), all of them shielded through high *ad valorem* tariffs and many of them subject to measures that further mitigate the operation of free markets (as state trading commodities, the use of tariff-rate quotas, and in the case of pork, also through the use of the gate price system[8]), though more than 10 percent of Japanese tariffs (mostly representing primary commodities) have been off limits in trade negotiations. These domestic sensitivities dictated a defensive FTA approach as Japan largely avoided negotiations with its largest trade partners—who were also its main

*Figure 8-1.* Japan's Trade Covered by FTAs, 2014

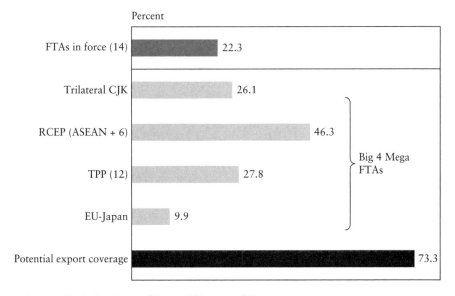

Source: Trade Statistics of Japan, Ministry of Finance.

Note: FTA=free trade agreement; CJK=China-Japan-South Korea Free Trade Agreement; RCEP=Regional Comprehensive Economic Partnership; TPP=Trans-Pacific Partnership.

agricultural suppliers (United States, China)—and maintained a firm line on agricultural exclusions in all its negotiations. The hope of reformers that successive FTAs would result in ever larger dents in agricultural protectionism was dashed as the string of Japanese FTAs that came into force failed to meet the WTO standard of 90 percent tariff elimination (see table 2-2).

Hampered by these political constraints, Japan developed a low-yield FTA strategy, both in terms of trade coverage and estimated income gains. Figure 8-1 shows the modest results of Japan's painstaking negotiation of fourteen FTAs, which, together, covered only 22 percent of the country's trade in 2014. A cross-national comparison shows Japan lagging behind several other countries in securing preferential access through its FTA network: Mexico (82 percent), Singapore (70.5 percent), South Korea (40.3 percent), the United States (40.1 percent), and the EU (28.6 percent) (see table 2-1). In particular, South Korea's trade agreements with the United States and the EU put strong competitive pressure on Japanese firms in the automobile and electronic sectors, prompting

*Figure 8-2.* Japan's Real GDP Gains from Trade Liberalization

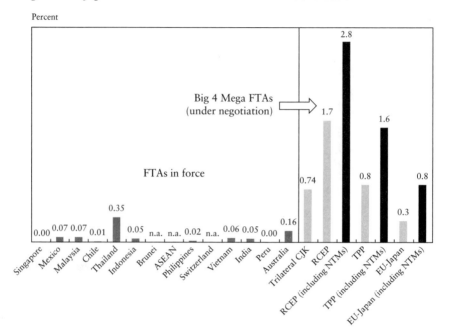

Percent

Source: Data collected from Kenichi Kawasaki, "Determining Priority among EPAs: Which Trading Partner Has the Greatest Economics Impact," col. 218, Research Institute of Economy, Trade and Industry (RIETI), May 31, 2011; Kenichi Kawasaki, "Rise of the Mega EPAs: A Comparison of Economic Effects," col. 284, Research Institute of Economy, Trade and Industry (RIETI), March 4, 2014; Kenichi Kawasaki, "The Relative Significance of EPAs in Asia-Pacific," *Journal of Asian Economics*, vol. 39 (2015), pp. 19–30. Kawasaki's estimates of the potential impact of the mega FTAs assume 100 percent tariff elimination, and 50 percent nontariff measure reduction with 50 percent spillover effects. Hence, these are upper-bound estimates of liberalization effects, different from actual negotiation outcomes.

Note: CJK=China-Japan-South Korea Free Trade Agreement; FTA=free trade agreement; NTM=nontariff measures; RCEP=Regional Comprehensive Economic Partnership; TPP=Trans-Pacific Partnership.

the Japanese business sector to demand countervailing FTAs with these industrialized countries.[9] Japan's entreaties, however, went nowhere. The United States was cool toward the possibility of launching a bilateral trade negotiation due to the perceived inability of Japan to open the agricultural sector, and the European Union showed interest only in rule harmonization, not tariff elimination through an FTA, since it feared a massive inflow of car imports.[10]

Because Japan bypassed its largest economic partners, the gains from trade from the first wave of FTA negotiations were very small, as can be seen in figure 8-2. Moreover, since many of Japan's FTA counterparts were developing countries that depended on Japanese aid and investment, they were not in a position to demand significant change to Japan's agricultural regime, as reformers had hoped. The flip side was that despite Japanese promises of broader economic cooperation in lieu of agricultural market opening and accepting larger flows of foreign workers, many Southeast Asian counterparts were reluctant to make substantial commitments on the WTO-plus rules that Japan advocated. The most dramatic case was the trade agreement with the Association of Southeast Asian Nations, which generated no new commitments on investment, services, intellectual property, and government procurement.[11] China's trade policy appeared poised to gain more traction in the region. Not only had China moved first in signing an FTA with ASEAN (and had made well-received agricultural concessions through the Early Harvest program), there seemed to be a shared preference with developing Southeast Asia for more limited rules and nonbinding commitments. Moreover, the disagreement between Japan and China on the membership configuration for an East Asian trade grouping also stalled efforts on that front.[12]

## THE TPP EFFECT IN JAPAN'S TRADE STRATEGY

As the first decade of the twenty-first century came to a close, there was serious concern among Japan's trade stakeholders that Japan would play a marginal role in the ever-growing surge of preferential trade agreements. Japan had not been able to keep up with South Korea in securing preferential access in European and American markets, it feared that China could eclipse its trade diplomacy in the Asian region, and the string of small FTAs coming into force had not been useful levers on domestic structural reform and had only moderate results in disseminating ambitious rules.

At this critical juncture, TPP membership acted as a catalyst, energizing Japan's trade policy. The TPP opened the way for a high-yield FTA policy by essentially closing the credibility gap that had hamstrung previous Japanese initiatives.[13] As a condition for TPP admission, prospective members had to commit to a high level of tariff elimination, could not carve out a priori sensitive commodities, and had to demonstrate willingness to tackle nontariff barriers. Through a TPP bid, Japan was, for the first time, capable of signaling a far more consequential commitment to market opening (and in so doing, boosting its own efforts at domestic reform and international rulemaking). For the United States, admitting Japan into the TPP also presented singular advantages: the prospect of securing much better market access in the world's third largest economy and the elevation of the economic significance of the TPP to qualify as a mega trade agreement (with 40 percent of world GDP); the boost to the Obama administration's Asian rebalance policy by incorporating a major Asian power and close security partner; and the ability to advance on the rules agenda with a like-minded partner such as Japan.[14]

The effect of the TPP on Japan's trade strategy was felt far and wide. Crucially, it brought about a major recalibration in China's trade initiatives vis-à-vis Japan. Concerned that with Japan on board the TPP would become the predominant trade grouping in the region (and fearing substantial trade diversion losses), China swiftly moved on two fronts. In spring 2011, it accelerated the conclusion of the feasibility study for the China-Japan-Korea FTA, and in the summer of that year, it endorsed the sixteen-member configuration for the East Asia trade negotiation that Japan had favored. This new China-Japan understanding compelled ASEAN to rollout a new framework—ASEAN-plus-plus (inviting ASEAN's six FTA partners to join a trade negotiation)—with the aim of ensuring ASEAN's centrality and influencing terms of negotiation (for example, special and differential treatment provisions). In this manner, the Regional Comprehensive Economic Partnership trade negotiations were launched.

Europeans reacted swiftly to Japan's potential entry into the TPP. Out of concern that the United States and Japan would move ahead in defining the new rules on trade and investment, the EU finally agreed to open trade talks with Japan.[15] Japan became a pivotal state capable of influencing the viability of long-stalled trade schemes with its TPP move.[16] Figures 8-1 and 8-2 eloquently depict the transformation in expected outcomes from Japan's new proactive trade strategy.

Nevertheless, the road to TPP admission was far from easy for Japan. It was a protracted process (Japan's first signal of interest took place in October 2010 in a speech by then Prime Minister Naoto Kan, but it took until July 2013 for Japan to sit at the negotiation table). It was a long road full of uncertainty and reversals (two Democratic Party of Japan prime ministers made TPP admission a high priority for their administrations but were unable to formally seek membership; and in the

December 2012 election that returned the Liberal Democratic Party to power, the party ran on a platform that opposed TPP participation if the talks were predicated on full tariff elimination). Japan's TPP entry was a reachable goal only after intense pre-accession negotiations with the United States. At the operational level, this meant that Japan agreed to deliver on three confidence-building measures (a standstill on new cancer insurance products from Japan Post until a level playing field was created,[17] easing sanitary restrictions on beef, and expanding the number of car imports under simplified certification rules), and consented to the launch of parallel TPP talks on autos and NTMs. At the highest political level, Japan's TPP entry was forged through a carefully crafted political compromise. The Obama-Abe summit statement released in February 2013 to officially welcome Japan into the TPP acknowledged that both countries had sensitive sectors and a prior commitment to unilaterally eliminate all tariffs was not required (at Japan's insistence). It also stated that no good could be taken off the negotiation table and Japan would work with others to ensure a comprehensive agreement was reached (at the insistence of the United States).

The road to the TPP was predicated on a realignment of Japanese domestic political dynamics, and the summit compromise structured the trade talks and defined what it would be possible to achieve through the TPP. These issues are discussed in the next two chapters.

## CHAPTER NINE

# Decisiveness/Inclusiveness Dilemmas in Japanese Trade Policy

**JAPAN'S PATH** to the Trans-Pacific Partnership was enabled by a concurrent process that centralized decisionmaking. As Japan moved away from a deeply fragmented process of policy formulation, its level of ambition in trade negotiations increased. Japan's progression toward greater decisiveness was far from linear, however, with doomed institutional attempts at centralization hindering more forceful trade initiatives. The Shinzo Abe administration was, finally, able to assert executive leadership and accomplish both entry into the TPP and reform of core policies and institutions of the agricultural regime. Nevertheless, this centralization was not achieved through formal institutional reforms (as attempted by Abe's predecessors), but rather by capitalizing on favorable political trends (for example, the decimation of the opposition after the Democratic Party of Japan's [DPJ] ouster from office) and by effectively elevating the prime minister's office to act as the control tower in decisionmaking. These bold policy departures carried a heavy dose of political pragmatism regarding the terms of TPP admission, the award of subsidies to secure the position of part-time farmers, and the calibration of agricultural cooperatives reform. To understand the pattern of "negotiated decisiveness" that has characterized the Abe administration, it is important to realize that the limits of the reform agenda were set by the political imperatives of preserving party unity and prevailing at the election booth to regain control over the legislative agenda.

Japan's TPP entry was also possible because of the gradual but real weakening of the most formidable veto player in Japanese trade policy, the agricultural lobby. Demographic and electoral changes have transformed the role played by the agricultural lobby in the conservative alliance. At the height of interparty competition, farmers were able to reward the party that offered the most generous subsidies and toed the line on the limits of agricultural market opening. Even during the period of the Liberal Democratic Party's (LDP) dominance post-2012, the agricultural lobby retained enough clout to protect its most vital interests in TPP negotiations and in domestic reform initiatives. But major change has, indeed, happened; the agricultural lobby is no longer able to altogether veto policy departures that threaten the status quo.

Greater decisiveness on trade policy has brought the challenge of delivering on inclusiveness. In the TPP, the battle over the legitimacy of trade policy crystallized, with opponents and supporters engaged in a robust debate to sway public opinion. The battle over TPP participation was unlike any other before in Japan. It brought together an expanded coalition of opponents from across the ideological spectrum, it was fought on new (online) platforms, and it tapped into fears of Americanization. This anti-TPP mobilization compelled the government to develop an outreach strategy to win over public opinion and assuage critics that Japan would not embark on unwanted economic and social transformation.

This chapter's analysis unfolds in three parts. It first traces the long and winding road toward greater concentration of policymaking authority in the executive office and the impact of this domestic process on Japan's positioning in trade negotiations. Next, it analyzes the evolution of the agricultural lobby's electoral clout and its redefinition of the redlines of agricultural trade policy. The third segment discusses the legitimacy challenges triggered by the TPP negotiation and the path toward ratification.

## IN SEARCH OF A "CONTROL TOWER" IN JAPAN'S TRADE POLICY DECISIONMAKING

Greater centralization of policymaking was indispensable for Japan to join the big leagues of preferential trade negotiations and avoid the pitfalls of a dispersed decisionmaking system, as discussed in chapter 6. As the following analysis shows, the display of executive leadership in trade policy was a reflection of broader trends in Japanese politics toward the "presidentialization" of the prime minister.[1] The quest for greater executive authority was far from a linear process, however. It experienced significant setbacks, and it involved both formal institutional reforms (some successful, others fruitless) as well as the skillful adaptation of existing institutional structures to new political realities.

### Traditional Japan: Conditions Ripe for State Indecisiveness

Japan's traditional trade policymaking system was severely fragmented. Organized interest groups exercised clout over trade policy in their respective issue areas. Bureaucratic sectionalism was intense, with coequal ministries operating under the unanimity rule and no effective interministerial coordination mechanisms. The cabinet was bypassed as the main locus of decisionmaking by the policy tribes of the ruling LDP and the bureaucracy. These institutional traits extinguished the potential for prime ministerial leadership and created ideal conditions for the success of iron triangles (policy tribe politicians, bureaucrats, and economic interests) that resisted market liberalization.

Two major factors conspired against the emergence of top-down executive decisionmaking in Japan. First, the postwar electoral system (multimember districts with a single nontransferable vote) fostered intraparty competition and encouraged individual LDP politicians to affiliate with factions to secure the party nomination and funds to court the personal vote. Factional balance determined the selection of the prime minister as well as the distribution of posts in the cabinet. Hence, the competence of the prime minister was judged not by displays of executive leadership but, rather, by his ability to coordinate among different factions and keep the party united.[2] Moreover, executive strength was sacrificed to frequent cabinet reshufflings to reward senior politicians and regulate factional competition through a promotion system.[3]

Second, an informal party-bureaucracy decisionmaking system (known as *seifu-jiminto seido*) overshadowed both the cabinet and the Diet. The cabinet could submit bills to the Diet only if they had received prior approval from the LDP's policymaking organ, the Policy Affairs Research Council or PARC, and the meeting of administrative vice-ministers.[4] This horizontal policymaking system, therefore, lacked transparency, diminished the importance of Diet deliberations (since in a dominant party system, Diet approval of PARC-sanctioned bills was considered almost automatic), and established an array of policy subgovernments where powerful vested interests, LDP policy tribes, and line agencies could act as effective veto points.

Trade policy was no exception. Although the Japanese constitution grants the cabinet the authority to conclude international treaties (including trade agreements) that must be approved by the Diet, de facto the *seifu-jiminto seido* was at the center of the domestic political accommodation process, shaping Japan's position on trade negotiations.[5] Traditionally in Japan, politicians certainly delegated trade negotiation authority to bureaucrats, but this delegation had two distinctive characteristics: (1) it lacked formalization (no specific vote was required as it is with Trade Promotion Authority in the United States, and (2) it was highly compartmentalized by issue area. In other words, the degree of autonomy of bureaucrats was determined by the extent to which politicians deemed a sector to be a core political constituency. Politicians in the agricultural policy tribe kept a tight leash on the Ministry of Agriculture, Forestry and Fisheries (MAFF), but Ministry of International Trade and Industry (MITI) bureaucrats dealing with manufacturing had a much greater degree of freedom in international negotiations.[6] It follows that cross-sectoral negotiations involving both primary and industrial goods frequently resulted in domestic impasse and greatly complicated trade talks. In essence, Japanese trade negotiators were not only negotiating across the table with their foreign counterparts but also with the other Japanese ministries in their delegation sitting alongside them at the negotiation table.

## *Toward a "Presidential Prime Minister"?*
## *Institutional Reforms Under the LDP*

The launch of Japan's FTA policy coincided with incipient efforts to centralize policymaking around the political executive. The 1994 electoral reform (introducing a mixed system of single-member electoral districts and proportional representation seats) did not produce the much-anticipated emergence of a two-party system, but did affect Japanese politics in some significant ways, and consequently, the reform affected policymaking. By easing intraparty electoral competition, the new electoral rules weakened the role of factions and encouraged parties to develop policy platforms and rely on electoral manifestos to appeal to voters. In conjunction with the growing role of mass media and the larger ranks of floating voters, those reforms increased the importance of the prime minister's popularity to the party's electoral fortunes.[7] Displays of executive leadership became a valued asset for the party label.

The hand of the prime minister was also strengthened through reforms to the Cabinet Office in 2001. The amendments to the Cabinet Law for the first time explicitly gave the prime minister the power of initiative to send proposals to the cabinet, expanded the operations of the cabinet secretariat to include not only coordination but also policy planning, and established a new Cabinet Office that enabled the prime minister to direct the bureaucracy in areas requiring interministerial coordination without requiring prior authorization from the cabinet.[8] Prime Minister Junichiro Koizumi (2001–06) made further strides by establishing a high-level advisory board, the Council on Economic and Fiscal Policy (CEFP), which sought to make the Cabinet Office the locus of policymaking and the prime minister the arbiter of policy conflicts.

In fact, the Koizumi years saw an unprecedented display of executive initiative. The reformist prime minister refused to bow to party factions in cabinet appointments and battled politicians in his own party who vehemently opposed his signature economic reform policy: postal privatization. Koizumi engineered a landslide electoral victory in the snap election of 2005, as he successfully appealed to voters to help him battle "the forces of resistance" in his own party and proceeded to expel Diet members opposed to postal reform.

In the area of trade policy, Koizumi tinkered with intraparty decisionmaking by establishing an FTA subcommittee in PARC to vocalize more market-friendly views. He attempted to deal with the problem of bureaucratic sectionalism by establishing a Meeting of FTA-Related Ministers and Bureaus in 2003, while proclaiming himself "FTA Minister."[9] The impact of Koizumi's actions on trade policymaking, however, was modest. The FTA subcommittee was eventually phased out by agricultural politicians, and the FTA ministerial meeting did not provide effective coordination given that the prime minister himself was mostly concerned with his domestic reform program and did not intervene decisively in favor of major trade initiatives.

No major dent was made in the clout of the agricultural lobby over trade policy, and the problem of bureaucratic sectionalism continued unabated. Demands from the private sector to establish a single institutional window in charge of FTA negotiations akin to the Office of the United States Trade Representative or to create an "External Economy Strategy Headquarters" to emulate the success of CEFP went unanswered.[10]

More broadly, it was not possible to consolidate and institutionalize the changes Prime Minister Koizumi had made toward greater executive-led decisionmaking. The postal rebels were soon admitted back to the party, nullifying the potent message that opponents to the prime minister's reform campaign could lose party membership. His three immediate successors (Shinzo Abe, Yasuo Fukuda, and Taro Aso) suffered very low approval rates and oversaw short-lived administrations, so it was not possible to engage in long-term strategic planning and to revive the CEFP.

### The DPJ's Failed Institutional Reforms and Policy Paralysis

The victory of the DPJ in August 2009 seemed to herald the dawn of regime change in Japan, not only due to the novel political dynamic of alternating parties in power but also because the new party in power appeared determined to change the essence of Japanese policymaking. The DPJ's intention was to bring about "cabinet-led policymaking" by asserting the primacy of politicians over bureaucrats, and by ensuring that the cabinet would prevail over the party's policy tribes in decisionmaking.

Upon his inauguration, Prime Minister Yukio Hatoyama proceeded to swiftly dismantle the core tenets of traditional policymaking in Japan. He eliminated the party's Policy Research Council and the meeting of administrative vice-ministers, increased the number of political appointees in the bureaucracy, and created a triumvirate of political appointees at the top of each ministry to ensure bureaucratic compliance with politicians' directives. Hatoyama replaced the CEFP with a National Policy Unit (NPU) to provide overall directives in the budget-making process and further diminish the clout of the Ministry of Finance (MOF).[11]

However, the abrupt elimination of established decisionmaking structures without instituting effective mechanisms to tap into bureaucratic expertise and to ensure that the NPU was well prepared to undertake its hefty responsibilities soon resulted in policy overload and the breakdown of politician-bureaucrat communication. Moreover, suddenly marginalized from the policy input process, disgruntled party backbenchers pushed back, adding to intraparty tensions. Combined with the fumbling of issues surrounding the relocation of the U.S. military base in Futenma, the position of Prime Minister Hatoyama became untenable and he resigned less than a year after his inauguration.

His successors, Prime Ministers Naoto Kan and Yoshihiko Noda, gradually reinstated the party-bureaucracy decisionmaking apparatus. Prime Minister Kan restored the Policy Research Council (although without the right of prior screening of bills) and sought to ease communication with bureaucrats. Prime Minister Noda brought the process full circle when he granted the party's policy deliberation body the right of prior screening of bills and reinstated the meeting of administrative vice-ministers. Far from replacing bureaucratic influence, the NPU was staffed with seconded personnel from the ministries and ceased to operate when the DPJ lost power.[12]

The DPJ's botched centralization campaign prevented the government from displaying decisiveness. Old patterns of decisionmaking were not substituted with effective lines of top-down policy formulation and implementation. The three-plus years of DPJ rule saw the rules on policymaking and the roles of the cabinet, bureaucracy, and party in constant flux, adding confusion and producing policy stasis. With their defeat in the July 2010 Upper House election, the DPJ's legislative agenda was furthered hampered, as it now required cooperation from opposition parties to enact bills. Ironically, core problems that plagued the LDP also paralyzed the DPJ once in office: political instability at the highest level with frequent replacement of prime ministers, deep intraparty rifts, and divided government (known in Japan as the "twisted Diet").

These broader problems in carrying out the tasks of government also curtailed the party's ambitions on trade policy. As an urban party, Hironori Sasada points out, the DPJ had long championed market liberalization, but on its road to power it increased its reliance on rural voters (by 2009, 25 percent of DPJ Lower House members hailed from rural districts).[13] During the 2009 general election, longtime political strategist Ichiro Ozawa successfully courted the rural vote by offering to introduce direct income payments to all farmers. The shift in the domestic basis of support for the party greatly complicated the prospects of hammering out a cohesive party strategy on international trade. The first sign of trouble appeared when the elected party quickly backtracked from its proposal to conclude a trade agreement with the United States. Facing an uproar from agricultural groups, the DPJ amended its policy manifesto to settle for the possible initiation of trade talks with the United

States and assured the farm lobby that all key commodities would be protected.[14]

When Prime Minister Kan suddenly announced in the fall of 2010 his interest in Japan joining the TPP, the party quickly polarized among supporters and detractors. The anti-TPP group with 140 members represented close to half the party's lawmakers in the Lower House and included powerful party bosses like Ozawa and Hatoyama. Sharp bureaucratic disagreements acquired a new pitch with the TPP discussion. MAFF and the Ministry of Economy, Trade and Industry (METI) adopted diametrically opposed positions. MAFF forecasted a 90 percent reduction in rice production, a drop in the food self-sufficiency ratio from 39 percent to 13 percent, and the loss of 3.4 million jobs. In contrast, METI estimated the cost of foregoing TPP participation to be around $128 billion—equivalent to 1.5 percent of GDP—with an estimated job contraction of eight million jobs.[15] Facing stiff opposition from the agricultural lobby, an ever-widening party rift, and opposing estimates on the economic consequences of the TPP, trade policy indecisiveness ensued. Prime Minister Kan was unable to commit to Japan's TPP entry at the 2010 APEC leaders' summit. Although the Kan administration promised a decision on the TPP by June 2011, the massive earthquake that hit Japan in March of that year forced a postponement of the decision and contributed to the demise of the Kan government a few months later due to dissatisfaction with his administration's response to the disaster.

Prime Minister Noda also proved unable to hammer out a cohesive stand on TPP membership, both within the party and the bureaucracy. The "cautious faction on the TPP" once again flexed its muscle and turned in a letter opposing participation signed by close to two hundred DPJ lawmakers. To build a party consensus in favor of TPP entry, Noda established a special project team within PARC on the TPP. The effort was fruitless, however, as the group reached deadlock and was unable to give clear advice to the prime minister.[16] To avoid a party split, Noda could only announce the initiation of consultations with TPP member countries, not a membership bid, at the 2011 APEC meeting. The weakness of the bureaucratic setup (with line ministries that cannot be overruled and the Ministry of Foreign Affairs playing a weak coordinator role) also led Prime Minister Noda to set up a new fifty-member team for TPP talks, to improve coordination and infuse prime ministerial leadership in the process: "We will select negotiating staff regardless of past practices. I am going to be the control tower."[17]

The goal to assert executive leadership on trade policy, however, proved to be a mere aspiration, since Prime Minister Noda presided over a short-lived administration. Intraparty tensions finally triggered a party split, followed soon after by a major electoral loss in the December 2012 general election. Frictions with the Ozawa group over TPP participation were compounded by an intraparty rift over one of the most heated domestic policy issues: a hike in the consumption tax. Determined to restore Japan's fiscal health, Noda reached out to opposition parties (the LDP and Komeito) to ensure the legislative passage of the consumption tax bill. The political cost was high; Ozawa denounced the move and split from the party with forty-nine of his supporters in July, and the opposition parties attached a hefty price tag to their cooperation on tax policy, the convocation of a snap election later that fall, which brought about the end of DPJ rule.

The DPJ years were characterized by bouts of prime ministerial initiative curtailed by the failure of institutional reforms to decisionmaking. The constant writing and rewriting of the rules on the role of the party and the bureaucracy in crafting policy prevented the emergence of top-down decisionmaking. Prime Ministers Kan and Noda were the first Japanese leaders to articulate the important benefits of TPP participation for Japan, but neither managed to execute a membership bid. In the end, powerful centrifugal forces thwarted their efforts: lack of party unity with DPJ backbenchers pushing against TPP membership; a farm lobby asserting its influence over a DPJ that had intensified its dependence on rural support; sparring ministries with sharply contrasting assessments of the implications for Japan of joining the TPP; and legislative gridlock due to the twisted Diet.

### The Abe Kantei: *Centralization Without Wholesale Institutional Reform*

After more than three years out of office, the LDP, with its coalition partner Komeito, once again took the reins of political power with a landslide victory (the LDP alone increased its number of seats in the Lower House from 119 to 294) and the decimation of the DPJ (the party's seats declined from 308 to a mere fifty-seven) in December 2012.[18] Most surprising was the comeback of Shinzo Abe, who had abruptly resigned as prime minister due to illness in 2007 and had been the unlikely winner of the LDP's presidency just two months prior to the snap election. In sharp contrast to his first tenure as prime minister, this time around Prime Minister Abe immediately launched ambitious plans for economic revitalization and followed later with a more proactive foreign policy, including reinterpretation of the constitution to allow for the exercise of collective self-defense.

Announcing that exit from the deflationary economy was his first priority, Abe pressured then Bank of Japan Governor Masaaki Shirakawa to adopt a 2 percent inflation targeting policy and was instrumental in the selection of his successor Haruhiko Kuroda, a strong advocate of monetary easing. Prime Minister Abe proceeded to lay out his strategy for economic revitalization, popularly known as Abenomics, to move along three tracks (or arrows): monetary expansion, flexible fiscal policy, and economic growth through productivity-enhancing measures. Recognizing that structural reform in a contracting economy could quickly exacerbate zero-sum politics (and as seen in the charges of market fundamentalism that were leveled against his predecessor Prime Minister Koizumi), the aim of Abenomics has been to combine stimulus and reform. One of the hardest challenges throughout has been to demonstrate that genuine economic reform will match the expansionary efforts.[19]

To advance the critical third arrow, Prime Minister Abe buttressed the role of the prime minister's office (known in Japanese as *Kantei*) in several familiar ways. He relied on the advisory councils to shape the discussion of important economic initiatives, incorporate private sector members to break the monopoly of the bureaucracy, and enable the prime minister to be the final arbiter in deciding a course of action. To this effect, Prime Minister Abe revived the Council on Economic and Fiscal Policy, but with the new twist of circumscribing its role to macroeconomic issues, as he established a new Economic Revitalization Headquarters to address microeconomic policy issues through the Industrial Competitiveness Council and the Regulatory Reform Council.

The prime minister also resorted to the tried and true formula of designating special portfolio ministers to promote priority policy issues and named his longtime ally Akira Amari as economic revitalization minister in charge of the namesake headquarters, de facto becoming his point man in the pursuit of the economic reform agenda. The emergence of the Abe *Kantei* leadership owed much to the competence of Chief Cabinet

Secretary Yoshihide Suga, who skillfully managed cabinet appointments, maintained internal unity, and went beyond the traditional role of policy coordinator to enforce adherence to policy directives from recalcitrant ministries.[20]

Two fundamental differences emerged in the campaigns to empower the chief executive of the DPJ and the Abe *Kantei*. They derive from the contrasting emphasis and distinct strategies to promote "political leadership" and "*Kantei* leadership." As Ushio Shioda explains, in the former, the DPJ identified the bureaucracy as the main adversary as it sought to assert the preeminence of politicians in decisionmaking.[21] In the latter approach, followed by the Abe administration, the main targets are the policy tribes within the party that oppose the prime minister's initiatives. The Abe *Kantei* has not sought the marginalization of the bureaucracy, being keenly aware of the breakdown of communication and atrophy in policymaking experienced during the DPJ period. Instead, the Abe *Kantei* has tapped into bureaucratic expertise to achieve its goals, and senior officials from one ministry in particular (METI) have been appointed to leading advising positions in the *Kantei*.[22] Rather, the goal has been to ensure a responsive bureaucracy. With Suga as its enforcer, the *Kantei* has contravened influential ministries when policy decisions were deemed to be of utmost political importance. A case in point is the fallout with the Ministry of Finance, when Prime Minister Abe first decided in the fall of 2014 to postpone the second increase in the consumption tax after the economy took a bigger dip than expected.[23] And in late 2015, Suga—guided by the imperative of securing the cooperation of coalition partner Komeito in the upcoming July 2016 Upper House election—quelled MOF and the LDP tax policy tribe's objections to the exemption of food purchases from the planned second increase in the consumption tax. As Takao Toshikawa notes, Suga considered the tax decision a "matter of political strife requiring a high level political decision, not a technocratic policy debate."[24]

Even though influential party leaders lost the battle over the consumption tax exemption, the Abe *Kantei* took a different approach from the DPJ's in dealing with the party's policy tribes. The restoration of the LDP to power meant the reactivation of PARC, the party's policymaking machinery—not its abrogation as the DPJ originally attempted to do, only to gradually bring the traditional system back. To be sure, the economic reform agenda of the Abe administration pits the *Kantei* against many of the vested interests whose positions are defended by policy tribe politicians. But these voices have not been completely shut out of policy deliberations, especially when their support is essential to the continued electoral clout of the government. The decision to accommodate rather than marginalize foes of reform reflects the need to preserve internal unity and to expand the party's control over the Diet. It is also the result of Prime Minister Abe's central concern with elevating Japan's security profile. Political capital is a finite commodity, and the prime minister's willingness to devote heavy doses of it to the pursuit of his security agenda (for example, the loss of public support during the passage of the security legislation reforms in early fall 2015) counsels some compromises on economic reforms.

The prime minister has undoubtedly moved the needle in areas long resistant to change, but he has incorporated the views of these interests regarding their most vital concerns. The most appropriate descriptor for the Abe approach is "negotiated decisiveness," with all the possibilities and contradictions implied in the term. The combination of centralized decisionmaking (enabling significant policy departures) with political pragmatism (moderating the reach of reforms) is evident in the decision in March 2015 to seek TPP membership, and in the subsequent reforms to the pillars of the agricultural regime (the set-aside program and the Japan Agriculture [JA] network) as the government sought to give traction to the liberalization *cum* reform agenda without sacrificing its political imperatives (see table 9-1 showing the political chronology of the Abe administration).

SEEKING TPP MEMBERSHIP

Prime Minister Abe's early push for TPP membership came as a surprise. There were a host of compelling factors suggesting he would wait in making a risky move until after the July 2013 Upper House election because securing a majority in that chamber, to end the divided government, was key to his entire legislative agenda. In its campaign manifesto, the LDP had adopted a defensive attitude on the TPP, listing six preconditions that would guide any decision to join: no prior commitment to abolish all tariffs, no numerical targets on automobile imports, no investor-state dispute settlement (ISDS) provisions that would undermine sovereignty, regulation on government procurement and financial services should reflect Japan's special characteristics, maintenance of the universal health

*Table 9-1.* Chronology of the Abe *Kantei*: TPP and Agricultural Reform

| | |
|---|---|
| *2012* | |
| Dec 16 | Landslide LDP victory in general election, coalition government with *Komeito* |
| *2013* | |
| Jan 23 | Relaunch of economic headquarters, CEFP; launch of Economic Revitalization Headquarters |
| Feb 22 | Abe-Obama summit, bilateral understanding clearing Japan's TPP participation |
| Mar 1 | Appointment of Koya Nishikawa as chairman of LDP's TPP Committee |
| Mar 14 | LDP's TPP Committee resolution on five sacred commodities |
| Mar 15 | Prime Minister Abe announces Japan's TPP membership bid |
| Apr 5 | Cabinet decision to establish TPP Headquarters with Minister Akira Amari in charge |
| Apr 19 | Diet resolution on five sacred commodities |
| Jul 21 | LDP victory in Upper House election: end of twisted Diet |
| Jul 23 | Japan formally joins the TPP negotiations |
| Nov 6 | Government announces reform of *gentan* (set-aside program) |
| *2014* | |
| Apr 1 | First tranche of consumption tax increase (from 5 to 8 percent) |
| May 14 | Regulatory Reform Council proposes far-reaching JA reform |
| Jun 1 | *Kantei* and LDP agree on principle of JA self-reform |
| Nov 18 | Prime Minister Abe announces postponement of second tranche of consumption tax increase |
| Dec 14 | Snap general election; LDP and *Komeito* victory |
| *2015* | |
| Feb 1 | Compromise package on JA reform adopted |
| Feb 23 | Farm minister Koya Nishikawa resigns over political funding scandal |
| Apr 1 | Unified local elections |
| Oct 5 | TPP negotiations conclude |
| Oct 9 | Prime Minister Abe establishes the TPP Taskforce |
| *2016* | |
| Jan 14 | Supplementary budget for 2015 fiscal year approved |
| Jan 28 | Resignation of Minister Amari over graft claims |
| Mar 29 | Budget for 2016 fiscal year approved |
| Apr 5 | Lower House deliberations on TPP begin |
| Apr 8–18 | Diet deliberations suspended and resumed due to Nishikawa book scandal |

Table 9-1. *(continued)*

| | |
|---|---|
| Apr 19 | TPP ratification vote postponed until after the Upper House election |
| Jul 10 | Upper House election; ruling coalition keeps majority |
| Nov 10 | Lower House ratifies TPP |
| Dec 9 | Upper House ratifies TPP |
| *2017* | |
| Jan 20 | Japanese cabinet finalizes all domestic TPP ratification procedures |

CEFP = Council on Economic and Fiscal Policy; JA = Japan Agriculture

care system, and protection of the country's strict food safety standards. As they campaigned for the 2012 general election, a vast majority (84 percent) of LDP candidates stated opposition to the TPP. After the election, the ranks of the LDP's anti-TPP caucus swelled to 250 (more than half of the party's Diet members).

A fractious party debate and the lack of resolution on TPP entry (replicating the DPJ experience) seemed to be in store. Yet Prime Minister Abe made the decision to join the negotiations in the early spring. The prime minister had powerful motives to seek Japan's participation. In the policy speech announcing his decision, Abe addressed the range of national interests at stake in joining such an ambitious trade grouping.[25] He referred to the transformation of the Pacific Ocean into a vast inland sea for commerce, key to Japan's prosperity and to its ability to address adverse demographic trends, stubborn deflation, and, in particular, to avoid becoming an inward-looking nation. He drew a direct connection between TPP membership and Japan's national security interests: working together with its ally (the United States) and other countries that shared values of democracy, human rights, and the rule of law would enhance peace and stability in the region. He asserted Japan's rule-making penchant, noting that Japan had to be at the "heart of the Asia Pacific Century" with participation in the TPP as its "provident masterstroke."

In tandem with this announcement, the prime minister proceeded to establish a TPP headquarters with Minister Amari concurrently serving as minister in charge of TPP negotiations, and Deputy Foreign Minister Koji Tsuruoka designated as chief negotiator. One hundred elite bureaucrats from different ministries were tapped to work in the new headquarters so they would no longer represent the narrow interests of their sending ministries. Signaling a unified front, the government released a whole-of-cabinet assessment of the TPP's (positive) impact on the Japanese economy. The TPP staff was divided into two teams: one to participate in the international negotiations and the other to focus on domestic measures and reach out to LDP members and organized interests—the first time the government had launched such an outreach program.[26] With this new setup, the prime minister had created a far more coherent negotiating arm with a strong political mandate to the TPP minister, clear lines of delegation to bureaucratic actors, and with the *Kantei* as the locus for hammering out positions at the negotiation table and coordinating with domestic interests. American negotiators with long experience in dealing with Japan noted a marked contrast with past trade talks and attributed Japan's ability to achieve results to the new negotiating structure.[27]

Before announcing the membership bid and altering the negotiating setup, Prime Minister Abe ensured that the manner of Japan's entry would not adversely affect his two central political priorities: to avoid major party division and to secure a majority in both houses of the Diet to avoid policy gridlock. To this end, he first secured an understanding with President Barack Obama in their February summit meeting that both countries had sensitive sectors and that no prior commitment to eliminate all tariffs was required for Japan's participation—meeting the LDP's campaign pledge. Next, he enlisted an agricultural policy tribe politician, Koya Nishikawa, to create a party consensus as chairman of the LDP's TPP committee.

The day before the prime minister's announcement, the committee issued a resolution identifying five "sacred" commodities (rice, wheat, beef and pork, dairy, and sugar) as off-limits from full tariff elimination. The prime minister vowed to endorse the party's resolution, maintaining party unity on the decision to join the TPP. Hence, Japanese trade officials received a negotiating mandate to protect these core agricultural interests.

The LDP went on to win a handsome victory in the July 2013 Upper House election. The ability to secure TPP membership and win a major election underscored the political strengths of the Abe administration. His high approval ratings, a product of his focus on economic revitalization, gave him some immunity from TPP foes.[28] Moreover, LDP party members were less tempted to defect when they expected the Abe government to finally break the cycle of one-year prime ministerships. Last, the decimation of the opposition camp after the DPJ lost power left the agricultural lobby bereft of a large national party that could champion its anti-TPP crusade. The pragmatic choice was to work within the LDP to minimize the impact of trade liberalization. The electoral victory, in turn, strengthened the hand of the prime minister, as opposition parties could no longer use the Upper House as a roadblock to stall government bills.

REFORMS TO THE AGRICULTURAL REGIME

After securing TPP entry and passing the electoral test, Prime Minister Abe directed his reform efforts toward pillars of the agricultural regime that had long been deemed obstacles to modernization and liberalization efforts: the rice set-aside policy (known in Japanese as *gentan*), which restricts rice output to maintain high prices, and the status and prerogatives of the nationwide agricultural cooperative organization Japan Agriculture.

JA is one of the most powerful organized interests in Japan, one that has long enjoyed a semi-official status. In the reconstruction effort after World War II, the government enlisted the agricultural cooperatives for the collection and distribution of staple commodities, and in exchange it awarded JA several prerogatives, such as an exemption from the anti-monopoly law and the ability to diversify into other business sectors, like banking. Organizationally, the JA group evolved into a complex and far-ranging system. At the top of the JA pyramid sit four major national organizations: Zenchū, the central decisionmaking and political lobbying organization; Zen-noh, the group's marketing company in charge of sales of fertilizers and other agricultural inputs; Norinchūkin, its banking arm; and JA Kyosai, offering insurance products.

JA benefited enormously from its core position in all aspects of agricultural production. Operating as a quasi-monopoly on the government food control system, and in the sale of agricultural inputs such as fertilizer and machinery, JA reaped hefty profits from rice distribution fees and from the higher prices it charged farmers for its products.[29] Later, it took over the administration of the set-aside program for rice cultivation established in 1969. Diversification into other economic activities, especially banking and insurance, generated substantial profits for JA. In the late 1980s, Zen-noh ranked as the seventh largest Japanese trading company, and Norinchūkin was the largest bank in the country and ranked seventh in the world in 1992.[30]

However, the golden years of JA as a quasi-official monopoly on rice distribution, financial mammoth, and key pivot in the conservative electoral machine have passed. Since the 1990s, a number of challenges diminished JA's organizational, economic, and political leverage. With financial deregulation in the mid-1990s (known as the Big Bang), Norinchūkin lost the preferential treatment enabling it to pay higher interest rates on deposits than commercial banks and to open branches with greater ease. Once these privileges were removed, the agricultural bank had difficulty keeping up with its competitors.[31] Norinchūkin turned to risky investments in real estate, and when the Japanese real estate bubble burst in the early 1990s it suffered major losses, which required a large and unpopular government rescue package.[32] A second major setback for Norinchūkin took place in the aftermath of the 2008 global financial crisis when the value of the bank's securities dropped by half.[33] Given this, it became difficult for the financial arm of JA to cross-subsidize the less profitable economic activities of the group, such as farming. Indeed, deregulation of the food distribution system had eliminated the monopolistic rents that JA had enjoyed. Prior to the enactment of the 1995 Staple Food Law, farmers had only two channels to sell their rice, the government or JA. With the new law, the so-called freed rice was legalized and JA's share of the rice distribution market decreased to a 50 percent market share.[34]

The contraction of agricultural output and the drop in the number of farmers presented a steep challenge to JA. In addition to shifting its business portfolio (with financial services becoming more important to its economic fortunes), JA also responded by diversifying its membership base. The total number of JA members has, in fact, increased over time, from 7.67 million in 1975 to 9.97 million in 2012. This was due to the rise of associate members (nonfarming rural residents) who, in 1975, represented only 24.8 percent of membership, but in 2012 were up to 53.75 percent of members.[35]

Even though the identity of JA as a farmer cooperative became diluted over time, JA remained a central cog in the agricultural iron triangle (with LDP politicians and MAFF), deciding the core tenets of the agricultural regime. Among them, JA was a staunch supporter of the set-aside program, which eventually diverted one-third of all paddies in the country away from rice production. By decreasing supply, the set-aside program has been instrumental in boosting the price of rice, especially after the government eliminated its policy to set producer prices in the mid-1990s. For JA, the economic and political stakes of *gentan* are high. It can charge a higher commission on rice distribution transactions, and the higher prices help shore up part-time farmers, a bastion of JA support.[36] Artificially high prices mandated border barriers (tariffs and quotas) to avoid imports undercutting Japanese farmers. Hence, JA fiercely opposed trade liberalization (more on this later).

Agricultural modernization figured prominently in Prime Minister Abe's plans for third-arrow reforms. A major step forward in this direction seemed to be the announcement in November 2013 that the decades-old *gentan* system would be abolished within five years. However, agricultural experts doubted that this step would bring about the purported change. They noted that with the announcement of the phase-out of *gentan* subsidies came the phase-in of subsidies for livestock feed rice production and farmland management. In other words, part-time farmers will remain in business as they switch production to receive financial support for feed rice and as they benefit from the price boosting effect of the decreased supply of staple rice.[37] Despite the symbolism of eliminating a mainstay of the agricultural policy regime, the net effect will be a preservation of the status quo: part-time farmers operating in miniscule plots.

A far more substantive battle took place when the Abe *Kantei* put reform of the JA system itself on the reform agenda. In May 2014, the Regulatory Reform Council announced a proposal for far-reaching change to the structure of the agricultural cooperative organization. Among the proposed changes was stripping JA Zenchū from the Agricultural Cooperatives Law. This would result in defunding the political arm of JA by taking away its right to collect levies from local cooperatives and eliminate its top-down control through its auditing prerogatives. The council also proposed to turn JA Zen-noh into a regular joint stock company, no longer immune from the anti-monopoly law and no longer qualifying for perks such as lower tax rates. Finally, the council aimed to curtail the membership expansion drive by limiting the share of associated members to less than 50 percent, with the aim of returning the organization to its farmer origins.[38]

If implemented, the council's proposals would have triggered a substantial loss of economic and political power for JA. Not surprisingly,

JA and LDP agricultural policy tribe politicians pushed back, endorsing the notion of "self-reform" (that is, letting JA define the terms of change). While Prime Minister Abe agreed to let JA put forth its own proposed reforms, he eventually found them insufficient and demanded greater change. With the *Kantei* acting as the final arbiter, a compromise was struck among foes and proponents of reforms. Kazuhito Yamashita captures the contours of this compromise well: JA Zenchū will become a general incorporated association and will not be able to directly collect levies from local units. But the prefectural cooperatives do retain this prerogative, and will likely continue to funnel the funds to the central organization. On the other hand, JA local cooperatives can now choose to seek out independent auditing firms, which could dilute the power of the national organization. JA Zen-noh was given the discretion to decide on its own whether to turn itself into a joint stock company (unlikely), and the issue of JA membership composition will be revisited in the future.[39]

In securing TPP entry and pursuing JA reform, Prime Minister Abe achieved goals that long eluded his predecessors. The policy departures, while unprecedented, were essentially political compromises that upheld the most vital interests of the agricultural lobby. Moreover, the Abe administration succeeded in making the prime minister's office the locus of decisionmaking. This was not achieved through institutional changes (such as the Hashimoto or DPJ reforms) but, rather, through skillful adaptation to new political realities. The decimation of the DPJ and the fragmentation of the opposition camp strengthened the hand of the LDP as disaffected interest groups found it harder to credibly threaten defection. Moreover, the high rates of public approval of Prime Minister Abe and his ability to deliver a string of electoral successes (starting with the Upper House election in the summer of 2013) quieted down potential challengers within his own party. That victory in the Upper House election also closed the twisted Diet cycle and the opposition lost the ability to stall the Abe government's legislative agenda. In this way, Prime Minister Abe has been able to stay in power for an extended period of time, avoiding the blow of a party split, the paralysis of divided government, and a crippling loss of confidence from voters. The array of negotiated agricultural reforms and liberalization commitments is guided by these political imperatives.

## JAPAN'S AGRICULTURAL LOBBY: A WEAKENING— BUT STILL FORMIDABLE—VETO PLAYER

The reform accomplishments—and limits—of the Abe government are also influenced by the shifts in the electoral clout of the agricultural lobby and the consequent renegotiation of the terms of the veto it exercises over trade policy.

### Farm Power: Shifting Electoral Clout

In the postwar period, JA became a bastion of conservative politics by consistently delivering the agricultural vote to the LDP. Equally important to JA's influence was its ability to electorally punish the party when it deviated from core JA preferences. JA's power rested on the importance of the farming vote to the Japanese electoral process. In the early postwar period, agricultural households represented the single most important electoral constituency (47.7 percent of eligible voters in 1950). With the twin forces of industrialization and urbanization, the share of the rural vote decreased to 25.4 percent in 1972 and to 17.4 percent in 1986.[40] The weakening of electoral influence brought about by these economic and demographic changes was, however, mitigated by the traits of the electoral system. The multi-member electoral districts allowed politicians to win elections by targeting narrow electoral groups (as opposed to appealing to the median voter, increasingly in the cities), and the malapportionment of electoral districts substantially over-represented the rural vote. Consequently, the LDP's early electoral dominance was based on farmer (and small business) support; even as the party transitioned into a catchall party it did not shake off its rural roots.[41]

As the LDP lacked its own grassroots organizational network, it relied on JA for the delivery of the rural vote.[42] Like other organized interests recruited to perform state functions (such as food distribution or postal service), JA developed a vast national network reaching deep within localities, and it became an efficient machinery to mobilize the vote. JA displayed great zeal in backing candidates who pledged support for its key policies.[43] These "contracts" extracted a pre-commitment from candidates to support JA's policies and helped the farm lobby monitor compliance once these politicians were elected. The LDP, therefore, could not take farmer backing for granted, since the support of this constituency was contingent on the maintenance of the system of agricultural subsidization and protection. Any deviation from core JA policies would result in withdrawal of support. The most dramatic example took place in the aftermath of the 1988 beef and citrus liberalization deal negotiated with the United States. In the Upper House election of the following year, the LDP lost six out of seven electoral districts producing these commodities, and the rural protest vote was a major factor behind the party losing, for the first time ever, its majority in this chamber.[44] Politicians were, therefore, forewarned that unwanted trade liberalization could result in a significant electoral backlash.[45]

Nevertheless, unrelenting demographic trends, growing rifts in the farming community, and the electoral reforms in 1994 began to erode JA's electoral grip. As rural depopulation continues unabated, the share of farm households over the total population has dropped at a fast rate, from 8.3 percent in 2000 to 5.1 percent in 2010.[46] At the same time, JA's ability to reach this shrinking constituency has been curtailed by its own rationalization campaign eliminating many of the local cooperatives that had provided the day-to-day contact with farmers. Moreover, JA's ability to deliver the agricultural vote has been hampered by the growing split between part-time and full-time farmers. The latter complain about the high distribution fees and inflated equipment prices, and many believe JA is driven by its own organizational interests and not the welfare of farmers. They criticize JA's support for cumbersome land regulations that prevent commercial agricultural concerns from buying agricultural land to increase economies of scale; and they argue that, instead of heavy subsidization (which has done nothing to improve efficiency), what Japanese agriculture needs is the introduction of managerial know-how and corporate-style farming that only full-time farmers can supply.[47] Many of these full-time farmers do not see participation in trade agreements as an unmitigated disaster, but rather as an opportunity to tap overseas markets in areas where they compete based on product quality.

The electoral reforms of 1994 further diminished the power of the farm vote and made it more difficult for JA to play its role as intermediary in delivering the organized rural vote to the LDP. The introduction of single member districts (SMDs) meant that politicians could no longer hope to get elected by offering particularistic benefits to narrow constituencies but, rather, had to appeal to the median voter. Moreover, as the new system eliminated intraparty competition among candidates in

multimember districts, Japanese elections have become more party ori-
ented and less based on appeals to loyalty to individual candidates.[48]
While politicians' personal support groups (known in Japanese as
*kōenkai*) have certainly not disappeared as politicians rely on them to
win elections in SMDs, their relative importance has decreased.[49] Thus,
the electoral reform weakened a cornerstone in JA's mobilization strategy that relied on these interpersonal networks in rural communities to
turn out the vote.

Still, political parties in Japan keenly compete to secure the agricultural vote, and for very good reasons: (1) JA may no longer be able to
ensure the victory of a candidate given the dwindling number of farmers, but it can still deny a win in tight races; and (2) JA shed its sense of
loyalty toward the LDP and exploited interparty competition to secure
policy benefits. In other words, the famed hard rural vote went soft with
remarkable volatility from one election to the next. The rural swing vote
was particularly evident at the height of interparty competition (2007–
10), but even a resurgent LDP post-2012 has no assurances regarding
JA's electoral allegiance.

The LDP began to lose ground with agricultural voters during the
Koizumi years, when structural reforms threatened to curtail pork-barrel
practices, the decision to privatize the postal service alienated the local
postmasters (raising alarm about the future of ties to organized interests),
and the administrative reform campaign reduced the number of local
municipalities.[50] The party was hard pressed to fight the label of "market
fundamentalism" to regain its ground in the countryside.

In the 2007 Upper House and 2009 Lower House elections, it was
the DPJ that captured most seats in rural districts. The loss of control
of the Upper House during the first Abe administration was due, in
part, to the profound disenchantment of the agricultural lobby with the
launch of FTA talks with Australia. To show its rejection, JA convened
3,000 farmers and a truck parade in downtown Tokyo, but the electoral results spoke louder. Farmers' desertion of the LDP in the all-
important general election in 2009 was striking; while the LDP had
always won seventy-four of the one hundred most rural districts in general elections, in 2009 it only prevailed in forty-two districts.[51] The
DPJ outbid the LDP to cultivate the agricultural vote by offering an
individual household income support program that would extend to
all farmers (while the LDP's decoupled payments program was earmarked only for full-time farmers of a certain scale), yet a few months

later, in the July 2010 Upper House election, it was the DPJ who took a beating at the polls as rural residents came to resent the cutbacks on local infrastructure projects. In the twenty-nine most rural prefectures, the LDP won twenty-one seats and the DPJ a mere eight, whereas three years before, the opposite had been true, with the LDP winning only six and the DPJ twenty-three.[52] Rural voters, therefore, were quite willing to exploit interparty competition by rewarding the party offering the most income compensation, pork-barrel projects, and trade protection for core commodities.

By the general election of December 2012, DPJ support from the countryside had evaporated, in particular as JA decried the willingness of the DPJ Prime Ministers Kan and Noda to seek TPP membership. The LDP recaptured its rural base, winning eighty-two of the one hundred most rural districts, and continued to lead in rural districts in subsequent elections (in the 2013 Upper House election it captured all but two of the thirty-one most rural districts, and in the 2014 Lower House election it won forty-five of fifty-nine rural single-member districts).[53]

But this is no reemergence of the hard farm vote. The strategies of both JA and the LDP underscore a brittle electoral alliance. In the past few elections, JA has asked its members to vote not based on party affiliation but based on a candidate's position on core issues: opposition to the TPP (2012), withdrawal from TPP talks if the five sacred commodities were compromised (2013), and support for JA self-reform and protection of the sacred commodities (2014).[54] Organized agriculture once again reminded the LDP of its ability to mete out electoral punishment with the defeat of then Minister of Agriculture Koya Nishikawa in the SMD race (he retained his Diet seat only through the proportional representation list) and the loss of the LDP candidate in the Saga Prefecture governorship race in January 2015.[55]

The LDP under Abe has treaded carefully to avoid alienating the farm vote as it moved forward with TPP participation and JA reform. As it geared up for the 2013 Upper House election, the commitment to protect the five sacred commodities was elevated through Diet resolutions in April, and the LDP followed suit with a new agricultural plan aiming to double farmers' incomes in the next ten years, with provisions for doubling agricultural subsidies.[56] In the 2014 general election, the LDP downplayed both agricultural reform and the TPP in its electoral manifesto to avoid alienating rural voters.[57] Not surprising, after the conclusion of the TPP talks, and with the next Upper House election (July 2016) in mind, the Abe government put forth a hefty budget for agricultural countermeasures (analyzed in the next chapter).

But agricultural politics of yesteryear are no more; the LDP brought Japan into an unprecedented trade negotiation and escaped a major electoral setback. This sets an important precedent and shows that the agricultural lobby's veto over trade policy is not ironclad; in fact it has been molded over time to reflect new political realities

### Shrinking Veto: Renegotiating Red Lines in Agricultural Trade Policy

JA did not approve of the launch in the late 1990s of a multitrack trade strategy incorporating preferential trade negotiations through FTAs. Despite the fact that the Uruguay Round negotiations had extracted liberalization commitments on the most sensitive agricultural commodity, rice, JA still insisted trade liberalization be handled exclusively at the WTO. This "multilateralism-only" position was informed first and foremost by the incorporation of the "multifunctionality" principle in the WTO.[58] This principle upholds the notion that trading rules should be different for manufactured goods than for agricultural commodities because of agriculture's nonmarket functions: environmental protection, regional development, cultural preservation, and so on. Therefore, JA objected to the fact that FTAs have not endorsed the multifunctionality concept.[59]

There was also widespread concern in agricultural circles that FTAs would bring about the complete elimination of tariffs and affect other core policies of agricultural support (import quotas, state trading items, tariff-rate quotas, and price stabilization mechanisms).[60] It was not clear if a hefty compensation package to cope with FTA liberalization would be provided to farmers. Whereas in the past the Japanese government had made side payments to farmers when it committed to some market opening in sensitive products (most recently agreeing to a six trillion yen payment in the aftermath of the Uruguay Round commitments), the prospects for a repeat side payment were not bright in the late 1990s. The compensation package had been controversial not only for its size but because of misuse of funds, which were directed toward pork-barrel projects and away from agricultural modernization.[61] This time around, bureaucrats were not eager to support a similar scheme, and many argued that it was not feasible to compensate agriculture for every bilateral trade agreement signed.[62]

Consequently, the agricultural lobby adopted a defensive position vis-à-vis the first FTAs contemplated by the Japanese government. During exploratory talks with Mexico in 1999, the Japanese delegation acknowledged that agricultural interests wanted to completely exclude the sector from FTA talks; and in the negotiations launched with Singapore in 2001, Japan agreed to "liberalize" only 486 agricultural tariff lines that were already de facto duty-free.[63] This initial hardcore line would have nixed FTA policy, since outright sectoral exclusions would preempt compliance with WTO rules on preferential trade agreements and countries with larger agricultural sectors would have been uninterested in Japan's "Singapore formula" of nominal liberalization with no real market access concessions.

### Conditional Yes: FTAs and Controlled Liberalization

JA's FTA position, however, softened as it acquired more information on the treatment of agriculture in other FTAs. Particularly important was the realization that, instead of insisting on the total exclusion of agriculture from FTA talks (and paying the political cost at home of torpedoing the new trade policy), the key agricultural commodities could remain protected under exclusion or renegotiation clauses. The Mexico-European Union FTA signed in 2000 was widely cited as a key reference point since 28.6 percent of the agricultural lines were not liberalized.[64] It was this "flexibility" that persuaded JA to drop its absolute opposition to FTAs. Importantly, JA's acceptance of the new FTA policy was predicated on the notion of "controlled liberalization." In other words, Japan's FTA commitments could not compromise the regime of protection and subsidization of Japanese agriculture.

Therefore, in the aftermath of trade negotiations with Mexico, where Japan made its first—although modest—WTO-plus concessions on agriculture, JA insisted that agricultural negotiations take place ahead of market access talks for industrial goods.[65] Given the modest concessions that Japanese trade negotiators were able to make on agriculture, they had to resort to pledges of economic cooperation instead as they attempted to open the markets of FTA counterparts. This dynamic was evident in Japan's FTA negotiations with the Philippines, Malaysia, and Thailand. But by weakening the cross-sectoral exchange of concessions (long identified as a powerful driver of market opening), the overall results of these trade negotiations were modest.[66] JA's position on negotiating FTAs with smaller trading partners in Southeast Asia that were willing to let Japan exclude sensitive agricultural commodities in return for economic cooperation, in effect relegated FTA policy to a low-yield trade strategy.

The negotiation of preferential market access with large agricultural exporters was deemed off-limits by JA. However, its ability to veto these FTA negotiations was tested at different times: the launch of FTA negotiations with Australia (2007) and the discussion and eventual decision to participate in the TPP (2010–13). JA had long insisted that negotiations with Australia were out of the question because it is a major producer of the most sensitive agricultural commodities for Japan (beef, wheat, rice, sugar, dairy products, and so on). However, as the administrations of Prime Ministers Koizumi and Abe sought to improve security cooperation with Australia, the chances of a bilateral FTA dramatically increased. Prime Minister Koizumi decided to commission an official FTA feasibility study to reciprocate for Australia's dispatch of troops to protect the Japanese Self-Defense Forces in Iraq.[67] In the spring of 2007, Prime Minister Abe announced the launch of trade talks at the same time Japan and Australia signed a joint declaration on security cooperation that significantly upgraded bilateral relations. JA swiftly condemned this move as an example of market fundamentalism in disregard of agriculture's multifunctionality and insisted that sensitive commodities be excluded from the agreement. They warned that failure to do so would result in JA demanding that the Diet Agricultural Committee stop the trade negotiations with Australia.[68]

The largest threat to JA's stance on trade policy emerged in the fall of 2010, when Japan's participation in the TPP was first seriously considered under the DPJ government. JA immediately rejected Prime Minister Kan's expression of interest in joining the TPP, arguing that this trade negotiation would destroy the Japanese farming community. JA prognosticated a dire economic outcome based on its view that Japanese agriculture could never achieve the economies of scale of the United States and Australia, and further predicted that a collapse of the food self-sufficiency ratio would ensue.[69]

For JA, the TPP was a nonstarter because it violated the two core principles of its policy on preferential trade agreements: the exclusion of key agricultural commodities and the veto on trade negotiations with large agricultural exporters. TPP countries vowed to maintain the very high levels of tariff elimination of their predecessor trade grouping—the

Trans-Pacific Strategic Economic Partnership or P4, short for Pacific-4—in the range of 99 percent, which JA deemed unacceptable. Moreover, among the TPP members were major exporters of primary commodities (Australia, New Zealand, Chile, the United States, and later, Canada). For these reasons, JA insisted on vetoing the TPP talks.

JA went as far as to appeal to the United States to reject Japan's TPP participation. In a January 12, 2012, letter to the USTR, JA outlined how Japan's participation would run counter to U.S. economic and geo-strategic interests.[70] It argued that the TPP-induced devastation of dairy and meat production would hurt American exporters of soybeans and corn, that the decimation of agricultural production in marginal areas would promote depopulation and lead to prohibitive costs to provide security for uninhabited islands, and that the elimination of Japanese agricultural tariffs would increase world hunger for hundreds of millions of people by tightening international food supplies if Japan was compelled to import most of its rice.

In a second submission to the USTR, dated June 7, 2013, a significant change in JA's position was evident.[71] Citing the LDP and Diet Agricultural Committees' resolution on the exclusion of the five sacred commodities from full tariff elimination, JA asserted this negotiation guideline was the only way to prevent the dire consequences highlighted in its previous letter to the USTR. The rest of JA's letter was devoted not to opposing Japan's participation but to influencing the terms of the negotiation. It pressed for the introduction of "nontrade concerns" (code for multi-functionality) to justify a separate treatment of agricultural commodities in the trade talks. JA insisted on the protection of intellectual property for food products in the form of trademarks and geographical indicators, upholding Japan's standards on food safety, and banning export restrictions on food and energy.

The terms of JA's veto over trade policy have shifted. It lost the battle in rejecting preferential trade negotiations with large agricultural exporters but succeeded in shielding the most sensitive agricultural products. JA did not easily consent to this renegotiation of the "redlines" of Japanese trade policy. It relied on well-tested methods (extracting pledges from candidates, bringing the base to the street, circulating petitions), but it also forged new partnerships with other groups in Japan's society and launched entirely new lines of attack to try to stop—and later mitigate—the effects of Japan's TPP participation.

## THE QUEST TO EXORCISE THE TPP GHOSTS: VYING FOR PUBLIC OPINION

When the debate opened in Japan in late 2010 on the merits of joining the Trans-Pacific Partnership, JA launched a robust anti-TPP crusade. The DPJ's early attempts to shut down PARC—the venue through which agricultural policy politicians had asserted their weight in policymaking—and the prospect that Japan would join a trade negotiation with large agricultural exporters that aimed for full tariff elimination created strong incentives for JA's all-out mobilization. JA's anti-TPP message resonated in the countryside. Local governments weighed in on the discussion around a potential FTA negotiation. Forty-six local assemblies (representing 70 percent of the total) issued statements of outright rejection (fourteen) or of caution against (thirty-two) the TPP.[72]

The anti-TPP campaign was like no other trade policy battle. It mobilized new groups and gave birth to unlikely partnerships. It relied on new tools as the Internet became a powerful source of both information and misinformation. It revolved not just around the perennial problem of agricultural protectionism but broader issues that had never before been in the public eye in connection to an FTA negotiation: investor lawsuits and regulatory sovereignty, the impact of deep liberalization on Japan's economic revitalization, and the responsiveness of government officials to concerns from civil society.

The lines of the antiliberalization campaign were redrawn when JA Zenchū established a broader coalition with a constellation of other forestry and fishery cooperatives and consumer groups by creating the "Network to protect Japan's food, livelihood and lives from the TPP" (*Nihon no shoku to kurashi inochi wo mamoru nettowāku*). Among the groups that joined the fray to oppose the TPP were the Japan Medical Association and the Consumer Union of Japan (Nisshoren). In its coalition-building strategy, JA (long a bastion of conservative support) crossed traditional political lines by joining hands with groups closely affiliated to the Japanese Communist Party, such as Seikyo (a consumer cooperative).[73] It was possible to build a broader anti-TPP coalition by tapping into the greater degree of uncertainty over how a comprehensive trade agreement like the TPP would affect other groups in Japanese society.[74] JA made an eloquent display of its strength in numbers by submitting an anti-TPP petition to the Diet with 11.6 million signatures just as Prime Minister Noda prepared to make his decision on whether to join the TPP negotiations.[75]

*Figure 9-1.* Online Interest in the TPP, 2009–15

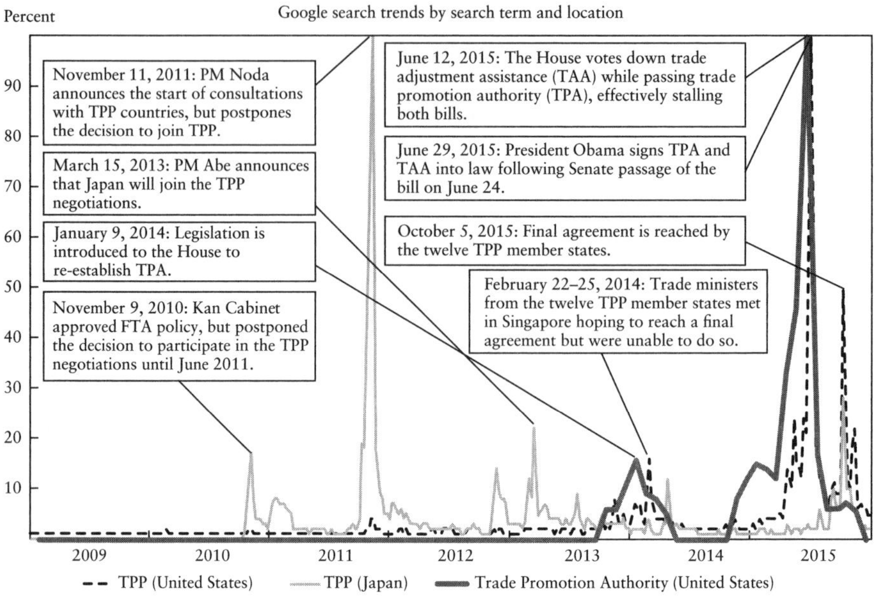

Percent                    Google search trends by search term and location

November 11, 2011: PM Noda announces the start of consultations with TPP countries, but postpones the decision to join TPP.

March 15, 2013: PM Abe announces that Japan will join the TPP negotiations.

January 9, 2014: Legislation is introduced to the House to re-establish TPA.

November 9, 2010: Kan Cabinet approved FTA policy, but postponed the decision to participate in the TPP negotiations until June 2011.

June 12, 2015: The House votes down trade adjustment assistance (TAA) while passing trade promotion authority (TPA), effectively stalling both bills.

June 29, 2015: President Obama signs TPA and TAA into law following Senate passage of the bill on June 24.

October 5, 2015: Final agreement is reached by the twelve TPP member states.

February 22–25, 2014: Trade ministers from the twelve TPP member states met in Singapore hoping to reach a final agreement but were unable to do so.

- - TPP (United States)    —— TPP (Japan)    ■■■ Trade Promotion Authority (United States)

Source: Google Trends, March 10, 2016 (www.google.com/trends).

Explanation of data: These numbers do not represent absolute search volume; they represent search interest relative to the point of highest search volume during the specified time span. The point where there are the most searches for the specified term is considered 100.

The battle over the TPP was not only fought through petition drives, the creation of like-minded networks, and protest rallies. The debate was also carried out in the virtual world, with the Internet providing a platform for Japanese citizens to form their opinions on the merits and demerits of this trade agreement. Figure 9-1 uses Google search trend data to document the rapid rise of the TPP in Japanese public awareness. Online interest in the TPP among the Japanese public peaked in November 2011, at a moment of high drama, when Prime Minister Noda seemed on the verge of announcing his decision to seek Japan's participation in the TPP during the APEC summit meeting only to backtrack because of intraparty discord and initiate only consultations with TPP countries. More generally, the waves of interest in this trade agreement tracked potential decision points (in the fall of 2010 and 2011 with the expression of interest to have Japan join the TPP from Prime Ministers Kan and Noda) and actual turning points in Japan's TPP involvement

(Prime Minister Abe's decision to join in March 2013 and the conclusion of TPP negotiations in October 2015).[76]

As online interest in the TPP grew, opponents of the agreement launched websites such as *Think TPP* and *TPP for Dummies* to make the case against Japan's participation by predicting far-ranging and devastating consequences for the country's future. Takaaki Mitsuhashi, for instance, argued that while the government and mass media insisted in portraying the TPP discussion as an "agricultural problem," the negative effects would be keenly felt in the medical sector and financial and insurance industries.[77] The Japan Medical Association argued that the TPP would bring about the collapse of Japan's universal health-care system (by lifting the ban on mixed medical treatment, allowing the entrance of for-profit enterprises into the medical sector, and encouraging the international migration of doctors).[78] Many critics also posited that beef tainted with bovine spongiform encephalopathy (commonly known as mad cow disease) could reach Japanese consumers and that food safety would be compromised by the scrapping of sanitary standards.[79] More generally, opponents argued that the TPP could result in the abrogation of Japan's public safety laws and regulations if foreign investors (most notably large American companies) challenged them through the ISDS mechanism.[80]

A running theme for the anti-TPP camp was that Japan was acting under pressure from the United States, and through the TPP it would surrender core social and economic institutions. A prominent critic, Takeshi Nakano, articulated this concern: "The world has been forced to accept domestic systems that are convenient for the United States in the name of nontariff barrier elimination. This is what globalization is all about."[81] As Saori Katada points out, this argument resonated with the public because of lingering memories of bitter trade negotiations where the United States had pressured Japan to change its ways.[82] Skeptics argued that while the Japanese government pursued the "Americanization of Japan" through the TPP, it failed to listen to the concerns of its citizens. A prominent news outlet in agricultural circles editorialized about concerns over Prime Minister Abe's hastiness in making monumental decisions for Japan's future. It listed, for instance, the approval of the State Secrets Law; changes to Japan's foreign and defense policies; the consumption tax raise; and the introduction of market principles to the fields of medicine, labor, and agriculture. It also complained about the secrecy of the TPP talks and the lack of accountability of negotiators as Japan embarked on a trade negotiation that could compromise its sovereignty.[83] As the government moved forward with reforms to the *gentan* system and the agricultural cooperative structure, it indicted Prime Minister Abe's leadership for displaying "excessive decisiveness" generating confusion and distrust in farming communities and rural areas.[84]

For proponents of Japan's participation in the TPP it became essential to launch a public awareness campaign to dispel the "TPP ghosts." A group of prominent academics and policy researchers offered a point-by-point rebuttal of the criticisms aimed at the TPP. For example, they noted that the TPP does not call for an elimination of food safety standards; on the contrary, it aims to strengthen them by requiring them to be based on scientific assessments. They dismissed fears of a regulatory overhaul through lawsuits by foreign corporations by noting that Japan has long included ISDS in its FTAs; corporations must prove discriminatory treatment, not just decreased profitability, to initiate a lawsuit; and corporations cannot demand regulatory changes even if they win an arbitral ruling. The academics and researchers also drove home the point that national health-care systems are not the subject of TPP negotiations, nor will the TPP bring about an avalanche of foreign capital in the medical sector. Japan already imposes no restrictions on foreign investment in this sector, but does bar the participation of for-profit corporations—domestic and foreign alike.[85]

The business community rallied in favor of the TPP and launched its own information dissemination campaign to correct distortions regarding the scope of TPP negotiations and the likely implications of TPP commitments for Japan. The business peak association, Keidanren, emphasized the risks of marginalization, noting that failure to join the TPP would mean Japan's abdication of any role in devising rules for the world economy. If Japan remained outside the TPP zone, this would minimize opportunities for exports of goods, services, and technology. It would be harder to crack open infrastructure markets abroad, achieve a seamless customs regime for imports and exports, promote e-commerce, prevent the piracy of Japanese products, nurture the export of Japanese agricultural products, and secure a stable supply of safe food imports.[86]

But as Aurelia George Mulgan notes, the TPP debate was not just a black-and-white discussion between opponents and proponents. There was, in fact, a lot of gray with several groups expressing caution or conditional support depending on how the final outcome of the agreement would affect them. Her review of 124 invited submissions to the government on the TPP shows that thirty-five groups were against (mostly from the primary sector, consumer groups, and the medical association), twenty-four were in favor (mostly industrial groups with export interests), and sixty-three were cautious (groups in the fields of health care, pharmaceuticals, and food processing, and professionals such as lawyers and accountants).[87]

This public comment mechanism underscores an effort by the Japanese government to broaden its base of consultation on trade agreements. Japan does not have a formalized private sector advisory committee akin to the one in the United States (see chapter 5). Instead, a bureaucracy-led informal consultation process with select producer groups operated in the past through FTA feasibility study groups, which gathered bureaucrats, representatives from different economic sectors, and academics.[88] While the public comment system used for the TPP gives many more groups the chance to present their views to the government, their input is more indirect since they do not interact with government officials and other affected groups in hammering out potential compromises to guide the negotiations (as was done through the FTA feasibility studies); nor do they offer ongoing input to trade negotiators or issue assessment reports on the merits or demerits of the concluded trade agreement (as is the case in the United States).

Mindful of the need to address the heated TPP debate through the dissemination of accurate information, the TPP headquarters' domestic section was charged with the task of outreach. While the trade talks were still unfolding, these efforts were rather modest, revolving around occasional symposiums and online discussions, as well as posting brief summaries of each TPP negotiation and the parallel talks with the United States.[89] Once the negotiations were concluded, the government embarked on a far more comprehensive dissemination campaign on negotiation results and planned countermeasures. The cabinet secretariat not only released the entire text but posted detailed information on the negotiation outcomes for Japan, fact sheets by economic sector, estimates of expected economic impacts, and a detailed listing of the budgetary allocations for TPP countermeasures.[90]

How has this "grand debate" on the TPP affected public opinion? Figure 9-2 highlights the focal points that galvanized public support or opposition to the TPP in Japan. On the latter, the TPP ghosts have fig-

*Figure 9-2.* Reasons for Support or Opposition of TPP in Japan

What is the main reason you support Japan's
participation in the TPP negotiations?
(NTV public opinion polls)

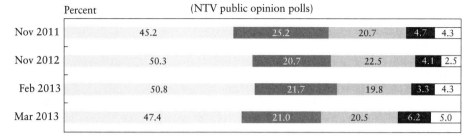

The further expansion of free trade will lead to the growth of Japan's economy
It is better to participate sooner rather than later in the establishment of a new trade framework
Domestic regulations will become relaxed and the economy will be invigorated
Other
Don't know / No answer

What is the main reason you oppose Japan's
participation in the TPP negotiations?
(NTV public opinion polls)

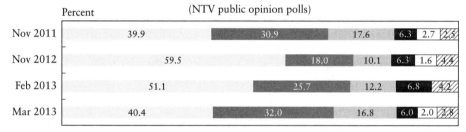

Japan's agriculture would take a devastating hit
Medical and food safety will be endangered
There is a risk of becoming subservient to the U.S. government
The current degree of free trade is sufficient
Other
Don't know / No answer

Source: "*Nihon telebi yoron chōsa*" [Nippon Television Network Corporation
Public Opinion Polls], Nippon Television Network Corporation (NTV) (www.ntv
.co.jp/yoron).

*Figure 9-3.* Public Opinion on Japan's Participation in TPP Negotiations

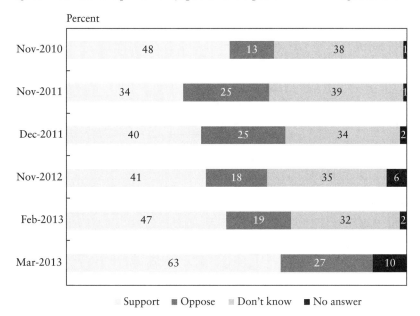

Source: *Mainichi Shimbun* public opinion polls, various dates, Maisaku (Mainichi Shimbun) database.

Note: The response option "Don't know" was not included in the March 2013 poll.

ured prominently in the minds of those who are against the TPP: the devastation of Japanese agriculture, the erosion of medical and food safety, and the "Americanization" of Japan. On the other hand, economic opportunity has galvanized support for the TPP: the chance to tap into overseas markets and to leverage domestic reforms to revitalize the Japanese economy, and to have a say in drafting the rules of the world economy. Opinion polls (see figure 9-3) show that support for the TPP has consistently surpassed opposition to the trade agreement, although a third of respondents had not made up their mind before Japan joined. At the time Prime Minister Abe announced entry into the TPP in March 2013, the balance of support was 63 percent in favor to 27 percent against. Even though the coalition opposing the TPP expanded, it did not generate a deep politicization of the trade agenda with mass protests, as seen, for example, in Korea over its trade agreement with the United States or in Japan regarding other hot-button issues such as the restart of nuclear reactors following the disaster at Fukushima

Daiichi Nuclear Power Plant and the Diet approval of new security legislation.

### Paving the Way to Ratification

On April 5, 2016, the Abe government initiated Diet deliberations on TPP ratification with the expectation of passing all related bills by the end of the Diet session in June. However, TPP deliberations did not proceed smoothly. Earlier, the Abe cabinet experienced a significant blow when Minister Amari, point man for the economic revitalization and TPP agendas, abruptly resigned on January 28 in the midst of a political scandal. Later, deliberations in the Lower House TPP Special Committee stalled when the Democratic Party accused the government of a double standard. Committee Chair Nishikawa—the former minister of agriculture—was preparing the publication of a book disclosing details of the TPP negotiation process that the government had not made available to lawmakers.[91] After a ten-day hiatus, deliberations restarted but ruling and opposition parties agreed to postpone the ratification vote until after the July Upper House elections to focus on the task of relief and reconstruction for the communities affected by the Kumamoto earthquakes, which struck on April 14 and 16 that year.

The political scandals and the decision to defer ratification until after the election did not, however, put in peril the ability of the Abe government to secure TPP ratification. As is usual in the Upper House election, all eyes were on the most rural, single-seat districts with speculation on whether disgruntled farmers would defect to the opposition. Aware of a potential opportunity, the Democratic Party changed its stance on the trade deal in its election manifesto. It noted that it could not support "this TPP" because it had come up short in meeting the Diet negotiation guidelines on the five sacred commodities. The LDP lost ground in the rural single-seat districts (it went from twenty-nine seats in the 2013 Upper House election to twenty-one in the last electoral cycle); and the losses in Tohoku (four out of five seats), in particular, generated some consternation in the party. The government's response was to redouble engagement on the TPP with local officials and to advocate for more rural support in the forthcoming supplementary budget.[92]

But the story line of the 2016 Upper House election is not one of an embattled LDP paying an electoral price for advancing the TPP. On the contrary, the ruling coalition expanded its lead in the Upper House by ten seats, for the first time creating the possibility that, through cooperation with other like-minded parties, it could secure the two-thirds majority in both Houses to embark on constitutional revision. It was with this commanding lead in the Diet that the Abe government faced no obstacle in ratifying the TPP on January 20, 2017, the exact same day that the Trump administration's inauguration called into question the fate of the trade agreement.

## CHAPTER TEN

# *Reform/Subsidization Dilemmas in Japanese Trade Policy*

**STRUCTURAL REFORMS** unleashing the forces of productivity, innovation, and entrepreneurship are essential to Japan's economic future. In the Trans-Pacific Partnership negotiations, the Japanese government has attempted to leverage its most ambitious trade commitments to date in the pursuit of far-reaching domestic reform. While the TPP agreement cannot tackle all areas in need of change in Japan, it can provide that rare and essential commodity, credibility. The TPP commitments stand as the litmus test of the resolve of Japan's political leadership to deliver on opening of the domestic market, pursuing the internationalization of lagging sectors, and shaking up existing iron triangles.

TPP negotiations marked a profound departure in U.S.-Japan trade relations. American and Japanese trade officials were finally able to find a compromise formula on sensitive market access issues, and they worked closely to disseminate new rules on the deep integration agenda. Indeed, the Trans-Pacific Partnership has underscored, like never before, the profound alignment of interests both in terms of geoeconomics (updating the international trading architecture) and geopolitics (anchoring the U.S. role in Asia's future and deepening the bilateral alliance in light of a rising China).

In the TPP agreement, Japan bested itself in eliminating/reducing agricultural tariffs (even in some of the five sacred commodities), although it still came last in overall tariff elimination compared to the rest of the TPP membership. The TPP, if enacted, is expected to generate handsome economic benefits for Japan by providing far more ambitious liberalization of services, promoting inward FDI through changes in corporate governance, and securing market presence disciplines in overseas markets that enhance the operation of Japan's supply chain—central to its future prosperity due to the projected contraction of the domestic market following demographic trends.

But the Trans-Pacific Partnership did not break the pattern of agricultural subsidization to deal with liberalization commitments. Given the small share of agriculture in Japan's GDP (1 percent), the modernization of this primary sector will not substantively alter Japan's growth trajectory. Nevertheless, the importance of agriculture derives from two inescapable facts. First, opposition from farmers had prevented Japan from embarking on ambitious trade negotiations that could have made a difference to its economic performance by opening the main export and investment markets and increasing international competition to improve the efficiency of the Japanese economy. Second, given that agriculture is Japan's core defensive interest, it very much sets the parameters of what Japan can hope to obtain in its offensive interests in trade negotiations. The focus on agriculture is also important to illustrate the lingering inertia in Japan's choices regarding the reform/subsidization dilemma. Japan's TPP countermeasures still display a strong inclination for stabilization measures and production-tied subsidies that blunt market signals and pork-barrel projects that have political resonance in the countryside.

The first section of this chapter discusses Japan's reform imperative with a focus on main impediments to growth and the significance of the structural agenda in the pursuit of productivity. The second section identifies the reasons behind the profound transformation in U.S.-Japan trade relations, which crystallized in the TPP negotiations as a vehicle to address old trade irritants and advocate new trade rules. The third section analyzes the reach and depth of Japan's TPP commitments on market access, services liberalization, and the parallel agreements with the U.S. on autos and nontariff measures (NTMs). The last section of this chapter discusses the unaddressed areas of Japanese agricultural modernization and the subsidization penchant of TPP countermeasures.

## JAPAN'S REFORM IMPERATIVE

Japan's low-growth era after the burst of the stock and real estate bubbles a quarter-century ago has been punctuated by episodes of modest recovery (for example, in the early 2000s) and sharp recession (in 1998 with the double blow of the Asian financial crisis and the consumption tax increase, and the global financial crisis a decade later), but the overall picture is one of underwhelming economic performance. The difficulties in overcoming stubborn deflation, promoting domestic demand, and leaving behind prolonged anemic growth are compounded by adverse structural trends in demographics, energy, and the utilization of human capital.

With one of the lowest fertility rates and highest life expectancy rates in the world, profound demographic change is afoot. In the next half-century, 40 percent of all Japanese will be above sixty-five years of age, and overall population levels will drop by 30 percent to approximately 87 million. The contraction of the working-age population, the increase in the elderly dependency ratio, and the effective management of the social security burden loom large in Japan's economic future.

Japan's growth prospects are also frustrated by a vexing energy challenge. In the aftermath of the tragic nuclear accident in Fukushima on March 11, 2011, the future of nuclear energy in Japan remains uncertain. As nuclear reactors across the country went idle, and only a few were brought back online at a protracted pace, the country has seen its bill for fossil fuel imports soar. In fact, Japan recorded its first trade deficit in more than thirty years in 2012. High-cost electricity hindered the competitiveness of Japanese companies and eroded the purchasing power of Japanese consumers. Although the recent drop in oil prices has brought some respite, the more fundamental task of weaning oil dependence through renewable sources of energy is slow going, and restoring public faith in the safety of nuclear power remains an elusive (some would say impossible) goal for the Japanese government.

Finally, Japan's human capital challenge is not about its ability to secure a highly educated workforce—it already has that. Rather, it is about overcoming its inability to offer productive and fulfilling employment to a large number of Japanese men and women and to meaningfully tap into the potential of individual creativity and entrepreneurship. Take for example the growing divide between regular and nonregular workers that underscores the rigidities of the Japanese labor market. Close to 40 percent of all Japanese workers are in the latter category, many of them working in dead-end jobs where they experience a significant wage gap, fewer training opportunities, and no job security. Labor market dualism is the main driver behind the rise in Japan's income inequality.[1] Figures from the Organisation for Economic Co-operation and Development (OECD) show that the Gini coefficient grew from 0.304 in 1985 to 0.336 in 2009.[2] The launch of new businesses remains saddled by the underdevelopment of venture capital and the enduring reality that the cost of failure in Japan is prohibitive. For example, in 2014 only 7 percent of survey respondents in Japan identified an opportunity to open a new business, and 55 percent said that fear of failing discouraged them from becoming entrepreneurs.[3]

Against these headwinds, Japan's path back to growth starts with the imperative of structural reform. This is the solution that fits T.J. Pempel's perceptive diagnosis of what ails the Japanese economy: the breakdown of the grand bargain between productivity and pork.[4] Japan's high-growth era (known as the 1955 system because it was ushered in by the consolidation of conservative Liberal Democratic Party rule in 1955) allowed for a virtuous cycle, whereby Japan's internationally competitive firms generated significant growth and, thus, enabled the compensation of low-productivity sectors. While exports' share of GDP in Japan has never been very high (for example, 16 percent in 2013), the "Japanese miracle" was based on an export-led growth model, as Japanese companies in different sectors succeeded in capturing world markets. The high growth period was a "no-losers" economy because growth propelled by internationally competitive industries was inclusive (creating a middle-class society) and export success created fiscal buoyancy to allow the LDP to target side payments to keep noncompetitive sectors afloat. In the post-bubble years, a shrinking economic pie meant that politicians skewed Japan's public resources increasingly in favor of low-productivity sectors through stimulus measures that had no efficiency gains and compromised Japan's fiscal health. Public debt levels soared from 70 percent of GDP in 1992 to 226 percent in 2014.[5] The grand bargain came undone and Japan transitioned to an "all-losers" economy, both because low-productivity sectors were prioritized in public outlays and because the performance of competitive sectors and the public's expectations of economic well-being were compromised by failed public policy choices.[6] What is needed now is a rebalancing in favor of productivity: deregulation, internationalization, and shaking off vested interests from the public coffer. Japan should transition to a "winners and losers" economy. As Richard Katz puts it, Japan needs creative destruction.[7]

## TRADE POLICY AND DOMESTIC REFORM:
## NO MORE OLD-STYLE *GAIATSU*

Today, trade policy, in particular the TPP, factors like never before in the attempt to achieve a transformation that unshackles the forces of productivity. The use of trade negotiations to channel foreign demands to leverage domestic reform is certainly not new in Japan, but the TPP negotiations are not just another iteration of *gaiatsu* (the widely used Japanese term for foreign pressure), despite superficial similarities to past U.S.-Japan trade negotiations. In the TPP talks, the United States and Japan again squared off on sensitive market access issues (such as agriculture and automobiles); and the United States insisted on parallel talks to address nontariff measures, long perceived as the most potent form of Japanese protectionism. But the discord that characterized the heyday of U.S.-Japan trade friction was in no way an indicator of TPP negotiation dynamics, despite efforts by opponents of Japan's entry into the TPP to cast the issue in this old framework.[8] Three main changes are in effect: changes in Japanese economic institutions and the structure of U.S.-Japan trade and investment relations over the past two decades; the shared geopolitical and rulemaking interests of the United States and Japan to use the TPP to build an Asia-Pacific economic architecture; and the display of a proactive Japanese strategy to use trade negotiations for foreign and domestic policy objectives, and not just to deflect unwanted demands from trade partners.

Japan's economy is in the midst of a transformation. The manifold challenges of the 1990s and 2000s—episodes of international financial shock; stress in the banking sector due to nonperforming loans, weak internal demand, and the increased costs of domestic production; plus the loss of competitiveness in traditional export markets like consumer electronics, to name a few—instigated significant change in core institutional features of Japan's capitalism. It is important to note that these were areas the United States had identified in the past as precluding a level playing field for American firms in the Japanese market: closed business groups (known in Japanese as *keiretsu*) and regulatory barriers in the areas of finance, capital transactions, and inward investment.

The postwar Japanese main bank system (embodied by the close ties of large firms to a commercial bank to meet their borrowing needs) no longer operates in Japan. A dramatic reconfiguration took place with a wave of mergers that consolidated thirteen city banks into four mega banks. The system of "implicit guarantees," whereby the government would keep ashore all major financial firms (known as the convoy system) and main banks would honor a commitment to rescue firms in distress, is gone. As Ulrike Schaede points out, large firms proceeded to diversify their funding strategies away from banks and into the stock market, with inter-firm ties weakening across the board.[9] For example, the ratio of cross-shareholdings decreased markedly from 45 percent in the mid-1990s to 24 percent in 2003; and the percentage of intra-group procurement and directorships also shrank from 11.7 percent to 6.4 percent and 8.6 percent to 4.2 percent, respectively.[10] The 1990s also witnessed a host of regulatory changes (known as the Big Bang reforms) with the aim of eliminating the segmentation of financial markets and foreign exchange controls, adopting international accounting standards, and liberalizing cross-border capital movements.[11] With this new institutional landscape, foreign financial investors rapidly increased their presence in Japan. As of 2006, they held one-third of the shares in the Tokyo Stock Exchange's first section.[12] Foreign direct investment has not increased as quickly, and judged by cumulative FDI stock as a share of GDP (more on this later), it is still miniscule. But as Kenji Kushida shows, in sectors as wide-ranging as finance, pharmaceuticals, telecom, and automobiles, foreign firms became prominent players in their own right and established business alliances with Japanese companies.[13]

None of this is to imply that nontariff barriers have ceased to be an irritant in U.S.-Japan relations. The American insistence on launching parallel talks on NTMs and automobiles with Japan alone among TPP counterparts should put that thought to rest.[14] It is also true that much has changed since the heyday of bilateral trade friction, not only because of the changes within Japan already discussed but also because of deep shifts in Japan's trade-investment nexus since the late 1980s. In the aftermath of sharp yen appreciation following the 1985 Plaza Accord, Japanese companies responded by rapidly expanding overseas production and developing regional production networks, spreading component manufacture across Asia and managing complex logistical operations tying together supply chains. As Japanese outward investment boomed, the nature of Japanese trade flows changed as well, with a much more prominent role for intra-industry and intra-firm transactions.[15] The consequences have been profound. Japanese companies report that as much as 35 percent of their production activities are carried out overseas, and they expect the foreign production ratio to grow to 40 percent in the next few years.[16] And Japan's rate of participation in global value chains (GVC) has only intensified; for example, its GVC participation index increased from less than 30 percent to 50 percent between 1995 and 2012.[17]

As the engines of trade and investment changed, a geographical reorientation ensued. The United States is still the top destination for Japanese direct investment (and Japan ranks number two in cumulative FDI stock in the United States). But whereas in the late 1980s half of all Japanese investment went to the United States, that share has been reduced more recently to a third. The retrenchment in relative shares has been far more pronounced in trade, essentially because China has become the main trading partner for both the United States and Japan. For example, Japanese exports to China in 1987 represented less than 4 percent but had grown in significance to nearly 20 percent in 2011.[18] In dethroning Japan as the main trade partner for the United States in Asia, China also became the source of the largest bilateral trade deficit for the United States. As depicted in figure 3-2, the trade deficit with China dwarfs that of all other U.S. trade partners, even when measured in value added terms (to take into account the weight of third-country components in China's exports). If bilateral trade deficits (misguidedly) animate friction among countries, then Japan is no longer the main focus of protectionist sentiment in the United States.

The significance of the trends highlighted here go well beyond the optics of the trade deficit. They underscore that Japan's current and future prosperity is intricately enmeshed in overseas markets given the significant relocation abroad of industrial capacity and the complex production networks that Japanese companies manage across borders. Traditional measurements of the importance of external demand, such as the share of exports to GDP, miss this important point. The revamped trade-investment nexus also accounts for the ambition of the Japanese government in negotiating deep integration FTAs, since behind-the-border disciplines on services liberalization or investment protection are deemed necessary to enhance the international competitiveness of Japanese global supply chains (see chapter 4). Japan's penchant for rule-making on international economic standards brought about a major convergence with the priorities of U.S. foreign economic policy.

In the TPP context, trade negotiations were no longer just a bilateral (and rancorous) affair. This multiparty negotiation demonstrated that the United States and Japan share the goal of disseminating multilateral disciplines on trade and investment to update and reinvigorate a languishing trade regime. The geopolitical alignment of such a multilateral trade initiative is even broader. China's economic rise has heightened the concern with being eclipsed (Japan) or edged out (United States) from the world's most dynamic region (Asia). The TPP addressed those concerns, both as a lever for Japan's economic revival and as an unequivocal demonstration of the United States's sustained presence as a Pacific power. As noted in chapter 2, supply of governance is a test of leadership for major powers. Notably, the TPP project has underscored how much the United States and Japan rely on one another to succeed in this endeavor. The TPP allowed Japan to scale up from modest accomplishments in trade policy to partake in the design of a new trade architecture. In turn, Japan's participation rendered the TPP a truly mega FTA and boosted U.S. efforts in the deep integration agenda. The TPP can be a powerful instrument of economic diplomacy, allowing the United States and Japan to define a proactive (not just reacting to institutional innovations from others, for example, the Asian Infrastructure and Investment Bank) and inclusive agenda (as China and others could seek admission).

This proactive Japan, seeking to elevate its international standing by boosting the competitiveness of its economy and partaking in the reform of the international economic architecture, is in sharp contrast to the reluctant Japan of the 1980s and 1990s, which grudgingly participated in heated negotiations with the United States and sought to deflect American pressure to change its institutions and embark on domestic reforms. Past U.S.-Japan sectoral and structural trade negotiations were carried out under the threat of retaliation (in the form of punitive tariffs through section 301 of the 1988 Trade Act).[19] The TPP negotiations moved Japan and the United States away from this counterproductive dynamic. The risk of failure in the TPP negotiations was not the ratcheting up of trade sanctions (as in the old *gaiatsu* pattern). Rather, the consequences of foregoing the TPP are measured by the missed opportunity to upgrade international economic governance, revive the global trade agenda, anchor the United States in the regional architecture, and add a new pillar to the U.S.-Japan alliance, all shared interests between the United States and Japan.

## GROWTH AND REFORM DIVIDENDS OF THE TPP

Departing from a passive trade policy, the Japanese government has sought to create synergies between its revitalization strategy and participation in deep integration agreements (the TPP and Japan-EU FTA). Launched in 2013 and revised a year later, Japan's Growth Strategy (known as the third arrow of Abenomics) has hinged upon three central axes: industry revitalization, human capital promotion, and global outreach. To increase productivity, enhance corporate profitability, stimulate venture capital, and turn Japan into a global business hub, the government has—among other measures—reformed the tax system to encourage crowdfunding and reduced corporate tax rates to bring them closer to international standards; established six National Strategic Special Zones to promote deregulation in areas such as employment, agriculture, and medical care; and made great strides in the area of corporate governance.

These include the adoption of a Stewardship Code, a Corporate Governance Code (using a "comply and explain" approach to increase accountability to stakeholders and encourage outside directors), and the launch of a JPX-Nikkei 400 index with exacting listing standards on profitability and governance standards (using a shaming strategy to incentivize companies that do not want to be seen as underperformers). To nurture human capital, the government has promoted the participation of women in the workforce; attempted to increase labor mobility by reversing the flow of subsidies from keeping redundant workers to rewarding for new hires; and sought to attract skilled foreign workers. As part of its global outreach strategy, the government set the ambitious goals of doubling inward direct investment stock by 2020 and expanding trade coverage under its FTA umbrella to 70 percent by the year 2018.

In many areas, however, the third arrow of Abenomics remains an aspirational goal. Other than in the area of corporate governance, progress in implementing measures has been slow. Some landmark reforms (for example, the agricultural cooperative system) have been blunted by political compromises, and the far-reaching reforms in agricultural modernization, gender equality, and labor market mobility remain largely on the drawing board. To be sure, many of the most pressing challenges in reactivating the Japanese economy are outside the scope of trade negotiations, including reforms in labor markets, energy mix, social security sustainability, and immigration policy, to name a few.

But high-level trade agreements do have an important role to play in advancing the reform agenda. Put simply, the Japanese government has not had a more effective credibility device to signal to private markets and the international community at large its commitment to market reform. The TPP can help close the internationalization gaps of the Japanese economy. As pointed out by Shujiro Urata, ambitious trade agreements that eliminate NTMs, promote deregulation, and expose protected sectors to international competition can help in areas where Japan's internationalization is clearly lagging. Its export share to GDP is low when compared to other industrialized economies; its stock of inward FDI as a share of GDP is the lowest among OECD nations (3.8 percent); and its exports of services as a share of GDP is at a very low level. At 2.5 percent, it is a little over half that of the United States and close to one-fifth of the UK's.[20]

Compared to its OECD peers, Japan still records significant pockets of tariff protection in agriculture as well as a host of other nontariff barriers to trade and investment. For example, at 54 percent, Japan's Producer Support Estimate (on government assistance for agriculture) is three times higher than the OECD average. In 2013, Japan scored above the OECD average on the barriers to trade and investment index and just below average in terms of product market regulation—an index that measures the impact of policies in encouraging or discouraging competition.[21] Regarding liberalization of communications services, a study of tariff equivalents of regulatory barriers ranks Japan at the top (tied with Singapore) at 63 percent compared to 37 percent for the United States.[22] This finding is corroborated in the OECD's Services Trade Restrictiveness Index, which shows Japan on par or above the OECD average in thirteen of eighteen service sectors.[23] Sectors where Japan scores higher than the OECD average include distribution, road, railway, maritime and air transportation, telecommunications, computer, insurance, and banking.[24]

Beyond these aggregate measurements, foreign companies have identified a number of obstacles to market access and investment operations in Japan: tariff sanctuaries and state trading practices in agricultural commodities, nontariff measures, high business costs, a closed and insular market, the difficulty in securing human capital, over-regulation, strict approval procedures, and insufficient incentives for direct investment.[25] Regulatory complexity, in particular, looms large in accounting for lower penetration ratios for foreign products and services and for the unbalanced pattern of FDI flows. Divergent technical standards, time-consuming product approvals, inadequate foreign input in the public comment process, and insufficient information on public contracts are responsible, according to a European Commission report, for increasing the costs faced by European exporters in the Japanese market by 16 percent. However, these are not one-way barriers, since NTMs in Europe are also deemed to result in a 13 percent cost increase for Japanese exporters.[26]

Regarding the difficulties of investing in Japan, foreign investors have long complained about Japan's weak corporate governance, which, until the adoption of the Corporate Governance Code in June 2015, had lagged behind global standards. Despite progress in that area, Japan's regulations on mergers and acquisitions (M&A) still remain a source of dissatisfaction for foreign investors.[27] The current formula for triangular mergers is only available to companies that already have affiliates in Japan. Thus, it does not facilitate new arrivals. Foreign investors have called for regulatory change to bring the level of M&A activity in Japan close to international standards as a most potent way to increase inward FDI.[28]

To the extent the TPP eliminates tariff barriers, enhances regulatory transparency and coherence as well as the adoption of international standards, and promotes widespread product market deregulation and more substantial opening of the services sector, it can help Japan overcome some of the obstacles to inward investment and close its internationalization gaps. Eliminating these NTMs also reduces business costs for Japanese companies, promotes the efficient allocation of resources across the economy, and incentivizes innovation. A well-established trend among OECD members is that nations that reduce their product market regulation index report increases in productivity, allocative efficiency, and patent activity.[29] The goals of internationalization and domestic competitiveness, therefore, go hand in hand.

In addition to the promotion of deregulation and competition in the domestic economy, the growth dividends of the TPP for Japan derive from enhancing its access to overseas markets, promoting Japanese outward investment, and upgrading Japanese global supply chains. As noted, Japan needs this strategy of outward engagement, since demographic trends and weak domestic demand dictate tapping into outside markets. Preferential access to the U.S. market certainly loomed large, but even if these gains are no longer available due to U.S. withdrawal,

Japanese companies also stand to benefit from improved access to other countries, some of which maintain relatively high tariff levels, do not participate in WTO government procurement agreement, and/or have not made substantial prior commitments on FDI liberalization. These benefits would translate into expanded opportunities for infrastructural exports and the opening of foreign markets to both Japanese products and investment. Cumulative rules of origin and market presence disciplines (encouraging investment, facilitating the management of complex logistical operations across borders, and improving regulatory transparency) would also help streamline and update Japanese production networks. A more indirect, but still powerful, benefit for Japanese companies derives from the TPP's effect in energizing other mega trade negotiations Japan is participating in, thereby improving access to other overseas markets.

### TPP Negotiation Outcomes and Estimated Impact

An analysis of the TPP's negotiation outcomes is essential to answer three important questions: In what areas did Japan and the other TPP members display resolve in opening markets (slashing tariffs, tackling NTMs), and in which others did sensitive sectors reassert their political clout to frustrate liberalization efforts? How did Japan in particular compare to the other TPP countries in the level of ambition achieved? And, based on the actual negotiation outcomes, what are the potential economic benefits of enacting the TPP?

Given the sheer complexity of the TPP deal, a full assessment of liberalization outcomes across all areas is beyond the scope of this analysis. However, a snapshot of the most common markers of Japan's unfinished liberalization process (overall tariff elimination targets, the evolution of Japan's agricultural sanctuary, commitments on services liberalization, and U.S.-Japan parallel negotiations on nontariff measures) should provide a good basis to understand the level of ambition in Japan's TPP diplomacy.

MARKET ACCESS

Table 10-1 compares Japan's tariff elimination commitments to the rest of the TPP membership. It is not a flattering comparison. Japan has the lowest level of overall tariff elimination among TPP countries, with 95 percent, compared to the 99.6 percent average for the other eleven

*Table 10-1.* Comparison of Tariff Elimination Commitments in the TPP

| | Overall tariff elimination (% of tariff lines) | Industrial goods (%) | | Primary agricultural commodities (%) | |
|---|---|---|---|---|---|
| | | Immediate tariff elimination | Total tariff elimination | Immediate tariff elimination | No tariff elimination |
| United States | 100 | 90.9 | 100.0 | 55.5 | 1.2 |
| Canada | 99 | 96.9 | 100.0 | 86.2 | 5.9 |
| Australia | 100 | 91.8 | 99.8 | 99.5 | 0.0 |
| Mexico | 99 | 77.0 | 99.6 | 74.1 | 3.6 |
| Malaysia | 99 | 78.8 | 100.0 | 96.7 | 0.4 |
| Singapore | 100 | 100.0 | 100.0 | 100.0 | 0.0 |
| Chile | 100 | 94.7 | 100.0 | 96.3 | 0.5 |
| Peru | 99 | 80.2 | 100.0 | 82.1 | 4.0 |
| New Zealand | 100 | 93.9 | 100.0 | 97.7 | 0.0 |
| Vietnam | 100 | 70.2 | 100.0 | 42.6 | 0.6 |
| Brunei | 100 | 90.6 | 100.0 | 98.6 | 0.0 |
| Average of TPP member countries besides Japan | 99.6 | 86.9 | 99.9 | 84.5 | 1.5 |
| Japan | 95 | 95.3 | 100.0 | 51.3 | 19.0 |

Source: *Naikaku kanbō TPP seifu taisaku honbu* [Governmental Headquarters for the TPP], "*TPP kyōteikōshō no oosuji gōi kanren shiryō*" [Materials Related to the Basic Points of Consensus for the TPP Agreement Negotiations], November 2015 (www.cas.go.jp/jp/tpp/pdf/2015/13/151109_tpp _setsumeikai_siryou.pdf).

participants. It is also true that, in the TPP, Japan went further than in other trade agreements in its efforts to eliminate tariffs. As noted in chapter 2, Japan had never met the WTO standard of 90 percent tariff elimination in previous trade agreements (including its recently con-cluded FTA with Australia, with a tariff elimination rate of 89 percent). Evoking a familiar dynamic, Japan negotiated very differently on market access for industrial goods and primary agricultural commodities. On the former, Japan went beyond the average for TPP countries in offering immediate tariff elimination (95.3 percent versus 86.9 percent) and eventually scrapping all industrial tariffs. Agriculture continues to be the Achilles' heel of Japanese trade policy. Japan's level of immediate tariff elimination is much lower (51.3 percent) than the TPP average

(84.5 percent), but more striking is the high level of agricultural tariffs that would not be subject to elimination: 19 percent. Canada, a country also known for its refusal to dismantle its dairy supply management system, comes in at a distant second (5.9 percent) and the TPP average is a much lower 1.5 percent.

Even so, the agricultural sanctuary has not remained intact. Figure 10-1 graphically depicts the narrowing down of the share of products never subject to tariff elimination from 10.3 percent to 4.9 percent. At the same time, the five sacred commodities have emerged more than ever as the remaining bastion of protectionism, representing the bulk of tariffs exempted from elimination. Japan's TPP commitments mandate liberalization for all manufactured products, and the share of remaining tariffs for forestry, fishery, and other agricultural products (beyond the core five) will be a mere 0.3 percent. Even within the agricultural sanctuary, the number of tariff lines exempted from elimination was reduced from 586 to 412, and some expanded market access opportunities were granted in these most sensitive products.

The central compromise behind Japan's negotiation strategy can be grasped by looking at table 10-2. Japanese negotiators had to align demands from TPP counterparts for meaningful market access with domestic resistance to the unraveling of decades-old policies of state protection and subsidization of key commodities. The end result was the preservation of core institutional features of the agricultural regime, managed liberalization through tariff rate quotas in staple products, and more significant tariff reductions in meats (coupled with newly instituted safeguards to temper market disruption in case of rapid import increases). Rice, wheat, and dairy continued to be designated as state trading commodities, the price adjustment mechanism in sugar was preserved, and none of the hefty, out-of-quota tariffs for these products were affected.

Calibrated market access opportunities were created through country-specific or general tariff rate quotas. For example, a duty-free country-specific quota for rice (to grow to 78,400 metric tons [MT] by year thirteen) and for wheat (to expand to 253,000 MT by year seven) were established, with the lion's share earmarked for the United States. On dairy, tariff rate quotas (of 3,719 MT by year six) were established for skim milk powder and butter, but in-quota tariffs were scheduled for reduction, not elimination. The beef tariff was reduced to the single digits for the first time (9 percent in sixteen years), and for pork, the gate

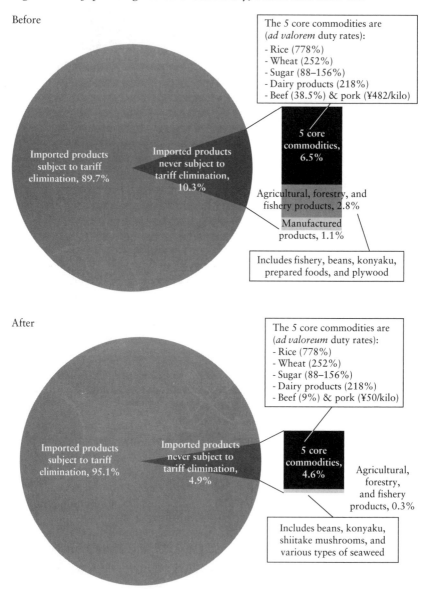

*Figure 10-1.* Japan's Agricultural Sanctuary, before and after TPP

Before

> The 5 core commodities are (*ad valorem* duty rates):
> - Rice (778%)
> - Wheat (252%)
> - Sugar (88–156%)
> - Dairy products (218%)
> - Beef (38.5%) & pork (¥482/kilo)

Imported products subject to tariff elimination, 89.7%

Imported products never subject to tariff elimination, 10.3%

5 core commodities, 6.5%

Agricultural, forestry, and fishery products, 2.8%

Manufactured products, 1.1%

> Includes fishery, beans, konyaku, prepared foods, and plywood

After

> The 5 core commodities are (*ad valoreum* duty rates):
> - Rice (778%)
> - Wheat (252%)
> - Sugar (88–156%)
> - Dairy products (218%)
> - Beef (9%) & pork (¥50/kilo)

Imported products subject to tariff elimination, 95.1%

Imported products never subject to tariff elimination, 4.9%

5 core commodities, 4.6%

Agricultural, forestry, and fishery products, 0.3%

> Includes beans, konyaku, shiitake mushrooms, and various types of seaweed

Sources: *Naikaku kanbō TPP seifu taisaku honbu* [Governmental Headquarters for the TPP], "*TPP kyōteikōshō no ōsuji gōi kanren shiryō*" [Materials Related to the Basic Points of Consensus for the TPP Agreement Negotiations], November 2015 (www.cas.go.jp/jp/tpp/pdf/2015/13/151109_tpp_setsumeikai_siryou.pdf); Ministry of Agriculture, Forestry and Fisheries, "*Norinsuisanbutsu hinmokubetsu sankō shiryō*" [Reference Materials for Agriculture, Forestry and Fisheries Items], November 2015 (www.maff.go.jp/j/kanbo/tpp/pdf/151224_sankou.pdf); U.S. Department of Agriculture, "Fact Sheet: Trans-Pacific Partnership and Japan: Key Outcomes for Agriculture," Release no. 0322.15, November 2015 (www.usda.gov/wps/portal/usda/usdamediafb?contentid=2015/11/0322.xml&printable=true&contentidonly=true).

*Table 10-2.* Sensitive Products in U.S.-Japan Trade: TPP Market Access Outcomes

| Japan agriculture | Status quo | TPP commitments |
|---|---|---|
| Rice | State trading commodity | No change |
| | Out-of-quota *ad valorem* tariff: 778% | No change |
| | Japan's WTO minimum-access commitments: 770,000 tons | Duty-free CSQ of 56,000 MT to increase to 78,400 MT by year thirteen (U.S. 70,000 MT) |
| Wheat | State trading commodity | No change |
| | Out-of-quota tariff: 55 yen/kg | No change |
| | | Duty-free CSQ of 192,000 MT to increase to 253,000 MT by year seven (U.S. 150,000 MT) |
| Dairy | State trading commodity | No change |
| | *Skim milk powder* | |
| | Out-of-quota tariff: 21.3% + 396 yen/kg | No change |
| | | TRQ of 3,188 MT to increase to 3,719 MT by year six In-quota tariff of 25% + 130 yen/kg to be reduced to 25% + 13 yen/kg by year ten |
| | *Butter* | |
| | Out-of-quota tariff: 29.8% + 984 yen/kg | No change |
| | | TRQ of 3,188 MT to increase to 3,719 MT by year six In-quota tariff of 35% + 290 yen/kg to be reduced to 35% + 29 yen/kg by year ten |
| Sugar | Sugar price adjustment mechanism | No change |
| | Out-of-quota *ad valorem* tariff: 379% | No change |
| | | Duty-free TRQ of 500 MT |
| Beef | 38.5% tariff | To be reduced to 9% in sixteen years Beef safeguard established |

(*continued*)

*Table 10-2.* (*continued*)

| Japan agriculture | Status quo | TPP commitments |
|---|---|---|
| Pork | Gate price system<br>Tariff on low-quality pork: 482 yen/kg<br>Tariff on high-quality pork: 4.3% | No change<br>To be reduced to 50 yen/kg by year ten<br>Reduced immediately to 2.2%, abolished by year ten<br>Pork safeguard established |

| U.S. autos | | |
|---|---|---|
| Cars | 2.5% tariff | Backloaded, long tariff phase-out by year twenty-five (tariff cuts to start in year fifteen) |
| Trucks | 25% tariff | Backloaded tariff elimination in year thirty |
| Auto parts | 2.5% tariff | Immediate elimination on 87% of tariff lines, 100% by year fifteen |
| Rule of origin | NAFTA standard: 62.5% using net cost method and tracing rules to determine share of regional value in list of components (equivalent of 53% with no tracing rules) | TPP standard: 45% using net cost method or 55% using build down method<br>No tracing rules |

Sources: *Naikaku kanbō TPP seifu taisaku honbu* [Governmental Headquarters for the TPP], "*Kantaiheiyō Patonashippu Kyōtei (TPP Kyōtei) no gaiyō*" [Outline of the Trans-Pacific Agreement (TPP Agreement)] (http://www.cas.go.jp/jp/tpp/pdf/2015/10 /151005_tpp_gaiyou_koushin.pdf); Trans-Pacific Partnership Agreement, Chapter 2. National Treatment and Market Access, Annex 2-D: Tariff Commitments, Japan Annex A. Tariff Rate Quotas, February 4, 2016 (https://ustr.gov/sites/default/files/TPP -Final-Text-Japan-Appendix-A-Tariff-Rate-Quotas.pdf); Cullen Hendrix and Barbara Kotschwar, "Agriculture," in *Assessing the Trans-Pacific Partnership, Volume 1: Market Access and Sectoral Issues*, PIIE Briefing 16-1 (Washington: Peterson Institute for International Economics, February 2016), pp. 41–59; Sarah Oliver, "Auto Sector Liberalization," in *Assessing the Trans-Pacific Partnership, Volume 1*, pp. 60–65.

CSQ = Country-Specific Quota; TRQ = Tariff Rate Quota; MT = Metric Tons

Note: Net cost method deducts value of marketing and shipping from vehicle value before assessing regional content.

price system was retained but tariffs were lowered on low-quality cuts and eliminated in the span of a decade for high-quality cuts.

Not surprisingly, agricultural policy experts do not expect a significant impact on Japanese agriculture from TPP commitments. For example, the price gap between domestic and foreign rice has closed in recent years, so even the WTO rice quota for human consumption has gone unfilled. Hence, the effect of the new TPP quota would likely be limited. Japanese beef producers have successfully specialized in higher-end production of *wagyu* beef, and pork importers have already been mixing cuts to benefit from the lower tariff, all moves that further limit the TPP's impact.[30] On wheat, government-administered price markups on imported wheat are set to continue, although they would be reduced by 45 percent by year nine. The dairy quotas on skim milk powder, in fact, reflect a small share of total milk consumption,[31] and the new butter tariff rate quotas would still be insufficient to address the large shortages in butter production of recent years. Political viability (neutralizing the opposition of key veto players) trumped the reform agenda in Japan's negotiation strategy for agriculture.

Exceptional treatment of sensitive sectors, however, was not Japan's prerogative alone. Table 10-2 discloses the defensive market access interests of the United States vis-à-vis Japan in the automobile sector. While tariff elimination on auto parts was mostly front-loaded, reflecting political realities on Capitol Hill, the United States had the dubious honor of securing the longest phase-out period for any product: the 25 percent truck tariff to be eliminated in year thirty (with no prior phase-out), while the 2.5 percent car tariff to be eliminated in a quarter century (with the first cuts scheduled for year fifteen).

SERVICES LIBERALIZATION

Through the TPP, Japan made greater strides toward service internationalization for two main reasons. First, the TPP agreement adopts a more liberalizing approach than the General Agreement on Trade in Services (GATS), a negative list where, in principle, all areas are subject to liberalization versus a positive list where only the enumerated sectors are subject to opening.[32] Second, Japan significantly narrowed the number of sectors to be kept off limits from liberalization. Gary Clyde Hufbauer offers a useful comparison of Japan's GATS and TPP commitments on services liberalization. He notes that, in GATS, of 138 nonfinancial services subsectors, Japan committed to national treatment in only twenty-six and had no commitments in fifty. In the TPP, however, Japan offered national treatment in eighty-five services subsectors and improved its GATS commitments in another forty-seven.[33]

The narrowing of Japan's defensive interests is underscored in table 10-3, which summarizes the main sectors where Japan lodged nonconforming measures from Annex I of the TPP text, which are subject to future renegotiation.[34] Japan filed fifty-six entries across twenty-eight subsectors on nonconforming measures. Almost half of those entries centered on two main areas: professional services (twelve entries for this sector) and transportation (fourteen entries across ten subsectors). On professional services, all nonconforming measures referred to cross-services trade and invoked exemptions to the disciplines of market access and local presence. The gist of these reservations was to require persons who offer services, such as lawyers, accountants, and so on, to have a local establishment and be licensed by the relevant Japanese authority. On transportation, most of the nonconforming measures on investment centered on national treatment (for example, mandatory prior notification and screening procedures will apply, using as a criteria whether the proposed investment will have an adverse effect on the Japanese economy); for cross-border services, they were focused on market access (for example, establishing limits in the number of licenses to be issued) and national treatment (for example, imposing a nationality requirement to provide the service).

NONTARIFF MEASURES IN U.S.-JAPAN PARALLEL TALKS
To what extent did the parallel talks deliver substantive results on long-standing U.S. concerns on nontariff measures blocking access to American products and firms in the Japanese market? The bilateral talks were divided in two broad categories (nontariff measures on automobiles and nontariff measures in several other sectors, including insurance, competition, and government procurement). It is important to note that the nature of commitments in each of these categories is very different. There is no dispute settlement on general nontariff measures, but there is a dispute settlement mechanism specific to the auto sector, which can be used not only for commitments on the parallel talks but all TPP obligations that relate to the automobile industry.

As can be appreciated in table 10-4, the outcomes of bilateral negotiations on the multisector nontariff measures range from the ambitious to the more modest. Among the former, postal insurance stands out as

*Table 10-3.* Japan's Services Liberalization

**Japan's nonconforming measures in TPP Annex I (56 entries across 28 sectors)**

**Professional services sector: 12 entries across the sector**

| Occupations and areas covered | Obligations (no. of entries applied to) | |
| --- | --- | --- |
| | Chapter 9: Investment | Chapter 10: Services |
| Architect, building engineer, land and house surveyor, attorney, patent attorney, handling of legal services by foreign lawyers, administrative scrivener, judicial scrivener, notary, certified public accountant, certified public tax accountant, certified social insurance and labor consultant, and maritime procedure agent. | | National treatment (1) Market access (12) Local presence (11) |

**Transport sector: 14 entries across 10 subsectors**

| Subsectors covered | Obligations (no. of entries applied to) | |
| --- | --- | --- |
| | Chapter 9: Investment | Chapter 10: Services |
| Air transport, customs brokerage, freight forwarding business, railway transport, road passenger transport, road transport, services incidental to transport, and water transport | National treatment (9) Most-favored-nation treatment (4) Senior management & boards of directors (5) | National treatment (6) Most-favored-nation treatment (3) Market access (9) Local presence (4) |

Source: Trans-Pacific Partnership Agreement, Annex I: Non-Conforming Measures, Schedule of Japan, February 4, 2016 (https://ustr.gov/sites/default/files/TPP-Final-Text-Annex-I-Non-Conforming-Measures-Japan.pdf).

an area where the concerns highlighted by the Office of the U.S. Trade Representative on the lack of a level playing field were effectively addressed through bilateral talks.[35] Some key changes include the onset of regulatory parity—by asserting the right of the Financial Services Agency to independently regulate Japan Post Insurance (JPI) and to

*Table 10-4.* Outcomes of U.S.-Japan Parallel TPP Negotiations: Nontariff Measures

| Issues | Long-standing U.S. concerns | TPP commitments |
|---|---|---|
| Insurance | • Level playing field for U.S. companies vis-à-vis JP before expansion into new products<br>• Avoid cross-subsidization of JP companies through arm's length rule and financial disclosure<br>• Increase transparency in JP regulation<br>• Ensure equal supervisory treatment for JPI/insurance cooperatives and private financial institutions | • GOJ will ensure JPI is not discouraged from distributing products of private insurance companies through its network<br>• GOJ will not adopt measures that give JPI competitive advantage<br>• GOJ will ensure JP publishes consolidated earnings statements once a year; JPI to publish financial statements with same level of transparency as private firms<br>• FSA will apply same standard for JPI new business applications that it uses for private insurance companies; FSA's ability to independently regulate JPI will be ensured |
| Express delivery | • Level the playing field for international express delivery providers vis-à-vis JP | • Greater transparency of JP's mail services through annual financial disclosures to prevent cross-subsidization |
| Transparency | • Advisory groups are opaque and there is no meaningful input from nonmembers<br>• Public comment procedure has short comment period and comments not sufficiently factored in rulemaking<br>• Double public comment period (to 60 days) | • GOJ will ensure access for interested persons to advisory councils, subject to reasonable regulations<br>• GOJ will provide meaningful opportunities to foreign companies to file statements<br>• GOJ will open meetings of advisory councils to the public<br>• Both governments will effectively implement public comment provisions of chapter 26 |
| Investment, M&A | • Provide meaningful investment access through M&As<br>• To do so, address these barriers: attitudes toward outside directors, inadequate corporate governance, cross-shareholdings, lack of transparency | • Amended Companies Act (effective May 2015) mandates companies to explain why they don't appoint an outside director<br>• Amended TSE listing requirements require companies to aim to ensure presence of at least one independent director (effective February 2014) |

*Table 10-4. (continued)*

| Issues | Long-standing U.S. concerns | TPP commitments |
|---|---|---|
| | • Ensure protection of shareholders when companies adopt anti-takeover measures | • TSE's Corporate Governance Code (June 2015) adopted "comply or explain" approach and established that companies should appoint two independent directors<br>• GOJ will receive recommendations on takeover defense measures |
| Intellectual property | • Strengthen copyright and technological protection<br>• Geographical indicators: uphold protection of prior trademark rights, safeguard use of generic terms, and due process | • In addition to effectively implementing chapter 18 (IP), GOJ will examine the scope of the private use exception for works downloaded from illegal sources |
| Standards | • Aim for greater transparency and flexibility<br>• Increase acceptance of international standards | • United States and Japan will establish working group on eliminating technical barriers to trade, regulatory cooperation, and good regulatory practice |
| Government procurement | • Take more effective measures to eliminate bid rigging and other practices that limit participation of U.S. companies in Japan's public works | • In addition to strict penalties on bid rigging, GOJ will adopt preventive measures, such as collusion training programs and enforcing the National Public Service Act<br>• GOJ will improve transparency in tendering process by increasing use of electronic bidding system and maintaining a data portal website with information on prior bids |
| Competition policy | • Maximize effectiveness of AMA by improving Japan Fair Trade Commission's economic analysis capabilities<br>• Strengthen due process protections | • Revisions to AMA (effective since 2015) provide for independent review of violation orders, enhanced access to evidence by defendants, and pre-order procedures |

*(continued)*

*Table 10-4.* (*continued*)

| Issues | Long-standing U.S. concerns | TPP commitments |
|---|---|---|
| Sanitary and phytosanitary measures | • Streamline risk management assessments for common food additives<br>• Fungicides and gelatin/collagen for human consumption | • Simplified approval process for fungicides<br>• Complete approval of four internationally used food additives<br>• MHLW eased restrictions on imports of gelatin and collagen |

Sources: Office of the U.S. Trade Representative (USTR), "Japan," in *2013 National Trade Estimate Report on Foreign Trade Barriers*, March 2013; USTR, "Fact Sheet: Toward the Trans-Pacific Partnership: U.S. Consultations with Japan," April 12, 2013 (https://ustr.gov/about-us/policy-offices/press-office/fact-sheets/2013/april/US-consultations-Japan); Trans-Pacific Partnership Agreement, U.S.-Japan Bilateral Outcomes, Japan Parallel Negotiations on Non-Tariff Measures, U.S.-Japan Letter Exchange on Non-Tariff Measures, February 4, 2016.

JP = Japan Post; JPI = Japan Post Insurance; FSA = Financial Services Agency; IP = Intellectual Property; AMA = Antimonopoly Act; MHLW = Minister of Health, Labor and Welfare; TSE = Tokyo Stock Exchange; GOJ = Government of Japan

employ the same criteria for new business applications already applied to private firms. Moreover, the agreement seeks to neutralize JPI's unfair competitive advantage not only through a commitment of the Japanese government not to adopt measures to that effect but also by opening JPI's vast network of post offices to distribute (rival) products of private companies. To avoid the problem of cross-subsidization among Japan Post companies, the USTR had called, among other measures, for greater financial disclosure,[36] and the parallel agreement delivers on this by mandating that Japan Post will publish consolidated earnings statements annually, that JPI will meet the transparency level of private firms in published financial statements, and that Japan Post mail services will be responsible for annual financial disclosures for the same purpose of preventing cross-subsidization through greater transparency.

When the United States and Japan launched the parallel talks, they agreed that negotiated outcomes on NTMs could be achieved through binding commitments, exchanges of letters, and/or new or amended regulation. It is through this last venue that the parallel agreement addresses American concerns on the administration of competition policy and on barriers to investment in Japan through mergers and acquisitions. On the former, the amended Anti-Monopoly Act (in effect since April 2015) offers improvements such as independent review of violation orders, improved access to evidence by defendants, and enhanced procedural fairness. Regarding the barriers to M&As, the USTR had identified the limited role of outside directors, inadequate corporate governance, cross-shareholdings, and lack of transparency.[37] As noted before, the amended Companies Act and Corporate Governance Code have lifted corporate governance standards and promoted the appointment of at least one outside director. The parallel agreement also has provisions to enhance regulatory transparency in advisory councils and improve the public comment procedure. While the reforms on corporate governance and transparency are significant, no concrete results were accomplished on the issue of ensuring shareholder protection when companies adopt antitakeover measures. The Japanese government merely committed to receiving recommendations for potential future action on this matter.

At the other end of the spectrum, modest accomplishments are evident in the areas of standards and the rooting out of bid rigging practices on government procurement. On the first issue, both countries will establish a working group to eliminate technical barriers to trade and promote good regulatory practices. Whether a working group can effectively make a dent in the maze of divergent product standards is an open question. The measures offered by the Japanese government to eliminate bid rigging on government procurement contracts appear as rather small steps for an enduring problem: collusion training programs, increased use of electronic bidding, and maintaining an online portal with data on prior bids. On the other hand, the steps to improve the bidding process (ensuring all bidders have access to the same information and prohibiting practices that prevent foreign participation such as consolidation of procurements into a single solicitation that unduly limits competition) may be more meaningful.

The second set of U.S.-Japan parallel talks focused exclusively on the auto sector (a key pillar of the trade and investment relationship and long an irritant in bilateral trade relations with charges by American auto firms of an impregnable Japanese market due to a host of nontariff measures).[38] Reflecting the sensitivity of the issue, both parties agreed at the outset that the parallel auto sector outcomes would be binding commitments incorporated into the bilateral market access schedule (table 10–5).

Regulatory divergence on safety and environmental standards is one of the most significant challenges American car companies face in tackling the Japanese market.[39] The parallel agreement addresses these

*Table 10-5.* Outcomes of U.S.-Japan Parallel TPP Negotiations: Auto Nontariff Measures

| | |
|---|---|
| Transparency | • Both parties shall ensure that advisory committees operate in transparent manner, with meetings open to the public and the opportunity for interested parties to have input |
| Standards | • Both parties shall ensure that technical regulations shall not be more trade restrictive than necessary to fulfill legitimate objectives<br>• GOJ will accept Worldwide Harmonized Light Vehicles Test<br>• GOJ will accept as equivalent seven safety regulations of the U.S. FMVSS<br>• Both parties will cooperate to harmonize standards on environmental performance<br>• Neither party will delay placing in the market a new motor vehicle on grounds that it incorporates a new technology |
| Preferential handling procedure | • GOJ shall not increase complexity or cost of PHP qualification<br>• GOJ will reduce the frequency of sampling tests for emissions and noise<br>• PHP vehicles remain eligible for any financial incentives offered by the central government |
| Distribution | • GOJ shall ensure that central government laws and regulations on zoning are applied in transparent and nondiscriminatory manner<br>• GOJ will pursue the establishment of a recommended standard processing period for local and regional governments to complete examination process<br>• JFTC to carry out survey on possible anticompetitive behavior in dealerships and distribution system |
| Auto safeguard | • Transitional safeguard that ends ten years after tariff elimination period<br>• Safeguard can be in effect for two years, with a two-year extension possible<br>• Parties will consult on appropriate trade liberalizing compensation |

*Table 10-5. (continued)*

| | |
|---|---|
| Dispute settlement | • Snapback mechanism: restore tariff if a dispute settlement panel rules on nonconforming measure<br>• Tariff delay mechanism: delay tariff phase-out if a dispute settlement panel rules on nonconforming measure (will operate during period before MFN tariff reduction/elimination starts)<br>• Formula to calculate trade retaliation in a dispute takes into account the ratio of bilateral auto exports and magnifies the amount of retaliation that the country with lower export volume can impose<br>• If a party already has zero MFN tariffs, it can impose trade retaliation on another product |
| New NTMs | • Rapid consultation mechanism on new NTMs, including those not yet implemented |

Sources: Office of the U.S. Trade Representative (USTR), "Fact Sheet: Toward the Trans-Pacific Partnership: U.S. Consultations with Japan," April 12, 2013 (https://ustr .gov/about-us/policy-offices/press-office/fact-sheets/2013/april/US-consultations-Japan); Trans-Pacific Partnership Agreement (TPP), Chapter 2. National Treatment and Market Access, Annex 2-D: Tariff Commitments, Japan Appendix D-1. Between Japan and the United States on Motor Vehicle Trade (https://ustr.gov/sites/default/files/TPP-Final-Text -Japan-Appendix-D-1-Appendix-between-Japan-and-the-United-States-on-Motor -Vehicle-Trade.pdf); TPP, Related Instruments, Market Access Related, U.S.-Japan letters related to the PHP, February 4, 2016 (https://ustr.gov/sites/default/files/TPP-Final -Text-US-JP-Letters-related-to-the-PHP.pdf); TPP, Related Instruments, Market Access Related, Japan to U.S. Letter on Safety Regulations for Motor Vehicles, February 4, 2016 (https://ustr.gov/sites/default/files/TPP-Final-Text-JP-to-US-Letter-on-Safety -Regulations-for-Motor-Vehicles.pdf); Sarah Oliver, "Auto Sector Liberalization," in *Assessing the Trans-Pacific Partnership, Volume 1: Market Access and Sectoral Issues,* PIIE Briefing 16-1 (Washington: Peterson Institute for International Economics, February 2016), pp. 60–65.

GOJ = Government of Japan; FMVSS = Federal Motor Vehicle Safety Standards; PHP = Preferential Handling Procedure; JFTC = Japan Fair Trade Commission; MFN = Most Favored Nation; NTM = Nontariff Measure

concerns in several ways. First, it consolidates and improves on Japan's Preferential Handling Procedure (PHP), which offers faster and stream-lined certification processes for American car companies. As part of Japan's bid to enter the TPP, the Japanese government announced the doubling of its PHP allocation (to 5,000 units per vehicle type annually). Through the parallel negotiations, the Japanese government agreed not to in-crease the complexity or the cost of PHP qualification, and that all PHP vehicles would remain eligible for any financial incentives. Second, the parallel auto agreement improves on mutual recognition of standards as Japan recognized the equivalence of seven U.S. safety regulations, the adoption of international standards (with Japan's acceptance of the Worldwide Harmonized Light Vehicles Test), and the promotion of future bilateral harmonization on environmental standards.

The lack of access to dealership networks has long been a complaint of foreign car companies. For instance, a survey of European auto producers noted that zoning laws make it very difficult to open service shops in metropolitan areas and that the costs of establishing sales sites in Japan are very high.[40] While the Japanese government agreed in the U.S.-Japan parallel agreement that central laws and regulations on zoning would be applied in a transparent and nondiscriminatory fashion, ensuring that local and regional governments actually do so remains a significant challenge. To expedite the process, the Japanese government agreed to develop a recommended standard processing period for zoning exemption applications by subnational authorities. Although more substantive commitments on distribution are certainly desirable, other factors limit the presence of American brands in the Japanese auto market. Compared to European car companies, American auto firms have a limited number of product offerings and have cut back on their investment in distribution networks over the past several years. For example, while the number of American dealerships in Japan dropped from 620 in 1996 to 159 in 2013, the number of European dealerships increased from 755 to 1,300. Compared to the 117 models offered by European car companies in the small-engine segment of the market, American firms offered ten in 2015.[41]

On the defensive side, the parallel agreement has a safeguard provision and a dispute settlement mechanism with novel elements. Similar to the U.S.-Korea Free Trade Agreement, when a dispute settlement panel rules that a party's nonconforming measure has impaired access, the claimant can snapback the tariff to the most-favored-nation (MFN) level. However, because the U.S. auto MFN tariff is scheduled to remain intact for fifteen and thirty years for cars and trucks, respectively, the United States could, instead, resort to a tariff delay during this period— in an already prolonged calendar for tariff elimination—if the panel ruled on a nonconforming measure. The other novel element of the safeguard provision is that it would enable the United States to impose significant trade retaliation in autos even though its export volume to

Japan in this sector is not very high. The adopted formula multiplies the amount of damage by the ratio of bilateral auto exports, enabling the country with the more modest export volume to significantly increase the retaliation amount.[42] Certainly these measures could give the United States a powerful deterrent against Japanese nonconforming measures, but they also were useful devices back home to allay concerns of stakeholders in the U.S. auto industry by introducing the possibility of further delays in tariff elimination and sizable penalties in the Japanese auto sector.

ESTIMATING THE TPP'S GROWTH DIVIDEND

What do economists forecast in terms of the TPP's growth dividend for Japan?[43] Peter Petri and Michael Plummer's econometric study of the TPP's economic effects revealed Japan to be one of the big winners.[44] Usually, the largest impacts of a trade agreement are experienced by smaller economies that are more reliant on trade as a share of GDP and/or are dismantling heftier tariff and nontariff barriers. The TPP assessment does confirm this dynamic in that Vietnam and Malaysia were deemed to reap very large real income gains, in the neighborhood of an 8 percent and 10 percent increase of GDP by the year 2030. As figure 10-2 shows, percentage gains for Japan were also significant across the board. Japan ranked sixth in terms of expected income gains (2.5 percent), but came second in exports (23.2 percent), first in inward FDI stock (30 percent), and third in outward FDI (4.0 percent). Certainly in the case of inward investment the relative increase is particularly large because of the low initial base of inward FDI stock in Japan.[45] The larger takeaway is that the Petri and Plummer study forecasted a significant contribution from the TPP to Japan's future economic performance compared to the baseline scenario (without the TPP).

The Japanese government also projected a sizable real income benefit from the TPP (increasing GDP by 2.6 percent). It identified a number of countermeasures to amp the TPP's effects to achieve three ambitious goals: Japan's rise as a "new export powerhouse" (through improved access to overseas markets), its emergence as a "global hub" (by reactivating the domestic economy), and the onset of a "new agricultural policy era."[46] Were these expectations realistic based on the outcomes of the negotiation and the set of complementary measures adopted?

As noted before, the TPP would enhance market access opportunities for Japanese products and investment. For example, industrial goods

*Figure 10-2.* Estimates of the TPP's Impact on the Japanese Economy by 2030

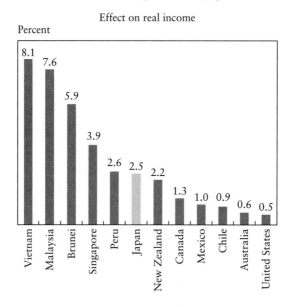

Effect on real income

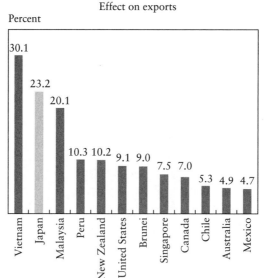

Effect on exports

Source: Simulations from Peter A. Petri and Michael G. Plummer, "The Economic Effects of the TPP: New Estimates," in *Assessing the Trans-Pacific Partnership, Volume 1: Market Access and Sectoral Issues*, PIIE Briefing 16-1 (Washington: Peterson Institute for International Economics, February 2016), pp. 6–30.

*Figure 10-2. (continued)*

Effect on inward FDI stock

Percent

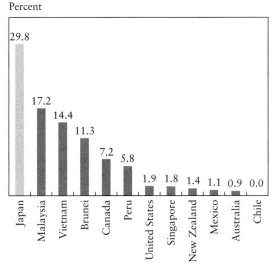

Effect on outward FDI stock

Percent

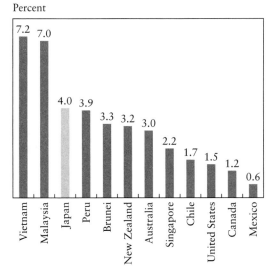

tariffs would eventually be eliminated (99.9 percent) within the TPP economic zone, and the Japanese auto industry would benefit from immediate tariff elimination in Australia, the elimination of the Canadian 6.1 percent tariff on passenger cars in five years, and the elimination of the hefty 70 percent tariff that Vietnam imposes on vehicles with engines over 3,000 cubic centimeters. On the investment front, the TPP deal established national treatment and most-favored-nation treatment in the pre- and post-establishment phase, and ruled out performance requirements. Moreover, Vietnam and Malaysia agreed to relax rules on foreign capital in sectors such as retail and banking, and in telecommunications in Vietnam.[47] The countermeasures identified by the Japanese government (that is, TPP user-friendly information centers and policies to incorporate small and medium-size enterprises [SMEs] in global value chains) seek to address limitations that have stymied the potential of other trade agreements (low rates of preference utilization and the limited internationalization of SMEs). As can be seen in table 10-6, 12 percent of government TPP countermeasure funds will be allocated to promoting the TPP's utilization and Japan's export drive.

The jury is still out on the chances for Japan to become a global hub aided by the TPP. As noted before, Japan agreed to the most significant liberalization of the services sector to date in the TPP (well beyond its GATS commitments), and has made strides in the area of corporate governance that foreign investors had long identified as a barrier to investment. But unleashing the forces of innovation, productivity, and efficiency in the Japanese economy will require much more than one trade agreement (as important as it may be). It will require bolder implementation of the complementary set of reforms of the third arrow of Abenomics to address bottlenecks to innovation and new business development, nurturing of human capital, and transformative reforms in labor markets, to name just a few. While the government has allocated 5 percent of its TPP countermeasures funds to the support of innovation, productivity growth through interfirm and interindustry cooperation, and inward direct investment, most of the funds to strengthen the economy will be geared toward improving regional earning power (32 percent). To this end, the government will promote tourism, sixth industry development, and the activities of regional public corporations, which do not directly speak to the industrial transformation agenda.[48]

Table 10-6. Budgetary Allocations for TPP Countermeasures

| | USD (millions)[a] | | | |
| --- | --- | --- | --- | --- |
| | 2015 Supplementary budget | 2016 Budget | Total | Share of combined budgets (%) |
| **TPP utilization promotion** | 453.4 | 273.5 | 726.8 | 12.1 |
| Information dissemination, consultation systems for SMEs | 11.1 | 0.9 | 12.0 | 0.2 |
| New market development, creation of global value chains | 442.2 | 272.6 | 714.8 | 11.9 |
| **Strengthen economy through TPP** | 1,047.6 | 1,165.4 | 2,213.0 | 37.0 |
| Policies to reactivate domestic economy through trade and investment | 71.4 | 227.1 | 298.5 | 5.0 |
| Strengthen regional earning power | 976.2 | 938.2 | 1,914.5 | 32.0 |
| **Agriculture, forestry, and fisheries industries** | 2,894.4 | | 2894.4 | 48.4 |
| Public works for agriculture | 1394.4 | (3,738.1)[b] | | (30.9)[c] |
| **Other** | 123.3 | 27.8 | 151.1 | 2.5 |
| **Total** | 4,519.6 | 1,466.7 | 5,986.3 | 100 |

Sources: *Naikaku Kanbō TPP Seifu Taisaku Honbu* [Governmental Headquarters for the TPP], "*Sōgōtekina TPP kanrenseisaku taikō wo jitsugensurutame no yosan uchiwake*" [Itemized Budget for the Implementation of the Comprehensive Outline of TPP Related Policies], 2016 (www.cas.go.jp/jp/tpp/torikumi/pdf/tpp-kanrenyosan.pdf); Ministry of Agriculture, Forestry and Fisheries, "*Heisei 28 nendo Nōrinsuisan yosan no jyutenjikō*" [Fiscal Year 2016 Ministry of Agriculture, Forestry and Fisheries Budget Priority Items], 2016 (www.maff.go.jp/j/budget/2016/pdf/28_kettei_juten.pdf).

a. Dollar budget amounts were calculated using a conversion rate of 107.86 yen per dollar. Numbers may not add up due to rounding.
b. Public works for agriculture in the FY 2016 budget were not counted as TPP countermeasures, but this number corresponds to the same budgetary lines funded in the supplementary FY 2015 budget to prepare the agricultural sector for TPP. It is listed for reference.
c. Share of public works for agriculture in the 2015 supplementary budget.

## REFORM/SUBSIDIZATION DILEMMAS
## IN JAPANESE AGRICULTURE

The goal of launching a new agricultural era through the TPP may be the hardest to realize. Japan's response to the reform-subsidization dilemma has not yet broken the old mold to allow for genuine agricultural modernization.

### The Reform Imperative in Japanese Agriculture

The structural decline of Japan's agriculture in the postwar era has been stark. Between 1960 and 2012, agriculture's share of national GDP dropped from 9 percent to 1 percent, while its share of employment contracted from 28 percent to 3 percent.[49] The number of agricultural households today (2.5 million) is just a third of their number in 1960, and the ageing of the farming population continues unabated (the average age of farm workers is sixty-five years old).[50] Agriculture in Japan has largely morphed into a part-time occupation (full-time farm households represented only 33 percent of the total in 2015), and throughout the postwar period progress in increasing the scale of operations of Japanese farms has been modest.[51] In 1960, the average farm size was one hectare, and today it stands at only 1.8 hectares.[52] This is in sharp contrast to the average farm acreage of large agricultural exporters such as the United States (63.8 hectares), Australia (99.4), and Canada (132.3), but also below European countries such as France (7.3) and the Netherlands (4.7).[53]

Painted in these broad strokes, this picture of Japanese agriculture fails to capture the diversity in Japan's primary sector. The levels of border protection to keep imports at bay, for example, vary a great deal. In contrast to the very high *ad valorem* duties of the five sacred commodities, tariff levels on vegetables are in the single digits, and average agricultural tariffs are not very high at 17 percent. These producers have already proven their resilience to international competition. There are also differences in the scale of production, with poultry, dairy, and pork registering a higher share of large-scale production (97 percent of their sales receipts are above ten million yen).[54] For these sectors, farm income represents the lion's share of total income, whereas rice farmers derive only 11 percent of their income from farming (the rest represents nonfarming income and pensions).[55] Rice farmers represent the bulk of agricultural votes (60 percent of all farming households), and this political clout ensured that the preferences of part-time farmers permeated Japan's agricultural regime.

Japan's agricultural policy framework has not been geared to increase productivity and modernization. Its defining traits include (a) price support through production restrictions (the set-aside policy) and stiff border measures, (b) restrictions on land transactions (private companies cannot buy land, only lease it, and the tax regime encourages farmers to maintain idle plots and to wait for changes in land use designation to sell their land at a more profitable rate for nonfarming purposes), and (c) the lack of decoupled direct payments targeting full-time farmers. In contrast to the United States and the EU, Japan's farm subsidies are tied to production for specific commodities; hence, they are more distortionary. The end result of these policy choices has been failure to scale up agricultural production to reap efficiency gains (part-time farmers have no incentives to sell their land and this prevents the emergence of full-time and commercial farming), the blunting of market signals to allow farmers to decide on their production mix and pursue new commercial opportunities inside and outside Japan, and the imposition of a heavy burden on Japanese taxpayers and consumers in footing a large subsidy bill and paying higher food prices.[56]

The decline of Japanese agriculture is not an inevitable result of geography or demography; rather it has been aided by flawed agricultural policies. Reform of the policy regime is an imperative for Japan's agricultural future, and it will require full elimination of production-restriction programs that sustain part-time farming through high prices (including the recently introduced set-aside policy for feed rice), reform of the land transaction regime (going beyond the current focus on leasing consolidated plots to actual land acquisitions), and support programs that are decoupled from production and are directed to full-time farmers. The shift to this productivity-enhancing policy framework has yet to happen.[57]

### Reform versus Subsidization in Japan's TPP Countermeasures

The TPP would subject Japanese agriculture to international competition to a larger extent than ever before. Japan agreed to immediately eliminate 50 percent of its tariffs on primary agricultural commodities (mostly in products already relatively open, such as vegetables), and in the longer term to eliminate 30 percent of tariff lines on the five sacred commodities.[58] Moreover, the TPP would create opportunities to expand Japanese agricultural exports to TPP countries, and the government has set up a target of increasing agricultural exports to ¥1 trillion by 2020 from its current level of ¥745.1 billion in 2015. As noted, Japan upheld its core defensive interests and no major adjustment in the agricultural sector is expected. The Ministry of Agriculture, Forestry and Fisheries' (MAFF) own estimates confirm the limited impact of the TPP on Japan's most sensitive sectors. While the ministry estimates that agricultural production will decrease by ¥130 billion, to ¥210 billion, an analysis of forty agricultural commodities shows that a major increase of imports is not expected, with only longer-term concerns for beef, pork, and dairy. Moreover, MAFF estimates no change whatsoever to Japan's self-sufficiency ratio, 39 percent on a calorie basis.[59]

Even so, organized agriculture has been deeply dissatisfied with TPP outcomes, denouncing a breach in negotiation mandate (by eliminating some tariffs in the five sacred commodities) and predicting much more dire consequences for agriculture. Support in agricultural circles for the Abe cabinet runs low (only 18 percent) according to a survey of farmers, who also believe in large numbers that the Diet resolutions on the TPP were not adhered to (69 percent).[60] To quell this dissatisfaction, the Japanese government announced the establishment of a TPP Task Force as soon as the negotiations wrapped up in October 2015. The Task Force rolled out a series of policy measures to both promote agriculture "on the offensive" and to allay concerns about the adjustment costs to market liberalization. This second consideration, in particular, weighed heavily in the design of TPP countermeasures. As the country geared up for an Upper House election in the summer of 2016, there were worries that farmer dissatisfaction in the single-seat rural districts could make a dent in the LDP's electoral performance.

Using the metrics of pro-reform adjustment measures laid out in chapter 7 (that is, the adoption of policies that help—not hinder—market signals; that offer temporary relief, not permanent subsidies; and that provide assistance that is commensurate to the expected adjustment burden, not inflated side payments), it is evident that Japan chose to navigate the reform/subsidization dilemma in familiar ways. The pull of political compensation is still strong in Japan, especially during an important electoral year. Four tenets of the TPP agricultural countermeasures underscore this point.

First, stabilization measures for all five sacred commodities figure prominently in the Japanese government's agricultural TPP policy. In fact, one of the first announcements from the government after the conclusion of the TPP talks was the use of stockpile purchases to match any increase in the supply of rice through the TPP quota to uphold the price of the grain (thereby blunting market signals to bring about change in rice production). Other stabilization measures were also announced to maintain farmers' incomes that will require greater budgetary outlays; for example, extending subsidies to all dairy products and compensating for the scheduled cuts in the price markup for wheat (45 percent by year nine).[61]

Second, these measures reinforce Japan's approach to support specific commodities, further setting it apart from the farmer policies of the EU and the United States, which favor general income support untied from production. This divergence may become fixed, as the government is moving toward legally institutionalizing the deficiency payments for pork and beef. While American pork producers complained about the increased subsidization rate (from 80 to 90 percent) in the support for hog farmers and cattle ranchers in case of price drops, the more problematic element could very well be their acquisition of legal permanent status.[62]

Third, the Japanese government has made hefty budgetary allocations to fund agriculture's TPP countermeasures despite the fact that the impact of the TPP will be limited. In December 2015 the government approved a $28.2 billion supplementary budget with $4.5 billion set aside for TPP countermeasures. The lion's share of TPP adjustment funds was destined to agriculture (64 percent). A few months later, a record-breaking budget of $851 billion was adopted for fiscal year 2016 (April 2016 to March 2017), which earmarked $20.3 billion for agriculture. TPP countermeasures were allocated $1.46 billion in the budget for fiscal year 2016 (see table 10-6)

Fourth, the agricultural countermeasures have brought about a revival of public works in the countryside reminiscent of the "scattered spending" (*baramaki yosan*) that characterized Japanese compensation in the aftermath of the Uruguay Round.[63] Agricultural circles saw in the TPP countermeasures an opportunity to increase spending for rural public works, which had decreased by more than 60 percent when the Democratic Party of Japan came to power.[64] One-third of the 2015 supplementary budget funds for TPP countermeasures were earmarked for agricultural construction works: land consolidation, irrigation, and readying plots for cattle clusters. The budget for fiscal year 2016 set aside an additional $3.7 billion for these land improvement projects (although they were not specifically labeled TPP countermeasures).

The process of Japanese agricultural reform during the TPP era displays important continuities: the preservation of a policy framework that protects the core interests of part-time rice farmers and the pull of political compensation in an important electoral year. Significant change is underway, as well: the shrinking of the agricultural sanctuary, the targeting of JA reform as part of the agricultural modernization process, and the redrawing of agricultural redlines on trade policy. Agriculture is no longer the obstacle preventing Japan from negotiating with its main trading partners. Japan's participation in the wave of mega trade agreements is key to its future prosperity and its ability to shape an emerging Asia-Pacific trade order.

## CHAPTER ELEVEN

# Conclusion

## Forging a New Economic Asia-Pacific Order

**THIS BOOK HAS UNDERSCORED** the hard choices inherent in trade policy design in a world of great complexity. The stakes are higher with the attempt to negotiate mega trade agreements, the more contested regulatory agenda at the center of trade negotiations, and the multilateral system unable to close the governance gap by updating international rules that match the reality of production and trade patterns in the world economy. At this critical juncture, the (in)ability of lead economies to successfully overcome their own domestic political hurdles to devise a proactive trade strategy that advances their national interests and shores up the rules-based international order will have profound consequences. As the analysis of this book has made clear, for Japan and the United States, three defining dilemmas on trade governance loom large in renewing their economic potential and their will to lead internationally.

### JAPAN: THE SEARCH FOR DECISIVENESS

In the postwar period, Japan emerged as an export powerhouse and, later, as one of the largest foreign direct investors. Despite its growing economic heft, Japan continued to play a passive role in international trade negotiations for most of the postwar period. At the onset of the twenty-first century, Japan was a latecomer to the negotiation of preferential trade agreements, and its first decade of free trade agreement negotiations yielded modest accomplishments in terms of the size of export markets covered or the dissemination of WTO-plus rules. This unimpressive record was mostly a self-inflicted wound, the need to play defensively due to the clout of the agricultural lobby, which effectively vetoed negotiations with large economic partners and undercut Japan's negotiation leverage with its refusal to entertain liberalization of agricultural commodities.

A policymaking system ripe for state indecisiveness was responsible for Japan's lackluster preferential trade strategy. Top-down executive leadership was prevented by the clout that vested interests exercised in their respective policy areas, by intense bureaucratic sectionalism, and by the ability of policy tribes to shape policy inside the ruling party's policymaking body—eclipsing the prime minister and the cabinet. Some reforms to strengthen executive leadership were adopted over the years, but Japan's quest to join the Trans-Pacific Partnership—a transformational initiative for its trade strategy and economic reform efforts— coincided with renewed efforts to centralize decisionmaking, which were at first unsuccessful during the Democratic Party of Japan's tenure. When the DPJ took office in 2009, it came determined to ensure that bureaucrats were responsive to directives from politicians and that the cabinet would prevail over the party. Hence, one of the first moves of Prime Minister Yukio Hatoyama was to dissolve the party's policymaking body and the meeting of administrative vice-ministers. The botched centralization campaign, however, prevented the government from displaying decisiveness while it suffered the backlash from curtailed inclusiveness. The two succeeding DPJ prime ministers tried, but failed, to make an effective bid for TPP membership. Deep opposition within the party, feuding bureaucratic assessments on the consequences of the TPP for Japan's economy, and concern that the Liberal Democratic Party would be able to capitalize on rural discontent foiled their efforts. The agricultural lobby, deprived of access to the party's policymaking body and fearing that its redlines on trade policy were about to be crossed, went all out in a mobilization campaign unlike any before. It gave birth to unlikely partnerships (among groups across the ideological spectrum), it relied on the Internet as a powerful source of both information and misinformation, and it revolved not just around the perennial problem of agricultural protectionism but around broader issues never before in the public eye in connection to an FTA negotiation: investor lawsuits and regulatory sovereignty, and charges that the TPP would bring about the Americanization of Japan.

Japan's eventual admission into the TPP was enabled by political change in Japan: much stronger prime ministerial leadership under the

Abe administration. Prime Minister Shinzo Abe was able to capitalize on high and sustained levels of public support (warding off challengers from within his party) and on the decimation of the opposition camp after the unsuccessful DPJ tenure to centralize decisionmaking and break away from the cycle of one-year prime ministerships. The Prime Minister's Office emerged as the arbiter of policy conflicts and acted as control tower in setting the directives of a new economic strategy and a more cohesive approach on trade negotiations through the establishment of a TPP headquarters. But there was a heavy dose of political pragmatism in the way Prime Minister Abe navigated Japan's way into the TPP. The trade agenda was not to come at the expense of core political priorities: to maintain party unity and to recapture the Upper House in July 2013 to overcome the twisted Diet phenomenon. Moreover, the premium attached by the prime minister to the security agenda (and his willingness to spend heavy doses of his political capital to move forward security reforms) also dictated some degree of accommodation with foes of economic reform rather than an all-out confrontation. On the trade front, this pattern of "negotiated decisiveness" was evident in the negotiation mandate to keep the five sacred agricultural commodities off-limits from full tariff elimination.

The Abe government chose a different path to navigate the decisiveness/inclusiveness dilemma. The political conditions enabling bold policy departures that had long eluded Japan are surely present today: high levels of support for the Abe cabinet, control by the ruling coalition of both houses of the Diet, a divided and weakened opposition camp, and the emergence of a control tower in the Abe *Kantei*. The prime minister has delivered on policy initiatives that, until recently, looked unobtainable: participation in the TPP and reform of the agricultural cooperative system. In pursuing these reforms, decisionmaking was not completely centralized; the agricultural lobby was able to weave its core preferences into the adopted policies. The political compromises helped lower the intensity of anti-TPP campaigns and prevented major electoral punishment from disgruntled farmers, but they also reduced the potential impact of these landmark steps in Japan's reform process.

## Japan: The Quest for Reform

Japan's efforts to overcome decades of deflation and slow growth largely depend on its ability to unleash the forces of productivity and innovation and to move away from a public policy framework that favored low-productivity vested interests through pork barrel practices. Structural reforms, therefore, are rightly seen as the most important element of the economic revitalization strategy known as Abenomics. In the TPP project, the Japanese government has proactively attempted to use a major trade negotiation to create positive synergies with its domestic reform agenda. The old-style pattern of *gaiatsu* (where Japan reluctantly engaged the United States in trade negotiations mostly to deflect pressures for broad economic change) does not apply to the description of TPP dynamics. The United States and Japan engaged in tough market access negotiations on agriculture and automobiles, and launched the only set of parallel talks in the TPP on nontariff measures to address long-standing bilateral issues. But Japan's ongoing economic transformation of the past quarter-century and the growing convergence of geopolitical interests with the United States produced not only compromise solutions on long-divisive market access and regulatory issues but a novel coordinated effort in the multilateral rules area of the negotiations.

Japan's deflationary era witnessed changes in core areas of Japanese capitalism, which had been focal points in the trade friction years of the late 1980s and early 1990s. Tight business group links have waned (for example, cross-shareholding) or disappeared (the main bank system), deregulation of capital flows has been completed, and even if aggregate levels of inward investment remain low, foreign multinational companies play a larger role in the Japanese market. At the same time, the nature of Japan's global economic footprint morphed in dramatic ways with the wave of outward direct investment in the aftermath of the Plaza Accord and the construction of elaborate regional production networks abroad. The negotiation of deep trade agreements that enhance the operation of global value chains and the desire to strengthen international economic governance in the midst of a profound power shift are shared interests for the United States and Japan.

Restoring Japan's growth potential is also a shared interest. Realistic expectations on the potential contributions of the TPP to Japan's renewal must factor in that many of the priority areas for Japan to tackle are outside the scope of a trade agreement (labor market reform, energy policy, or social security reform), and that the agricultural sector itself represents only 1 percent of gross domestic product (GDP). But the importance of agricultural reform goes beyond its economic weight; it is central to Japan's credibility, internally and externally. At home, it is the litmus test of the resolve to launch a new politics of productivity by eliminating the flow of subsidies and patronage to a major vested interest. Internationally, it was only when TPP participation signaled a potential breakthrough on agricultural protectionism that Japan's trade diplomacy gained traction.

The growth and reform dividends of the TPP promise to be substantial for Japan. Given demographic trends and the substantial relocation of productive capacity overseas, the TPP could play a large role in securing Japan's future prosperity by opening export markets on preferential terms and upgrading the management of its vast supply chain. The adoption of cumulative rules of origin and the further dissemination of WTO-plus rules would provide a more effective platform to reap those gains. The TPP would also help Japan close internationalization gaps in services and promote inward direct investment. In this negotiation, Japan agreed to the most far-reaching liberalization of services to date, and the reforms on corporate governance introduced as part of the parallel talks with the United States touched on issues that had long figured in the American list of barriers to investment.

Japan's defensive trade interests are still substantial. It scored the lowest level of overall tariff elimination among all TPP countries due to the political decision to keep the most sensitive agricultural commodities off-limits. Liberalization commitments in agriculture reveal a mixed picture: narrowing the agricultural sanctuary and expanded export opportunities for TPP partners by lowering tariffs in some products or expanding tariff-rate quotas. The most sensitive items were not subject to tariff elimination and remained state trading commodities. Beyond the TPP liberalization commitments, the hefty set of TPP countermeasures shows that the Abe government opted to navigate the reform/subsidization dilemma in familiar ways. Despite the limited impact that market opening through the TPP will have on Japan's agriculture, the government allocated generous amounts to compensate farmers. Targeted side payments to specific commodities tied to production levels continue to set Japan apart from the United States and the EU. The government also announced a number of stabilization efforts (such as the use of the rice stockpile program) to manage the TPP transition in ways that will blunt market signals. The large portion of funds allocated in the budget for TPP countermeasures to land improvement projects brings back reminiscences of the "scattered budget" of yesteryear.

The potential of the TPP to promote agricultural modernization has been watered down by the logic of political compensation. However, major change has certainly been afoot; the agricultural lobby no longer blocks Japan's participation in mega trade deals. The irony is that as Japan found the political will to use trade policy proactively, there are now fundamental doubts about the ability of the United States to solve its own trade governance dilemmas and continue to lead in upholding multilateral rules-based trade liberalization, as embodied by the TPP.

### *United States: Renewing Internationalism*

For the past quarter-century, the domestic consensus on trade policy has been strained by the legitimacy challenges highlighted in this book: the distributional consequences of liberalization, the domestic reach of the regulatory agenda in trade negotiations, and the representativeness of trade policy. The U.S. political system—based on checks and balances—deliberately fragments authority among different branches of government. However, in the past this diffusion of power did not prevent effective decisionmaking at home or the exercise of leadership abroad. Trade promotion authority (TPA) provided a balanced institutional compact that ensured the constitutionally mandated authority of Congress over trade (by identifying negotiation objectives, monitoring the trade negotiators, and deciding on the enactment of trade deals) and allowed the executive to advance national interests through the conduct of trade negotiations. Nevertheless, a growing division of purpose in the American political system brought to the surface the dysfunctions of a divided polity (partisan divides, polarization among branches of government, and erosion of intraparty cohesion) with important implications for the decisiveness of trade policy. In contrast to the periodic renewal of TPA with bipartisan support prior to the signing of NAFTA, over the last two decades the reauthorization of TPA or the ratification of free trade agreements became more uncertain as support waned, first among Democrats and, later, also among Tea Party Republicans, for these trade initiatives.

Skepticism on the merits of trade has deepened with the rising levels of income inequality and the hollowing out of the middle class during this period. The argument that trade with developing countries (especially China) is the main culprit for the loss of employment opportunities in the manufacturing sector and for deepening economic disparities has gained traction in public debates. While import competition from China has certainly put strong pressure on low value-added manufacturing employment, it has not compromised the overall health of the manufacturing sector, as can be seen in rising productivity levels and expanding industrial output. The overall level of job losses from NAFTA and other trade agreements is small when compared to the normal churn of U.S. labor markets, and these agreements also help support better paying jobs in the export sector. Technological change and the skill premium play a much larger role in the increase of wage inequality. Moreover, trade has a pro-poor bias in the larger reductions in the cost of living it affords for lower-income groups.

The adjustment costs for trade-displaced workers are steep, with long spells of unemployment, wage cuts, and/or diminished potential on future earnings. Support policies for redundant workers have not been effective enough. Trade adjustment assistance was born as a quid pro quo deal with organized labor to gain its acquiescence to trade liberalization. Although very early on unions became disenchanted with this deal, it remained essential to congressional voting dynamics. Renewal of trade negotiation authority was contingent on reauthorization of trade adjustment assistance. Hence, the American solution to the reform/subsidization dilemma was to opt for a targeted compensation program to get clearance from veto players in subsequent liberalization initiatives.

In its design, TAA is not well equipped to deal with the challenges of job displacement for American workers. It is only available to trade-impacted workers (creating a certification hurdle) so its expanded benefits are off-limits for the vast majority of the unemployed. In the past, many recipients opted out of training requirements, which are important to skill acquisition and reentry into the workforce. Impactful components of the program, such as wage insurance (which favors reemployment), are only offered to a subset of recipients. Relocation allowances are insufficient to facilitate geographical mobility. TAA recipients consistently report wage cuts upon reemployment even when compared with peer workers who did not receive benefits. Because TAA has come up short in delivering genuine worker adjustment, it has stopped working as a political device to facilitate trade liberalization. In a first, House Democrats voted down the TAA bill in June 2015 in an attempt to sabotage the accompanying TPA bill. Only by voting separately on each bill was it possible to renew trade negotiation authority, keeping alive the hope for an eventual passage of the TPP.

Trade politics in the United States have become more divisive with rising anti-trade populism on both the left and the right. Trade policy became a focal point in the 2016 presidential election, and the candidate with the harshest views on trade (rejecting the TPP, threatening to withdraw from NAFTA, and imposing punitive tariffs on China and Mexico) won the electoral college—though not the popular vote—to be elected president. At this critical juncture, renewing American internationalism calls for a fundamental reset. Making the traditional case for trade by focusing on projected increases in economic activity and improved living standards from liberalization will not be sufficient. Doubling down on incremental changes to TAA will not foster needed worker adjustment throughout the economy, nor will it be enough to deliver the congressional votes to enact landmark trade initiatives. A different approach is required. This policy framework must give priority to measures that ameliorate income inequality. A thriving middle class is the best antidote for populism and inward economic policies. To repair the frayed consensus on trade, it must also offer a different solution to the reform/subsidization dilemma: a pro-adjustment safety net for all workers facing difficult economic transitions. Trading nations demand deeper social compacts, and this is where the American project has come woefully short.

## POLICY RECOMMENDATIONS TO RECALIBRATE NATIONAL CHOICES ON TRADE

The national choices made by Japan and the United States in sorting out the vexing trade-offs of trade policy design will have global consequences. At stake is the ability of these leading economies to upgrade international economic governance arrangements and create incentives for emerging economies to converge toward these higher standards. At play is the reaffirmation of a rules-based international order that has been a source of postwar stability, the deepening of a bilateral alliance at the core of America's diplomacy in Asia, and the ability to reassure friends and rivals of the staying power of the United States. In the execution of trade policy today, we are witnessing an international leadership test dominated by domestic governance dilemmas. A successful recalibration of national choices on trade will require critical investments at home and abroad.

*Domestic Investments*

The future of a rules-based Asia-Pacific architecture will hinge on the ability of the United States and Japan to spur on domestic renewal. To that end, a number of impactful policies should be pursued.

### PURSUE COMPLEMENTARY DOMESTIC MEASURES
### TO AMPLIFY ECONOMIC BENEFITS

Trade policy is an integral component but not a substitute for an over-arching competitiveness strategy. The potential of trade liberalization to promote efficiency and innovation and to foster the upgrading of productive sectors will be contingent on the parallel implementation of supplementary policies. Certainly sound macroeconomic policies, rule of law, and enforcement of property rights are essential foundations, but other policies that correct underinvestment or create reform synergies are key. On the former, the United States has failed to modernize its transportation infrastructure, which is essential to improve connectivity and realize efficiency gains. On the latter, the future modernization of Japanese agriculture will be shaped not only by increased international competition but, more fundamentally, by the full elimination of the set-aside policy, reforms to the land transactions regime, and decoupled payments to full-time farmers. These examples do not exhaust the universe of desirable complementary policies, but they do illustrate the need to embed trade initiatives in a larger policy framework.

### EXPAND REPRESENTATIVENESS OF TRADE POLICY

The United States has the most far-reaching system of consultation with stakeholders in the formulation of trade policy. Nevertheless, the challenge of incorporating input from groups in civil society in tandem with the larger reach of trade agreements into domestic policy domains has not been fully met. Reforming the trade advisory system to promote dialogue among different stakeholders in cross-cutting committees on the regulatory agenda should be a priority. In the TPP negotiations, Japan did make improvements in its system of consultation by inaugurating a public comment system. However, in moving past the traditional system of consultation with a few stakeholders in the form of FTA feasibility studies, the Japanese government should consider a more formal trade advisory committee system that has broad representation across all sectors of society and the economy. In addition, the government should also ensure that Diet members with appropriate security clearances have access to trade negotiation texts.

## NURTURE HUMAN CAPITAL AND RENEW THE SOCIAL COMPACT

For both the United States and Japan, investments in human capital are a first-order priority. The challenges each country faces are different, though, and they will require a distinctive policy mix. Income inequality in Japan has not been driven by an outsized increase in the income share of the top 1 percent of the population but, rather, by the reduced earning potential of the growing legion of nonregular workers. These employees do not have a steady career path, do not benefit from on-the-job training, earn much lower wages, and receive fewer social security benefits. The current campaign of the Japanese government to secure "equal pay for equal work" is a step in the right direction. Ensuring training and ongoing skill acquisition for nonregular workers is also important to safeguard Japan's economic future. At the end of the day, however, ameliorating Japan's labor market dualism will require measures to increase labor flexibility. Among them, clarifying rules on job dismissal will help eliminate the incentive for companies to hire nonregular workers as a buffer for business fluctuations. In addition, the government should redouble efforts to promote the development of venture capital and facilitate business startups to open the path to entrepreneurship to many more individuals in Japan. This will be beneficial toward diversifying career paths and promoting innovation.

In the United States, economic prospects for workers performing routine tasks are not bright. Whereas in the past, it was possible to aspire to a middle-class job with this skill set, it is no longer so. The pushback against trade policy springs to a large extent from fear about its impact on jobs and wages, but the larger truth is that economic change spurred by technological waves has wider distributional consequences. The skill premium has grown in both tradeable and nontradeable sectors, and countries that fail to close the skill-demand gap report higher levels of wage inequality. Rather than foregoing the benefits of technological progress or retreating inward, the United States needs a different modality of supply-side economics, one that ensures a skilled workforce. At a time when labor-intensive manufacturing has seen large reductions in employment, a similar number of job vacancies go unfulfilled, pointing to the large costs of labor market rigidities and the skill gap. The United States is in need of a revamped safety net for displaced workers that promotes not only resilience (fall back programs such as unemployment insurance and affordable health care) but mobility (spring forward programs that emphasize training and reemployment). Skill acquisition and upgrading should be at the heart of this strategy, as this is essential to increase employability, avoid wage erosion, and manage relocations across regions and occupations. In particular, the United States should correct the record of underinvestment in active labor market policies and boost training opportunities through various platforms (for example, community colleges or apprenticeships). A skilled and mobile labor force is an imperative investment for the United States.

### International Investments: Uphold Free Trade and Multilateral Governance in the Asia-Pacific and Beyond

Abroad, leadership from the United States and Japan to shore up an open and multilateral trading regime is essential. The trading regime is facing stress with the death of the Doha Round and the marked slowdown in trade growth. Creeping protectionism and the lack of liberalizing initiatives have played a role in the weakening of trade flows.[1] At a time when the world economy is stuck in a low-growth inertia, we are losing steam in an important engine for economic development and connection among nations.

At this critical juncture, enacting the TPP would be one of the most impactful investments the United States and Japan could carry out. This trading framework offers a vehicle to rejuvenate the trading regime by offering fresh gains from liberalization and closing the rules gap. It also awards more effective leverage, compared to a trade war scenario, to encourage China to reform problematic trade and investment practices. Asymmetric reciprocity on foreign direct investment, rampant subsidization of state-owned enterprises, and mandatory technology transfers are prominent Chinese trade policies that cannot be effectively curbed with the WTO rulebook. In contrast, the TPP codifies standards that tackle state capitalism practices, and their enactment and global dissemination should be a priority.[2]

The payoffs of investing in the TPP for the United States and Japan are also geopolitical: (1) deepening the bilateral alliance by moving past trade friction to launch a new endeavor—global economic rulemaking; (2) reassuring allies and rivals that the United States is a multidimensional power fully anchored to the region and capable of supplying, in collaboration with Japan and others, novel institutions for regional co-operation; (3) preventing China from becoming the focal point of Asian regionalism with the consolidation of trade agreements like the Regional Comprehensive Economic Partnership that are unlikely to interdict Chinese mercantilist practices.

Nevertheless, the Trump administration has rejected the TPP, promising a sharp policy departure based on a trade philosophy that stands at odds with multilateral rulemaking. Central to this new approach is an understanding of international trade as zero-sum, an emphasis on fixing results (trade deficit) rather than setting the rules, a preference for bilateralism over multilateralism, and concern with enforcement rather than governance. American abandonment of the TPP will have negative consequences. Economically, notwithstanding the low liberalization commitments expected from RCEP, if this deal enters into force, the preferential access that Chinese firms will have in the Japanese market could put American companies at a disadvantage in thirty-five industries, which export $5.3 billion in goods to Japan every year and employ five million people.[3] Strategically, the United States's exit from the TPP will hand China the leadership baton in Asian economic diplomacy, offering it an opportunity to draw a contrast between a retreating United States and its stepped up multilateral diplomacy in a wide array of policy arenas, from trade to infrastructure finance.

Japan and the remaining TPP countries stand to define the ultimate fate of the Trans-Pacific Partnership. To give the trade agreement a new lease on life, they could amend the enactment rules so that American participation is no longer a prerequisite for its implementation. Relaunching the TPP *sans* the United States will not be an easy path. The original TPP is a carefully calibrated package, and many participating countries agreed to politically sensitive concessions lured by the prospects of access to the large American market. But the trading world changed with the American election, and it is time to see the TPP in a new light, as insurance to navigate the new—and harsher—realities of international trade in a world of rising economic nationalism.

American exit from the TPP will certainly reduce the footprint of the trade deal, but will not wipe out economic benefits for remaining countries. Market access negotiations in the TPP were carried out on a bilateral basis, at the insistence of the United States, which intended to largely maintain the same terms of access that six of the TPP countries already enjoyed in the United States through existing FTAs. These prior trade agreements will continue to provide these TPP countries access to the American market, unless the Trump administration follows through with the campaign pledge of paring down benefits through renegotiation of agreements like NAFTA. Under that scenario, the TPP may become an even more attractive proposition as a diversification strategy and an improved gateway to Asian markets.

The potential costs of American withdrawal from the TPP will be higher for members that counted on this trade deal to obtain preferential access to the American market for the first time. Although Japan is in this category, it will secure important benefits if, as the largest remaining economy, it engineers the rescue of the TPP agenda. The TPP's rulebook enhances the operations of Japanese production networks, which are central to the competitiveness of the Japanese economy, and the higher levels of agricultural and services liberalization that Japan pledged in the TPP help cement the credibility of the domestic reform program. As in the past, a revived TPP can provide Japan negotiation leverage for its trade strategy to gain traction: in concluding trade talks with the EU, pressing for greater ambition in East Asian trade talks, and in any future bilateral negotiation with the United States. Moreover, it is only by keeping the TPP alive that Japan can keep open the possibility of a future return of the United States to the TPP project, if and when the American government recommits to multilateral rulemaking. If such a scenario ever unfolds, it will be much easier to push for a reactivation of U.S. membership in a trade framework that embraces its economic standards than to start negotiations from scratch. At that moment, the full potential of the TPP in deepening the U.S-Japan alliance and supplying governance for the Asia-Pacific could be realized. The survival of the TPP could very well be Japan's litmus test in its quest to emerge as a proactive trading nation combating a protectionist backlash and revitalizing an open trading regime.

At this uncertain time, the premium for Japan and the United States to address the domestic dilemmas of trade policy design with renewed vigor and political will could not be higher. This is the path that holds the most promise in charting, together, a new Asia-Pacific economic order.

# *Notes*

## CHAPTER 1

1. Populism—with its complex mix of economic grievance, cultural back-lash, and anti-establishment message—is on the rise in the West; but it has yet to become a sizable national force in Japan. Deepening income inequality and attrition of the middle class, which is common to many OECD nations including Japan, increases the appeal of populist promises to deliver prosperity by dialing back liberalization and resorting to economic nationalism. The question then arises as to why Japan has, so far, been immune to pressure to retreat from the liberal international order. Some striking differences on the levels of income inequality between Japan and the United States may provide part of the answer, although the complexity of the topic requires deeper analysis. For example, while the top 10 percentile of the population in the United States holds 75.6 percent of wealth, the figure for Japan is a much lower 49.4 percent. See Credit Suisse, "Global Wealth Databook 2015," October 2015, p. 149 (http://publications.credit-suisse.com/tasks/render/file/index.cfm?fileid=C26E3824-E868-56E0-CCA04D4BB9B9ADD5). Moreover, the vast majority of Japanese still self-identify as middle-class (86.5 percent). See Cabinet Office, Government of Japan, "Public Opinion Survey on the Life of the People, 2014," figure 29 (Japanese) (http://survey.gov-online.go.jp/h26/h26-life/zh/z29.html). There is no room for complacency, however, in anticipating that Japan can escape the more divisive politics of populism. Consider the following socioeconomic trends: the high poverty rate (16 percent) and the concentration of income inequality in the lower rungs of the distribution ladder due to the ongoing plight of an expanding number of nonregular workers. See Toshiaki Tachibanaki, "Achieving Both Efficiency and Equity in Japan," *Global Asia*, vol. 11, no. 2 (Summer 2016).

2. Representative Gerald Connolly (D-Va.) offered a compelling assessment of the politics of grievance afflicting the United States in remarks at the Sasakawa Peace Foundation USA. See "American and Japanese Interests and the Future of the Alliance," Sasakawa USA Third Annual Security Forum, Washington, May 6, 2016 (http://spfusa.org/event/third-annual-security-forum-american-japanese-interests-future-alliance).

3. Peter Gourevitch, *Politics in Hard Times: Comparative Responses to International Economic Crises* (Cornell University Press, 1986).

4. David P. Baron, *Business and its Environment*, 6th ed. (Upper Saddle River, N.J.: Prentice Hall, 2010).

5. Helen V. Milner, *Interests, Institutions, and Information: Domestic Politics and International Relations* (Princeton University Press, 1997), p. 99.

6. Negotiated agreements that are abandoned or voted down in the internal ratification process matter for other reasons; they undermine negotiation credibility and harm relations with other members who invested political capital in a negotiation that came to naught.

7. Dani Rodrik offers a different interpretation of the tensions inherent to trade and financial liberalization by positing a trilemma between hyper-globalization, national sovereignty, and democracy. See Dani Rodrik, *The Globalization Paradox: Democracy and the Future of the World Economy* (New York: W.W. Norton, 2011).

8. George Tsebelis, "Decision Making in Political Systems: Veto Players in Presidentialism, Parliamentarism, Multicameralism and Multipartyism," *British Journal of Political Science*, vol. 25, no. 3 (July 1995).

9. As discussed in later chapters, Japan embodies well the first risk, and the United States the second.

### CHAPTER 2

1. Scott C. Bradford, Paul L. E. Grieco, and Gary Clyde Hufbauer, "The Payoff to America from Global Integration," in *The United States and the World Economy: Foreign Economic Policy for the Next Decade*, edited by C. Fred Bergsten (Washington: Institute for International Economics, 2005), p. 78.

2. Opportunity costs (the amount that a country must sacrifice in the production of one good to produce another) underscore that national resources are used most efficiently and consumer welfare is enhanced when nations specialize in products in which they are most competitive (have lower opportunity costs). See Adam Smith, *An Inquiry into the Nature and Causes of the Wealth of Nations* (The Strand, U.K.: William Strahan and T. Cadell, 1776); David Ricardo, *The Works of David Ricardo: With a Notice of the Life and Writings of the Author* (London: John Murray, 1881); Charles de Secondat Montesquieu, *De l'esprit des loix* [The spirit of the laws] (Geneva: Barrillot, 1748).

3. Regarding the growing weight of developing economies, in 1962 the share of developing countries in international trade flows was only 15 percent; today it is almost 40 percent. See World Economic Forum, "The Case for Trade and

Competitiveness," September 2015, p. 4 (www3.weforum.org/docs/WEF_GAC
_Competitiveness_2105.pdf).

4. World Economic Forum, "Case for Trade."

5. David Dollar and Aart Kraay, "Trade, Growth, and Poverty," *Economic Journal*, vol. 114, no. 493 (February 2004), pp. 22–49.

6. Antoni Estevadeordal and Alan M. Taylor, "Is the Washington Consensus Dead? Growth, Openness, and the Great Liberalization, 1970s–2000s," Working Paper 14264 (Cambridge, Mass.: National Bureau of Economic Research, August 2008).

7. Commission on Growth and Development, "The Growth Report: Strategies for Sustained Growth and Inclusive Development" (Washington: World Bank, 2008), pp. 2, 21 (http://siteresources.worldbank.org/EXTPREMNET /Resources/489960-1338997241035/Growth_Commission_Final_Report.pdf).

8. Cited in Jeffrey Frankel, "Assessing the Efficiency Gains from Further Liberalization," in *Efficiency, Equity, and Legitimacy: The Multilateral Trading System at the Millennium*, edited by Roger B. Porter and others (Brookings Institution, 2001), pp. 87–88.

9. Bradford, Grieco, and Hufbauer, "Payoff to America," p. 68. Josh Bivens considers these figures overblown. In his estimate, trade liberalization produced a much smaller increase in U.S. income (a quarter of the estimate by Bradford, Grieco, and Hufbauer). However, Bivens's calculations only focused on static gains from market opening (multiplying the decrease of import prices [14.5 percent] by the increase in import share [7.1 percent] to gauge the impact in the U.S. economy of lowering trade barriers). See L. Josh Bivens, "The Gains from Trade: How Big and Who Gets Them?" Working Paper 280 (Washington: Economic Policy Institute, December 17, 2007), p. 3 (www.epi.org/publication /wp280).

10. Pablo D. Fajgelbaum and Amit K. Khandelwal, "Measuring the Unequal Gains from Trade," *Quarterly Journal of Economics,* vol. 131 (August 2016), p. 3.

11. Francisco Rodriguez and Dani Rodrik provided a powerful critique of early econometric studies of the relationship between trade and growth by pointing to problems such as using trade share to GDP as an indicator of trade policy (since total trade volumes are affected by many other variables) or using measures of trade barriers that are strongly correlated with other growth retarding factors. The Rodriguez-Rodrik critique led to a wave of more sophisticated econometric research, such as the ones cited in the text that address these issues, and continue to find a positive contribution of trade to growth. See Francisco Rodriguez and Dani Rodrik, "Trade Policy and Economic Growth: A Skeptic's Guide to Cross-National Evidence," in *NBER Macroeconomics Annual 2000*, edited by Ben Bernanke and Kenneth S. Rogoff (MIT Press, 2001).

12. Richard Newfarmer and Monika Sztajerowska, "Trade and Employment in a Fast-Changing World," in *Policy Priorities for International Trade and Jobs*, edited by Douglas Lippoldt (Paris: OECD Publishing, 2012), p. 13.

13. World Economic Forum, "Case for Trade."

14. Llewelyn Hughes, Jeffrey S. Lantis, and Mireya Solís, "The Life Cycle of Regimes: Temporality and Exclusive Forms of International Cooperation," *Journal of International Organizations Studies*, vol. 5, no. 2 (2014).

15. In this regard, the lack of a common tariff schedule in the TPP is a significant missed opportunity since market access negotiations were carried out on a bilateral basis at the insistence of the United States.

16. Doo Bong Han, "Evaluation of FTA Negotiation Results, Economic Effects and Compensation Policies on the Korean Agricultural Sector: Focusing on Korea's FTAs with Chile, US and EU," Working Paper (Organization for Regional and Inter-Regional Studies, Waseda University, 2011) (www.waseda.jp /inst/oris/assets/uploads/2015/10/i4-1.pdf).

17. The figures in table 2-2 and 2-3 are not directly comparable because the ASEAN FTA table reports the average tariff elimination ratio for all participating countries to be achieved at the end of the transition period (which can be much longer than ten years, especially for the smaller developing economies in Southeast Asia).

18. Arata Kuno, "Constructing the Tariff Dataset for the ERIA FTA Database," in *Comprehensive Mapping of FTAs in ASEAN and East Asia*, edited by Chang Jae Lee and Misa Okabe, Report 2010-26 (Jakarta, Indonesia: Economic Research Institute for ASEAN and East Asia, March 2011), p. 20.

19. Not everyone agrees that the incursion of the trade agenda into "behind-the-border" issues improves the quality of trade liberalization. These views are discussed in chapter 4.

20. Andreas Dür, Leonardo Baccini, and Manfred Elsig, "The Design of International Trade Agreements: Introducing a New Dataset," *Review of International Organizations*, vol. 9, no. 3 (September 2014), pp. 6–7.

21. Masahiro Kawai and Ganeshan Wignaraja, "Evolving Trade Policy Architecture and FTAs in Asia," in *New Global Economic Architecture: The Asian Perspective*, edited by Masahiro Kawai, Peter J. Morgan, and Pradumna Bickram Rana (Cheltenham, U.K.: Edward Elgar, 2014), p. 151.

22. Dür, Baccini, and Elsig, "Design of International Trade Agreements."

23. Kawai and Wignaraja, "Evolving Trade Policy Architecture," p. 154.

24. Dür, Baccini, and Elsig, "Design of International Trade Agreements," p. 7.

25. Peter A. Petri, Michael G. Plummer, and Fan Zhai, *The Trans-Pacific Partnership and Asia-Pacific Integration: A Quantitative Assessment* (Washington: Peterson Institute for International Economics, 2012), pp. 36–39.

26. Csilla Lakatos and others, "Potential Macroeconomic Implications of the Trans-Pacific Partnership," in *Global Economic Prospects, January 2016: Spillovers Amid Weak Growth* (Washington: World Bank, 2016), pp. 227, 229 (www.worldbank.org/content/dam/Worldbank/GEP/GEP2016a/Global -Economic-Prospects-January-2016-Implications-Trans-Pacific-Partnership -Agreement.pdf).

27. Peter A. Petri and Michael G. Plummer, "The Economic Effects of the TPP: New Estimates," in *Assessing the Trans-Pacific Partnership, Volume 1:*

*Market Access and Sectoral Issues*, PIIE Briefing 16-1 (Washington: Peterson Institute for International Economics, February 2016), pp. 6–30.

28. Petri and Plummer attribute these higher TPP income gains, compared to their earlier analysis, to new data on nontariff measures.

29. United States International Trade Commission (ITC), "Trans-Pacific Partnership Agreement: Likely Impact on the U.S. Economy and on Specific Industry Sectors," Publication no. 4607, May 2016 (www.usitc.gov/publications /332/pub4607.pdf). Chapter 3 discusses the findings on trade's impact on jobs and income distribution in greater depth.

30. ITC, "Trans-Pacific Partnership Agreement."

31. Jeronim Capaldo, Alex Izurieta, and Jomo Kwame Sundaram, "Trading Down: Unemployment, Inequality, and Other Risks of the Trans-Pacific Partnership Agreement," Working Paper 16-01 (Global Development and Environment Institute, Tufts University, January 2016), p. 17 (www.ase.tufts.edu/gdae /Pubs/wp/16-01Capaldo-IzurietaTPP.pdf).

32. Robert Z. Lawrence, "Studies of TPP: Which is Credible?" *Trade and Investment Policy Watch* blog, Peterson Institute for International Economics, January 29, 2016 (https://piie.com/blogs/trade-investment-policy-watch/studies -tpp-which-credible).

33. Fredrik Erixon and Matthias Bauer also raise the issue that the model's equations and dataset have not been released to allow for peer verification of results. Fredrik Erixon and Matthias Bauer, "Capaldo Fails to Convince," *European Centre for International Political Economy* blog, May 13, 2015 (http:// ecipe.org/blog/capaldo-fails-to-convince).

34. Lakatos and others, "Potential Macroeconomic Implications," p. 228.

35. Gloria O. Pasadilla and others, "Key Trends and Developments Relating to Trade and Investment Measures and their Impact on the APEC Region: Do FTAs Matter for Trade?" APEC#215-SE-01.9, APEC Policy Support Unit, Asia-Pacific Economic Cooperation, May 2015.

36. Dür, Baccini, and Elsig, "Design of International Trade Agreements," p. 15.

37. Andrew Moravcsik, "Preferences and Power in the European Community: A Liberal Intergovernmentalist Approach," *Journal of Common Market Studies*, vol. 31 (December 1993).

38. Mireya Solís, "Business Advocacy in Asian PTAs: A Model of Selective Business Lobbying with Evidence from Japan," *Business and Politics*, vol. 15, no. 1 (April 2013).

39. Michael J. Gilligan, *Empowering Exporters: Reciprocity, Delegation, and Collective Action in American Trade Policy* (University of Michigan Press, 1997).

40. Manuel Pastor and Carol Wise, "The Origins and Sustainability of Mexico's Free Trade Policy," *International Organization*, vol. 48, no. 3 (Summer 1994).

41. Philip I. Levy, "The United States-Peru Trade Promotion Agreement: What Did You Expect?" Working Paper Series on Development Policy 1 (Wash-

ington: American Enterprise Institute, October 13, 2009) (www.aei.org/publication/the-united-states-peru-trade-promotion-agreement).

42. Nicholas R. Lardy, *Integrating China into the Global Economy* (Brookings Institution, 2002).

43. Ibid, p. 11.

44. Leonardo Baccini and Johannes Urpelainen, *Cutting the Gordian Knot of Economic Reform: When and How International Institutions Help* (Oxford University Press, 2014).

45. Mireya Solís, "Japan and East Asian Economic Regionalism," in *The Routledge Handbook of Japanese Politics*, edited by Alisa Gaunder (New York: Routledge, 2011).

46. Mireya Solís and Saori Katada, "Unlikely Pivotal States in Competitive Free Trade Agreement Diffusion: The Effect of Japan's Trans-Pacific Partnership Participation on Asia-Pacific Regional Integration," *New Political Economy*, vol. 20, no. 2 (2015).

47. Joanne Gowa and Edward D. Mansfield, "Power Politics and International Trade," *American Political Science Review*, vol. 87, no. 2 (June 1993).

48. Yul Sohn and Min Gyo Koo, "Securitizing Trade: The Case of the Korea-US Free Trade Agreement," *International Relations of the Asia-Pacific*, vol. 11, no. 3 (September 2011), p. 435.

49. Following this logic of trading with allies and shunning rivals, Ashley Tellis has advocated excluding China from future U.S. trade agreements in order to recoup the relative gains that China reaped upon entry into the WTO. See Ashley J. Tellis, "The Geopolitics of the TTIP and the TPP," in *Power Shifts and New Blocs in the Global Trading System*, edited by Sanjaya Baru and Suvi Dogra, Adelphi Series 450 (Abingdon, U.K.: Routledge, 2015). However, the mega trade deals the United States has pursued in Europe and Asia would not undo the deep levels of economic interdependence with China that already characterize the world economy. The creation of separate economic spheres through trade agreements is not in the cards (as there are overlapping memberships in the TPP and RCEP), but more important, an economic containment strategy has not been—nor should it be—a U.S. goal given the risks of promoting zero-sum competition.

50. Mireya Solís, "The Containment Fallacy: China and the TPP," *UpFront* blog, Brookings Institution, May 24, 2013 (www.brookings.edu/blogs/up-front/posts/2013/05/24-china-transpacific-partnership-solis).

51. On the connection between politics and economics, neither extreme holds. Deep economic interdependence will not rule out the eruption of war (witness the outbreak of World War I at a heyday of globalization), nor will deterioration in security relations doom economic exchange (the trough in Japan-China relations over disputed territories post-2012 did not result in an exodus of Japanese companies).

52. Albert O. Hirschman, *National Power and the Structure of Foreign Trade* (University of California Press, 1945), p. 31.

53. Mireya Solís, "Japan's Competitive FTA Strategy: Commercial Opportunity versus Political Rivalry," in *Competitive Regionalism: FTA Diffusion in*

*the Pacific Rim*, edited by Mireya Solís, Barbara Stallings, and Saori N. Katada (New York: Palgrave Macmillan, 2009), p. 209.

54. Mike M. Mochizuki, "Political-Security Competition and the FTA Movement: Motivations and Consequences," in *Competitive Regionalism*, p. 66; Sohn and Koo, "Securitizing Trade."

55. Mochizuki, "Political-Security Competition," p. 67.

56. Kevin O'Rourke, "Politics and Trade: Lessons from Past Globalisations," Bruegel Essay and Lecture Series, Bruegel, January 31, 2009, p. 8 (http://bruegel .org/2009/01/politics-and-trade-lessons-from-past-globalisations).

57. These design flaws emerge from the combined effect of unanimity voting rules, migration to the deep integration agenda, and rigorous enforcement (through the single undertaking and revamped dispute settlement mechanism). See Hughes, Lantis, and Solís, "Life Cycle of Regimes."

58. Richard Baldwin, "21st Century Regionalism: Filling the Gap between 21st Century Trade and 20th Century Trade Rules," Policy Insight 56 (Centre for Economic Policy Research, May 20, 2011) (http://cepr.org/active/publications /policy_insights/viewpi.php?pino=56).

59. Michael Froman, "Remarks by Ambassador Michael Froman at the CSIS Asian Architecture Conference" (Washington: Center for Strategic and International Studies, September 22, 2015) (https://ustr.gov/about-us/policy-offices /press-office/speechestranscripts/2015/september/remarks-ambassador -michael).

60. Peter van Ham, "The Geopolitics of TTIP," Policy Brief 23 (Clingendael Institute, October 2013), p. 6 (www.clingendael.nl/sites/default/files/The%20 Geopolitics%20of%20TTIP%20-%20Clingendael%20Policy%20Brief.pdf).

61. This difficulty has been evident in the Obama administration's messaging on China and the TPP. The oft-repeated talking point that "if the United States does not make the rules on trade, China will" has been interpreted by many as heralding an all-out competition. Although much less noticed, the Obama administration also stressed the importance of the TPP to launch a race to the top, and welcomed the possibility of China joining the TPP in the future if China was prepared to meet the agreement's standards. For an elaboration of the first point, see Michael Froman, "The Strategic Logic of Trade," *Foreign Affairs* (November-December, 2014); for the latter, see Susan Rice, "America's Future in Asia," remarks at Georgetown University (Washington, November 20, 2013) (www.whitehouse.gov/the-press-office/2013/11/21/remarks-prepared-delivery -national-security-advisor-susan-e-rice).

62. Edward N. Luttwak, "From Geopolitics to Geo-Economics: Logic of Conflict, Grammar of Commerce," *National Interest*, no. 20 (Summer 1990).

**CHAPTER 3**

1. Robert E. Scott, "No Jobs from Trade Pacts. The Trans-Pacific Partnership Could Be Much Worse Than the Over-Hyped Korea Deal," Issue Brief 369 (Economic Policy Institute, July 18, 2013), p. 2 (www.epi.org/publication/trade -pacts-korus-trans-pacific-partnership).

2. David E. Bonior, "Obama's Free-Trade Conundrum," Opinion Pages, *New York Times*, January 29, 2014.

3. Robert E. Scott, "NAFTA's Legacy: Rising Trade Deficits Lead to Significant Job Displacement and Declining Job Quality for the United States," in *Revisiting NAFTA: Still Not Working for North America's Workers*, Issue Brief 173 (Economic Policy Institute, September 28, 2006) (www.epi.org/files /page/-/old/briefingpapers/173/bp173.pdf); Scott, "No Jobs from Trade Pacts."

4. Ben Beachy, "NAFTA's 20-Year Legacy and the Fate of the Trans-Pacific Partnership," *Public Citizen's Global Trade Watch*, February 2014, p. 8 (www .citizen.org/documents/NAFTA-at-20.pdf).

5. An influential estimate of the offshorability of all U.S. jobs (both manufacturing and services) puts the figure at 25 percent. See Alan Blinder "Offshoring: The Next Industrial Revolution?" *Foreign Affairs*, vol. 85, no. 2 (2006); Alan Blinder, "On the Measurability of Offshorability," *Vox Column*, October 9, 2009 (www.voxeu.org/article/twenty-five-percent-us-jobs-are-offshorable). But Blinder explicitly dismisses the notion that the growth of offshoring will produce mass unemployment and rejects protectionist policies aimed at curbing offshoring.

6. Douglas A. Irwin, *Free Trade Under Fire*, 3rd ed. (Princeton University Press, 2009), p. 7.

7. Blinder, "Offshoring," p. 114.

8. J. Bradford Jensen, *Global Trade in Services: Fears, Facts, and Offshoring* (Washington: Peterson Institute for International Economics, 2011), pp. 3, 6.

9. Joseph Parilla and Alan Berube, "Metro North America: Cities and Metros as Hubs of Advanced Industries and Integrated Goods Trade," (Metropolitan Policy Program, Brookings Institution, November 7, 2013), p. 7 (www .brookings.edu/research/interactives/2013/metro-north-america).

10. Inu Barbee, "NAFTA at Twenty," commentary, *National Interest*, December 16, 2013 (http://nationalinterest.org/commentary/nafta-twenty-9569).

11. *NAFTA at Twenty: Accomplishments, Challenges, and the Way Forward*, hearing before the House Committee on Foreign Affairs' Subcommittee on the Western Hemisphere, 113th Congress (January 15, 2014) (statement by Carla A. Hills, chairman and chief executive officer, Hills & Company International Consultants) (http://foreignaffairs.house.gov/hearing/subcommittee -hearing-nafta-twenty-accomplishments-challenges-and-way-forward).

12. Theodore H. Moran and Lindsay Oldenski, "How US Investments in Mexico Have Increased Investment and Jobs at Home," *Realtime Economic Issues Watch* blog, Peterson Institute for International Economics, July 11, 2014 (https://piie.com/blogs/realtime-economic-issues-watch/how-us-investments -mexico-have-increased-investment-and-jobs).

13. David H. Autor, David Dorn, and Gordon H. Hanson, "The China Shock: Learning from Labor Market Adjustment to Large Changes in Trade," Working Paper 21906 (Cambridge, Mass.: National Bureau of Economic Research, January 2016) (www.nber.org/papers/w21906).

14. Ibid., p. 28.

15. Autor and his coauthors do not make any of these assertions, but trade opponents have seized upon the finding of job losses due to Chinese imports to advance these claims.

16. Lorenzo Caliendo, Maximiliano Dvorkin, and Fernando Parro, "The Impact of Trade on Labor Market Dynamics" Working Paper 21149 (Cambridge, Mass.: National Bureau of Economic Research, May 2015).

17. Philip Levy, "Did China Trade Cost the United States 2.4 Million Jobs?" *Foreign Policy* (May 8, 2016) (http://foreignpolicy.com/2016/05/08/did-china -trade-cost-the-united-states-2-4-million-jobs).

18. Agence France-Presse, "Reboot: Adidas to Make Shoes in Germany Again—but Using Robots," *Guardian* (Manchester), May 24, 2016 (www .theguardian.com/world/2016/may/25/adidas-to-sell-robot-made-shoes-from -2017).

19. Theodore H. Moran and Lindsay Oldenski, "The US Manufacturing Base: Four Signs of Strength," Policy Brief 14-18 (Washington; Peterson Institute for International Economics, June 2014), p. 3 (https://piie.com/publications /pb/pb14-18.pdf).

20. In fact, the TPP provides a lever to encourage China to reform its unfair trading practices—such as the asymmetrical access U.S. companies face when they try to invest in the Chinese market—as highlighted by David Dollar. See David Dollar, "The Future of U.S.-China Economic Relations," in *Brookings Big Ideas for America*, edited by Michael E. O'Hanlon (Brookings Institution, 2017).

21. Robert Z. Lawrence and Tyler Moran, "Adjustment and Income Distribution Impacts of the Trans-Pacific Partnership," Working Paper 16-5 (Washington: Peterson Institute for International Economics, March 2016), pp. 5–6 (https://piie.com/publications/working-papers/adjustment-and-income -distribution-impacts-trans-pacific-partnership).

22. U.S. International Trade Commission, "Trans-Pacific Partnership Agreement: Likely Impact on the U.S. Economy and Specific Industry Sectors," publication no. 4607 (May 2016).

23. Irwin, *Free Trade Under Fire*, pp. 107–08.

24. Surveys of this literature can be found in Bernard Hoekman and L. Alan Winters, "Trade and Employment: Stylized Facts and Research Findings," Working Paper 3676 (Washington: World Bank, August 2005), p. 16 (http:// documents.worldbank.org/curated/en/2005/08/6180806/trade-employment -stylized-facts-research-findings), and Görg Holger, "Globalization, Offshoring and Jobs," in *Making Globalization Socially Sustainable*, edited by Marc Bachetta and Marion Jansen (Geneva: International Labor Organization and World Trade Organization, 2011) (www.wto.org/english/res_e/publications_e /glob_soc_sus_e.htm).

25. Bruce Stokes, "Americans Agree on Trade: Good for the Country, but Not Great for Jobs," FactTank, Pew Research Center, January 8, 2015 (www .pewresearch.org/fact-tank/2015/01/08/americans-agree-on-trade-good-for -the-country-but-not-great-for-jobs).

26. Pew Research Center, "Faith and Skepticism about Trade, Foreign Investment," (Global Attitudes and Trends, September 16, 2014) (www.pewglobal
.org/2014/09/16/faith-and-skepticism-about-trade-foreign-investment).

27. Gallup's editor in chief, Frank Newport, cautions that the framing of the question largely shapes polling results, especially when referencing jobs. Opinion polls that frame trade as destroying jobs will generate largely negative responses. Framing issues also influence the results of the opinion poll cited in the text because the question references exports in asking about trade as an opportunity and references imports in asking about trade as a threat. In fact, however, trade implies both imports and exports. See Frank Newport, "American Public Opinion on Foreign Trade," *Gallup*, April 1, 2016 (www.gallup.com
/opinion/polling-matters/190427/american-public-opinion-foreign-trade.aspx).

28. This demographic largely supported the Donald Trump presidential campaign. Pew surveys show that 67 percent of Trump supporters view free trade agreements as a bad thing. In contrast, the majority of supporters for Bernie Sanders and Hillary Clinton view trade agreements as a good thing (55 percent and 58 percent, respectively), despite the fact that both politicians ran for the Democratic nomination opposing the TPP. See Bruce Stokes, "Republicans, Especially Trump Supporters, See Free Trade Deals as Bad for U.S.," FactTank, Pew Research Center, March 31, 2016 (www.pewresearch.org/fact
-tank/2016/03/31/republicans-especially-trump-supporters-see-free-trade
-deals-as-bad-for-u-s).

29. Carl Davidson and Steven J. Matusz, *International Trade with Equilibrium Unemployment* (Princeton University Press, 2010), p. 254.

30. Autor, Dorn, and Hanson, "The China Shock," pp. 35, 38.

31. The closer the number is to one, the worse the distribution of income.

32. Organisation for Economic Co-operation and Development (OECD), *Divided We Stand: Why Inequality Keeps Rising* (Paris: OECD Publishing, 2011), p. 22.

33. Alexandre Kolev and Catherine Saget, "Are Middle-Paid Jobs in the OECD Disappearing? An Overview," Working Paper 96 (Geneva: International Labor Organization, April 22, 2010), p. 8.

34. The increase in the market income of the top quintile includes labor, business, and retirement income as well as capital gains and other capital income. See OECD, "OECD Economic Survey: United States 2014," June 2014, p. 29.

35. Thomas Piketty, *Capital in the Twenty-First Century*, translated by Arthur Goldhammer (Belknap Press of Harvard University Press, 2014).

36. Jason Furman, "Global Lessons for Inclusive Growth," speech, Institute of International and European Affairs, (Dublin, Ireland, May 7, 2014), pp. 7–8 (https://www.whitehouse.gov/sites/default/files/docs/global_lessons_for
_inclusive_growth_iiea_jf.pdf).

37. Irwin, *Free Trade Under Fire*, p. 119.

38. William R. Cline, "Trade and Income Distribution: The Debate and New Evidence," Policy Brief 99-7 (Washington: Peterson Institute for Interna-

tional Economics, September 1999) (https://piie.com/publications/policy-briefs/trade-and-income-distribution-debate-and-new-evidence).

39. Paul R. Krugman, "Trade and Wages, Reconsidered," *BPEA*, no. 39 (Spring 2008), p. 104.

40. Robert C. Feenstra and Gordon H. Hanson, "The Impact of Outsourcing and High-Technology Capital on Wages: Estimates for the U.S., 1979–1990," *Quarterly Journal of Economics*, vol. 114, no. 3 (1999).

41. Robert Z. Lawrence, *Blue Collar Blues: Is Trade to Blame for Rising US Income Inequality?* (Washington: Peterson Institute for International Economics, 2008), p. 37.

42. Ibid., pp. 38–39.

43. Edward Gresser, "Trade and Inequality: Cause? Cure? Diversion?" (Progressive Economy, December 11, 2014) (http://progressive-economy.org/2014/12/11/trade-and-inequality-cause-cure-diversion).

44. Nina Pavcnik, "Globalization and Within-Country Income Inequality," in *Making Globalization Socially Sustainable*, p. 242.

45. Krugman, "Trade and Wages, Reconsidered."

46. L. Josh Bivens, "Globalization and American Wages: Today and Tomorrow," Briefing Paper 196 (Economic Policy Institute, October 11, 2007), p. 2 (www.epi.org/publication/bp196).

47. Avraham Ebenstein and others, "Estimating the Impact of Trade and Offshoring on American Workers Using the Current Population Surveys," Working Paper 5750 (Washington: World Bank, August 2011).

48. OECD, World Trade Organization (WTO), and World Bank Group, "Global Value Chains: Challenges, Opportunities, and Implications for Policy," report prepared for G20 Trade Ministers Meeting (Sydney, Australia, July 2014), p. 7.

49. Reflecting their active participation in production networks, the share of foreign content is also high for higher-income Asian countries: Taiwan, 44.9 percent; Korea, 41.8 percent; and Singapore, 40.4 percent.

50. Lawrence Katz, comment on "Trade and Wages, Reconsidered," by Paul Krugman, p. 146.

51. David Rosnick, "Gains from Trade? The Net Effect of the Trans-Pacific Partnership Agreement on U.S. Wages," report (Center for Economic and Policy Research, September 2013) (www.cepr.net/index.php/publications/reports/net-effect-of-the-tpp-on-us-wages).

52. Charles Lane, "Trade Measure is Anything but a Race to the Bottom for U.S. Producers," *Washington Post*, May 13, 2015.

53. Lawrence and Moran, "Adjustment and Income Distribution Impacts."

54. Center for American Progress, "Report of the Commission on Inclusive Prosperity" (January 2015) (www.americanprogress.org/issues/economy/report/2015/01/15/104266/report-of-the-commission-on-inclusive-prosperity).

55. Peggy Hollinger, "A Hollowing Middle Class," *OECD Observer* (2012) (www.oecdobserver.org/news/fullstory.php/aid/3660/A_hollowing_middle_class.html).

**CHAPTER 4**

1. Alan Tonelson, *The Race to the Bottom: Why a Worldwide Worker Surplus and Uncontrolled Free Trade Are Sinking American Living Standards* (Boulder, Colo.: Westview Press, 2000); Lori Wallach and Michelle Sforza, *Whose Trade Organization? Corporate Globalization and the Erosion of Democracy: An Assessment of the World Trade Organization* (Washington: Public Citizen, 1999); Herman E. Daly, "The Perils of Free Trade," *Scientific American*, vol. 269 (November 1993).

2. Daniel W. Drezner, "The Race to the Bottom Hypothesis: An Empirical and Theoretical Review," December 2006, pp. 14–15 (http://danieldrezner.com /policy/RTBreview.doc).

3. Arik Levinson, "Environmental Regulations and Industry Location: International and Domestic Evidence," in *Fair Trade and Harmonization: Prerequisites for Free Trade? Volume 1. Economic Analysis*, edited by Jagdish Bhagwati and Robert E. Hudec (MIT Press, 1996), p. 450.

4. Drezner, "Race to the Bottom Hypothesis," p. 8.

5. Geoffrey Garrett, "Global Markets and National Politics: Collision Course or Virtuous Cycle?" *International Organization*, vol. 52, no. 4 (Autumn 1998).

6. David Vogel and Robert A. Kagan, "Introduction: Dynamics of Regulatory Change: How Globalization Affects National Regulatory Policies," in *Dynamics of Regulatory Change: How Globalization Affects National Regulatory Policies*, edited by David Vogel and Robert A. Kagan (University of California Press, 2004), pp. 1–41.

7. David Vogel, *Trading Up: Consumer and Environmental Regulation in a Global Economy* (Harvard University Press, 1995).

8. Miles Kahler, "Modeling Races to the Bottom," paper prepared for the annual meeting of the American Political Science Association (Boston, Mass., September 1998).

9. Ibid.

10. Vogel and Kagan, "Introduction," p. 15.

11. Ibid., p. 12; Dale D. Murphy, *The Structure of Regulatory Competition: Corporations and Public Policies in a Global Economy* (Oxford University Press, 2004).

12. Kate O'Neill, "Globalization and Hazardous Waste Management: From Brown to Green?" in *Dynamics of Regulatory Change*, edited by Vogel and Kagan, pp. 156–82.

13. David G. Victor, "WTO Efforts to Manage Differences in National Sanitary and Phytosanitary Policies," in *Dynamics of Regulatory Change*, edited by Vogel and Kagan, pp. 227–68.

14. Daniel P. Gitterman, "A Race to the Bottom, a Race to the Top or the March to a Minimum Floor? Economic Integration and Labor Standards in Comparative Perspective," in *Dynamics of Regulatory Change*, edited by Vogel and Kagan, pp. 331–63.

15. Murphy, *Structure of Regulatory Competition.*

16. David Wheeler, "Racing to the Bottom? Foreign Investment and Air Quality in Developing Countries," Policy Research Working Paper (World Bank, November 1999) (http://elibrary.worldbank.org/doi/pdf/10.1596/1813-9450-2524).

17. Drezner, "Race to the Bottom Hypothesis," pp. 7–8.

18. Kahler, "Modeling Races to the Bottom."

19. Henrik Horn, Petros C. Mavroidis, and Andr Sapir, "Beyond the WTO? An Anatomy of EU and U.S. Preferential Trade Agreements," *The World Economy,* vol. 33, no. 11 (2010).

20. Iza Lejárraga, "Deep Provisions in Regional Trade Agreements: How Multilateral-Friendly? An Overview of OECD Findings," OECD Trade Policy Paper 168 (Paris: OECD Publishing, October 2014), pp. 9–10.

21. WTO, *World Trade Report 2011. The WTO and Preferential Trade Agreements: From Coexistence to Coherence* (Geneva: WTO, 2011), p. 133 (www.wto.org/english/res_e/publications_e/wtr11_e.htm).

22. WTO, *World Trade Report 2011,* p. 124. There are, however, wide variations by region (Africa's average most-favored-nation tariff in 2009 was a much higher 12 percent), by sector (agricultural tariffs are higher than manufacturing tariffs), and by specific product (take, for instance, the 1,706 percent Japanese tariff on *konnyaku* or yam cake).

23. WTO, *World Trade Report 2012. Trade and Public Policies: A Closer Look at Non-Tariff Measures in the 21st Century* (Geneva: WTO, 2012), p. 69 (www.wto.org/english/res_e/publications_e/wtr12_e.htm).

24. WTO, *Report on G20 Trade Measures 2016* (Geneva: WTO, 2016), p. 2 (www.wto.org/english/news_e/news16_e/g20_wto_report_june16_e.pdf).

25. IMF, *Global Trade: What is Behind the Slowdown?* (Washington, 2016), pp. 2, 74 (www.imf.org/external/pubs/ft/weo/2016/02/pdf/c2.pdf).

26. New Zealand Institute of Economic Research, "Quantifying the Costs of Non-Tariff Measures in the Asia-Pacific Region," Working Paper 4 (November 2016), pp. 7, 14 (http://nzier.org.nz/publication/quantifying-the-costs-of -non-tariff-measures-in-the-asia-pacific-region-initial-estimates-nzier-public -discussion-paper-20164).

27. Gary Clyde Hufbauer and Peter Draper, "Facts and Figures," in *Foreign Direct Investment as a Key Driver for Trade, Growth and Prosperity: The Case for a Multilateral Agreement on Investment* (Geneva: World Economic Forum, 2013), p. 11 (www3.weforum.org/docs/GAC13/WEF_GAC_GlobalTradeFDI _FDIKeyDriver_Report_2013.pdf).

28. Theodore H. Moran, "Foreign Direct Investment, Supply Chain Creation, and Structural Transformation: Lessons for APEC," in *Current Issues in Asia-Pacific Foreign Direct Investment* (The Australia APEC Study Centre, 2015), p. 21 (http://mams.rmit.edu.au/cwgz1keqt2r8.pdf).

29. Richard Baldwin, "21st Century Regionalism: Filling the Gap between 21st Century Trade and 20th Century Trade Rules," Policy Insight No. 56 (Centre for Economic Policy Research, May 20, 2011), p. 3 (http://cepr.org /active/publications/policy_insights/viewpi.php?pino=56).

30. Lejárraga, "Deep Provisions in Regional Trade Agreements," p. 15.

31. Baldwin, "21st Century Regionalism."

32. Richard Baldwin, "WTO 2.0 Governance of 21st Century Trade," *Review of International Organizations*, vol. 9 (2014).

33. Sébastien Miroudot, Dorothée Rouzet, and Francesca Spinelli, "Trade Policy Implications of Global Value Chains: Case Studies," OECD Trade Policy Paper 161 (Paris: OECD Publishing, December 2013) (www.oecd-ilibrary.org /trade/trade-policy-implications-of-global-value-chains_5k3tpt2t0zs1-en), pp. 38-40, 56. The authors created a network trade index (measuring how important country A is as a source of intermediate imports used in country B's production for export), a regional trade agreement index (measuring the depth of existing trade agreements), and a coefficient index (measuring the overlap among them). In 2009, the coefficient index results for headquarter economies were very different: Germany (0.79), the United States (0.59), and Japan (0.05).

34. Kenneth C. Shadlen, "Exchanging Development for Market Access? Deep Integration and Industrial Policy Under Multilateral and Regional-Bilateral Trade Agreements," *Review of International Political Economy*, vol. 12, no. 5 (2005).

35. Susan K. Sell, "TRIPS was Never Enough: Vertical Forum Shifting, FTAS, ACTA, and TPP," *Journal of Intellectual Property Law*, vol. 18, no. 2 (Spring 2011).

36. Kevin Gallagher, "Losing Control: Policy Space to Prevent and Mitigate Financial Crises in Trade and Investment Agreements," *Development Policy Review*, vol. 29, no. 4 (July 2011).

37. Thomas J. Bollyky, "A Dose of the TPP's Medicine: Why U.S. Trade Deals Haven't Exported U.S. Drug Prices," *Foreign Affairs* (March 2016).

38. Ibid.

39. Lee Branstetter, "TPP and the Conflict over Drugs: Incentives for Innovation versus Access to Medicines," in *Assessing the Trans-Pacific Partnership. Volume 2: Innovations in Trading Rules*, edited by Jeffrey J. Schott and Cathleen Cimino-Isaacs, PIIE Briefing 16-4 (Washington: Peterson Institute for International Economics, March 2016). Biologics are drugs derived from living organisms. Data protection refers to the period of time during which a generic manufacturer cannot use the test data submitted by the original producer to market its competing product. In the TPP, the data exclusivity period was set at eight years (or five years plus three years of other measures to deliver a comparable outcome in the market). The current standard in the United States is twelve years.

40. Branstetter, "TPP and the Conflict over Drugs."

41. Jörg Mayer, "Policy Space: What, for What, and Where?" *Development Policy Review*, vol. 27, no. 4 (July 2009), p. 377.

42. Leonardo Baccini and Johannes Urpelainen, *Cutting the Gordian Knot of Economic Reform: When and How International Institutions Help* (Oxford University Press, 2014).

43. Baldwin, "21st Century Regionalism."

44. Organisation for Economic Co-operation and Development, World Trade Organization, and World Bank Group, "Global Value Chains: Challenges, Opportunities, and Implications for Policy," report prepared for the G20 Trade Ministers Meeting (Sydney, Australia, July 2014), pp. 18, 26.

45. Michael Plummer, for instance, provides a list of best practices in regional trade agreements. See Michael G. Plummer, " 'Best Practices' in Regional Trading Agreements: An Application to Asia," *World Economy*, vol. 30, no. 12 (December 2007).

46. Gary Gereffi, "A Global Value Chain Perspective on Industrial Policy and Development in Emerging Markets," *Duke Journal of Comparative and International Law*, vol. 24, no. 3 (Spring 2014).

47. Daria Taglioni and Deborah Winkler, *Making Global Value Chains Work for Development* (Washington: World Bank, 2016) (https://openknowledge.worldbank.org/handle/10986/24426).

48. OECD, WTO, and World Bank Group, "Global Value Chains," p. 27.

49. Gereffi, "Global Value Chain Perspective," p. 456.

50. Taglioni and Winkler, *Making Global Value Chains Work*, p. 4.

51. Christian Tietje and Freya Baetens, "The Impact of Investor-State Dispute Settlement (ISDS) in the Transatlantic Trade and Investment Partnership," paper prepared for the Minister for Foreign Trade and Development Cooperation, Ministry of Foreign Affairs (The Netherlands, June 24, 2014), p. 25 (www.rijksoverheid.nl/documenten/rapporten/2014/06/24/the-impact-of-investor-state-dispute-settlement-isds-in-the-ttip).

52. Shayerah Ilias Akhtar and Martin A. Weiss, "U.S. International Investment Agreements: Issues for Congress," Report R43052 (Washington: Congressional Research Service, April 29, 2013) (https://www.fas.org/sgp/crs/row/R43052.pdf).

53. UN Conference on Trade and Development (UNCTAD), "Recent Developments in Investor-State Dispute Settlement," IIA Issue Note, no. 1, April 2014 (http://unctad.org/en/PublicationsLibrary/webdiaepcb2014d3_en.pdf).

54. Dan Ikenson, "A Compromise to Advance the Trade Agenda: Purge Negotiations of Investor-State Dispute Settlement," Free Trade Bulletin No. 57 (CATO Institute, March 4, 2014) (www.cato.org/publications/free-trade-bulletin/compromise-advance-trade-agenda-purge-negotiations-investor-state); Mary Hallward-Driemeier, "Do Bilateral Investment Treaties Attract FDI? Only a Bit . . . and They Could Bite," Working Paper 3121 (Washington: World Bank, August 2003); Productivity Commission, Australian Government, "Bilateral and Regional Trade Agreements," *Productivity Commission Research Report*, November 2010, p. 275 (www.pc.gov.au/inquiries/completed/trade-agreements/report).

55. Beth A. Simmons, "Bargaining over BITs, Arbitrating Awards: The Regime for Protection and Promotion of International Investment," *World Politics*, vol. 66, no. 1 (January 2014).

56. For example, in 2011 the tobacco company Philip Morris Asia Limited legally challenged Australia's plain packaging law for cigarettes using the

Australia-Hong Kong BIT. In December 2015, the arbitration panel ruled in favor of Australia, dismissing the case on jurisdictional grounds. In July 2016, Philip Morris International lost its lawsuit against Uruguay for its packaging laws. This last ruling may set a larger precedent since the arbitral tribunal ruled on the substantive elements of the case, determining that health-warning requirements on tobacco packaging did not constitute indirect expropriation. See Peter Leung, "Philip Morris Challenge to Uruguay Packaging Rules Rejected," *Bloomberg BNA*, July 14, 2016 (www.bna.com/philip-morris-challenge -n73014444729).

57. Jane Kelsey and Lori Wallach, " 'Investor-State' Disputes in Trade Pacts Threaten Fundamental Principles of National Judicial Systems," Working Paper (April 2012), pp. 2–3 (http://www.citizen.org/documents/isds-domestic-legal -process-background-brief.pdf).

58. Gus Van Harten, "Private Authority and Transnational Governance: The Contours of the International System of Investor Protection," *Review of International Political Economy*, vol. 12, no. 4 (2005).

59. José E. Alvarez, "The Evolving BIT," in *Investment Treaty Arbitration and International Law, Volume 3*, edited by Ian A. Laird and Todd J. Weiler (Huntington, N.Y.: JurisNet, 2010), p. 8; Scott Miller, "Investor-State Dispute Settlement: A Reality Check," Working Paper (Washington: Center for Strategic and International Studies, October 2014).

60. Roderick Abbott, Fredrik Erixon, and Martina Francesca Ferracane, "Demystifying Investor-State Dispute Settlement (ISDS)," ECIPE Occasional Paper No. 5 (Brussels: European Centre for International Political Economy, June 2014), p. 7 (http://ecipe.org/publications/isds).

61. Miller, "Investor-State Dispute Settlement."

62. Abbott, Erixon, and Ferracane, "Demystifying ISDS," p. 12.

63. Raymond Vernon, *Sovereignty at Bay: The Multinational Spread of U.S. Enterprises* (New York: Basic Books, 1971).

64. Abbott, Erixon, and Ferracane, "Demystifying ISDS," pp. 7–8, 10.

65. Ibid., pp. 15–18.

66. Susan D. Franck, "An Evidence-Based Approach to Investment Treaty Arbitration," presentation at "Investor-State Dispute Settlement: A Reality Check" (Washington: Center for Strategic and International Studies, October 31, 2014) (http://csis.org/event/investor-state-dispute-settlement-reality-check). These numbers are consistent with her earlier findings with a smaller dataset that covered up to 2006. See Susan D. Franck, "Empirically Evaluating Claims about Investment Treaty Arbitration," *North Carolina Law Review*, vol. 86, no. 1 (December 2007).

67. Miller, "Investor-State Dispute Settlement."

68. Daniel M. Price, "Chapter 11—Private Party vs. Government, Investor-State Dispute Settlement: Frankenstein or Safety Valve?" *Canada-United States Law Journal*, vol. 26 (2000), p. 111.

69. Tietje and Baetens, "Impact of ISDS," p. 57.

70. Miller, "Investor-State Dispute Settlement."

71. Tietje and Baetens, "Impact of ISDS," p. 43.

72. Jeremy Caddel and Nathan M. Jensen, "Which Host Country Government Actors Are Most Involved in Disputes with Foreign Investors?" *Columbia FDI Perspectives*, no. 120 (New York: Vale Columbia Center on Sustainable International Investment, April 28, 2014) (http://dx.doi.org/10.7916 /D8M32SWK).

73. Tietje and Baetens, "Impact of ISDS," p. 93.

74. Alvarez, "The Evolving BIT," pp. 9–11.

75. Leon E. Trakman, "Investor State Arbitration or Local Courts: Will Australia Set a New Trend?" *Journal of World Trade Law*, vol. 46, no. 1 (2012), p. 96.

76. Miriam Sapiro, "Transatlantic Trade and Investment Negotiations: Reaching a Consensus on Investor-State Dispute Settlement," *Global Views*, no. 5 (Washington: Global Economy and Development Program, Brookings Institution, October 2015), p. 9.

77. Gary Clyde Hufbauer, "Liberalization of Services Trade," in *Assessing the Trans-Pacific Partnership, Volume 1: Market Access and Sectoral Issues*, PIIE Briefing 16-1 (Washington: Peterson Institute for International Economics, February 2016).

78. Tietje and Baetens, "Impact of ISDS," pp. 96–106.

79. Further changes to the ISDS system may be in store, especially concerning the possible adoption of an appeals process. This has been a main feature of the EU's ISDS proposal to the United States in the context of Transatlantic Trade and Investment Partnership negotiations. The United States has not incorporated an appeals process in its ISDS provisions. As Miriam Sapiro notes, this could be an area of common ground since an appeals mechanism is contemplated as a possibility in both TPA's negotiation objectives and model BIT provisions, but the catch is that states could be the more frequent target of the appeal process since they win more cases. See Sapiro, "Transatlantic Trade and Investment Negotiations"; Office of the United States Trade Representative, "Upgrading and Improving Investor-State Dispute Settlement," TPP Fact Sheet (https://ustr.gov/sites/default/files/TPP-Upgrading-and-Improving-Investor -State-Dispute-Settlement10).

## CHAPTER 5

1. Sophie Meunier, "Trade Policy and Political Legitimacy in the European Union," *Comparative European Politics*, vol. 1, no. 1 (March 2003), p. 72.

2. David S. Levine, "Bring in the Nerds: Secrecy, National Security, and the Creation of International Intellectual Property Law," *Cardozo Arts and Entertainment Law Journal*, vol. 30, no. 2 (2012).

3. Lori Wallach and Ben Beachy, "Obama's Covert Trade Deal," Opinion Pages, *New York Times*, June 2, 2013.

4. Margot E. Kaminski, "Don't Keep the Trans-Pacific Talks Secret," Opinion Pages, *New York Times*, April 14, 2015.

5. Levine, "Bring in the Nerds."

6. Sean Flynn, "Learning from ACTA: TTIP Proponents Need to Embrace Democracy," *InfoJustice.org* blog, October 1, 2014 (http://infojustice.org /archives/33336).

7. Sean Flynn, "Kirk Responds to TPP Transparency Demands," *Infojustice .org* blog, May 10, 2012 (http://infojustice.org/archives/21385).

8. Sean Flynn, "WIPO Treaty for the Blind Shows That Transparency Can Work (and is Necessary)," *Infojustice.org* blog, June 26, 2013 (http://infojustice .org/archives/30027).

9. Susan Ariel Aaronson, "Trade Secrets. The U.S.-EU Free Trade Agreement Could be a Boon for the Global Economy, but Confidential Negotiations are a Dangerous Threat to Democracy," *Foreign Policy* (June 17, 2013) (http:// foreignpolicy.com/2013/06/17/trade-secrets).

10. Sean Flynn, "Law Professors Call for Trans-Pacific Partnership (TPP) Transparency," *Infojustice.org* blog, May 9, 2012 (http://infojustice.org /archives/21137).

11. Levine, "Bring in the Nerds."

12. Richard Steinberg, remarks at the conference "Trade and Transparency in the Internet Age" (Yale Law School, New Haven, Conn., February 10, 2014) (http://vimeo.com/86619442).

13. Oona A. Hathaway, remarks at the conference "Trade and Transparency in the Internet Age" (Yale Law School, New Haven, Conn., February 10, 2014) (http://vimeo.com/86619442).

14. A fuller discussion of executive-legislative relations and the politics of trade promotion authority (TPA) can be found in chapter 6.

15. "USTR Takes Steps to Boost Lawmakers' Access to TPP Negotiating Text," *Inside U.S. Trade,* March 20, 2015.

16. Alex Lawson, "USTR Aims to Improve Congressional Access to Trade Texts," *Law360,* October 29, 2015 (www.law360.com/articles/720599/ustr -aims-to-improve-congressional-access-to-trade-texts).

17. Vicki Needham and Mike Lillis, "Lawmakers Pass Up Chance to Read 'Secret' Trade Text," *The Hill,* April 27, 2015.

18. Office of the United States Trade Representative, "Fact Sheet: Transparency and the Obama Trade Agenda" (January 2015) (https://ustr.gov/about-us /policy-offices/press-office/fact-sheets/2015/january/fact-sheet-transparency -and-obama).

19. Brian J. Schoenborn, "Public Participation in Trade Negotiations: Open Agreements, Openly Arrived At?" *Minnesota Journal of Global Trade,* vol. 4, no. 1 (Winter 1995).

20. Hathaway, "Trade and Transparency."

21. Michelle Limenta, "Open Trade Negotiations as Opposed to Secret Trade Negotiations: From Transparency to Public Participation," *New Zealand Yearbook of International Law,* vol. 10 (2012), pp. 88–89.

22. The TPP confidentiality agreement can be found on the New Zealand Ministry of Foreign Affairs and Trade's website (www.mfat.govt.nz/assets/ _securedfiles/Trans-Pacific-Partnership/TPP-letter.pdf).

23. Anne Peters, "Towards Transparency as a Global Norm," in *Transparency in International Law*, edited by Andrea Bianchi and Anne Peters (Cambridge University Press, 2013), p. 577.

24. Mark Wu, remarks at the conference "Trade and Transparency in the Internet Age," Yale Law School (New Haven, Conn., February 10, 2014) (http://vimeo.com/86619442).

25. Barbara Koremenos, "Open Covenants, Clandestinely Arrived At" (unpublished manuscript under revision at *International Theory*, 2013).

26. Daniel Gervais, "Rethinking the International Intellectual Property System: What Role for WIPO?" in *Rethinking International Intellectual Property Law: What Institutional Environment for the Development and Enforcement of IP Law?* edited by Christophe Geiger and Xavier Seuba (Geneva: International Centre for Trade and Sustainable Development and Center for International Intellectual Property Studies, November 2015).

27. Maria Perez-Esteve, "WTO Rules and Practices for Transparency and Engagement with Civil Society Organizations," Working Paper ERSD-2012-14 (Geneva: World Trade Organization, September 2012).

28. Ibid., p. 24.

29. Gabrielle Marceau and Mikella Hurley, "Transparency and Public Participation in the WTO: A Report Card on WTO Transparency Mechanisms," *Trade, Law and Development*, vol. 4, no. 1 (2012).

30. Ibid., p. 39.

31. European Commission, "Communication to the Commission Concerning Transparency in TTIP Negotiations" (November 25, 2014) (http://ec.europa.eu/news/2014/docs/c_2014_9052_en.pdf).

32. Eugénia da Condeição-Heldt, "Explaining the Paradox of EU Transparency in TTIP Negotiations," paper presented at the 23rd International Conference for Europeanists (Philadelphia, Penn., April 14–16, 2016).

33. Joanna Raduszewksa, "TTIP: A Transparency Paradox," *My World, My Voice* blog, Polish Institute of International Affairs, February 2, 2016 (https://blog.pism.pl/blog/?p=1&id_blog=54&id_post=739); Peter van Hamm, "Communicating TTIP: Challenges for the European Union," Policy Brief (Clingendael: Netherland Institute of International Relations, March 2016).

34. Matthias Bauer, "Time to Challenge (German-Based) Anti-TTIP Propaganda Organisations," Debates, *E!Sharp*, September 2016 (http://esharp.eu/debates/external-action/time-to-challenge-german-based-anti-ttip-propaganda-organisations).

35. Sebastián Sáez, "Trade Policy-Making in Latin America: A Compared Analysis," Working Paper (Economic and Social Research Institute of the Cabinet Office, Government of Japan, and UN Economic Commission for Latin America and the Caribbean, January 2005), p. 10 (www.esri.go.jp/jp/workshop/050316/050316ECLA-R1.pdf).

36. Carlos Alba and Gustavo Vega, "Trade Advisory Mechanisms in Mexico," in "The Trade Policy-Making Process Level One of the Two Level Game: Country Studies in the Western Hemisphere," INTAL-ITD-STA Occasional Paper 13 (Buenos Aires: Inter-American Development Bank Integration and

Regional Trade Department, March 2002) (www.sice.oas.org/ctyindex/ARG /policymaking_e.pdf); Sáez, "Trade Policy-Making."

37. Robert O. Keohane and Joseph S. Nye Jr., "The Club Model of Multilateral Cooperation and Problems of Democratic Legitimacy," in *Efficiency, Equity, and Legitimacy: The Multilateral Trading System at the Millennium*, edited by Roger B. Porter and others (Brookings Institution, 2001).

38. Brian Hocking, "Changing the Terms of Trade Policy Making: From the 'Club' to the 'Multistakeholder' Model," *World Trade Review*, vol. 3, no. 1 (March 2004), p. 12.

39. Peter Newell and Diana Tussie, eds., "Civil Society Participation in Trade Policy-Making in Latin America: Reflections and Lessons," Working Paper 267 (Brighton, U.K.: Institute of Development Studies, 2006) (https://assets .publishing.service.gov.uk/media/57a08c46e5274a27b20010c7/1052734521 -newell_etal.2006-civil.pdf); Alba and Vega, "Trade Advisory Mechanisms."

40. Limenta, "Open Trade Negotiations," p. 93.

41. Hocking, "Terms of Trade Policy Making."

42. Schoenborn, "Public Participation in Trade Negotiations," p. 136.

43. Ann Capling, "Legitimacy Begins at Home: Overcoming the Democratic Deficit in Domestic Trade Policy-Making," paper presented at "Pathways to Legitimacy? The Future of Global and Regional Governance," Centre for the Study of Globalisation and Regionalisation conference (University of Warwick, Coventry, U.K., September 19, 2007) (www2.warwick.ac.uk/fac/soc/pais /research/researchcentres/csgr/csgr-events/conferences/conference2007/papers /capling.pdf).

44. Michelle Ye Hee Lee, "Warren's Claim that Advisory Committees 'Formed' During Drafting of Trans-Pacific Partnership," Fact Checker, *Washington Post*, July 18, 2016.

45. Christopher Ingraham and Howard Schneider, "Industry Voices Dominate the Trade Advisory System," *Washington Post*, February 27, 2014 (www .washingtonpost.com/wp-srv/special/business/trade-advisory-committees).

46. "Industry Trade Advisory Committees (ITACs) Meeting of the Committee Chairs, Public Session," Office of the United States Trade Representative, October 12, 2010 (www.ustr.gov/webfm_send/2449).

47. Margot E. Kaminski, "The Capture of International Intellectual Property Law through the U.S. Trade Regime," *Southern California Law Review*, vol. 87, no. 4 (May 2014).

48. Stephen Jacobi, "Secrets and Influence in Trade Negotiations," *New Zealand International Review*, vol. 38, no. 6 (November/December 2013).

49. Based on data from Ingraham and Schneider, "Industry Voices Dominate."

50. "USTR Allows Cleared Advisers to View TPP Texts as of July 9," *Inside U.S. Trade*, July 10, 2015.

51. Government Accountability Office, "International Trade: Prior Updates of the Trade Advisory System Offer Insights for Current Review," testimony of Loren Yager, director of Internal Affairs and Trade, before the Subcommittee on Trade, Committee on Ways and Means, House of Representatives (GAO: July 21, 2009).

52. Michael Froman, "A Values-Driven Trade Policy," remarks at the Center for American Progress (Washington, February 18, 2014) (https://ustr.gov/about -us/policy-offices/press-office/press-releases/2014/February/A-Values-Driven -Trade-Policy_Remarks-by-USTR-Froman-at-Center-for-American-P).

53. Sean Flynn, "USTR Accepts Business Proposal to Segregate Public Interest in Advisory Committees," *InfoJustice.org* blog, February 19, 2014 (http://infojustice.org/archives/32248); Kaminski, "International Intellectual Property Law."

54. "A Year After Unveiling, 'PITAC' Stalled Due to Fight Over Secrecy Rules," Daily Report, *Inside U.S. Trade*, February 25, 2015.

55. Cited in Institute for International Economic Policy, "5 Ways the U.S. Can Increase Trust, Responsiveness, and Transparency in Trade Negotiations," 2015 (www.internationaleconpolicy.com/international-trade/5-ways-the-u-s-can -increase-trust-responsiveness-and-transparency-in-trade-negotiations).

## CHAPTER 6

1. This is not to suggest that all policy innovations are superior to the status quo. But the general point still stands that a country unable to adapt its policies to match internal and external developments is at a disadvantage.

2. Stephan Haggard and Mathew D. McCubbins, "Introduction: Political Institutions and the Determinants of Public Policy," in *Presidents, Parliaments, and Public Policy*, edited by Stephan Haggard and Mathew D. McCubbins (Cambridge University Press, 2001), pp. 1–20.

3. George Tsebelis, *Veto Players: How Political Institutions Work* (Princeton University Press, 2002).

4. Haggard and McCubbins, "Introduction." Neither extreme (full concentration or complete fragmentation) is desirable. The former yields tyranny, where only one viewpoint informs policy and radical shifts in policy harm credibility; the latter yields anarchy with the inability to craft policies to address national problems. See Gary Cox and Mathew D. McCubbins, "The Institutional Determinants of Economic Policy Outcomes," in *Presidents, Parliaments, and Public Policy*, edited by Haggard and McCubbins, pp. 21–63.

5. Cox and McCubbins, "Institutional Determinants."

6. The next section draws from Mireya Solís, "Can FTAs Deliver Market Liberalization in Japan? A Study on Domestic Political Determinants," *Review of International Political Economy*, vol. 17, no. 2 (2010); and Mireya Solís, "Efficiency, Legitimacy, and Political Expediency: Governance Dilemmas in Korean and Japanese FTA Policy," paper presented at the International Studies Association Annual Conference (San Diego, Calif., April 1, 2012). Eric Batalla also applies the concept of state decisiveness to explain the evolution of trade policy in three Southeast Asian countries. See Eric Vincent C. Batalla, "Veto Players and State Decisiveness: Negotiating Bilateral Economic Partnership Agreements Between Japan and Southeast Asia," *Philippine Political Science Journal*, vol. 33, no. 1 (2012).

7. Sharyn O'Halloran, *Politics, Process, and American Trade Policy* (University of Michigan Press, 1994); Helen V. Milner, *Interests, Institutions, and Information: Domestic Politics and International Relations* (Princeton University Press, 1997).

8. Robert Baldwin notes that the chief executive usually supports open trade policies not only because standard-of-living gains appeal to his or her broad electoral constituency but also because of foreign policy considerations. See Robert E. Baldwin, "U.S. Trade Policies: The Role of the Executive Branch," in *Constituent Interests and U.S. Trade Policies*, edited by Alan V. Deardorff and Robert M. Stern (University of Michigan Press, 1998), pp. 81–82. This generalization does not apply, however, when the executive embraces a program of economic nationalism favoring specific sectors at the expense of aggregate economic gains from open markets. As a case in point, consider the early moves of President Trump to withdraw from the TPP and his threats to punish individual American companies with border taxes if they shift production abroad.

9. Sebastián Sáez, "Trade Policy-Making in Latin America: A Compared Analysis," Working Paper (Economic and Social Research Institute of the Cabinet Office, Government of Japan, and UN Economic Commission for Latin America and the Caribbean, January 2005), p. 12 (www.esri.go.jp/jp/workshop /050316/050316ECLA-R1.pdf).

10. Jacint Jordana and Carles Ramió, *"Diseños Institucionales y Gestión de la Política Comercial Exterior en América Latina,"* [Institutional Designs and Foreign Trade Policy Formulation in Latin America] *INTAL-ITD-STA Documento de Divulgación* 15 [Dissemination Documents 15] (Buenos Aires: *Banco Interamericano de Desarrollo Departamento de Integración y Programas Regionales*, June 2002), pp. 15–16 (https://publications.iadb.org/handle/11319 /6256).

11. Batalla, "Veto Players and State Decisiveness."

12. Mireya Solís, "South Korea's Fateful Decision on the Trans-Pacific Partnership," Foreign Policy Paper 31 (Foreign Policy Program, Brookings Institution, September 2013).

13. Stéphane Bergeron, "Another Perspective on Parliament and International Trade: Parliamentarians Are Not Puppets," *Canadian Parliamentary Review*, vol. 26, no. 4 (Winter 2003) and Cyndee Todgham Cherniak, "What are the Steps Canada Follows to Ratify and Implement a Treaty?" *Canada-U.S. Blog*, October 30, 2016 (www.canada-usblog.com/2016/10/30/what-are-the-steps -canada-follows-to-ratify-and-implement-a-treaty/). As these examples make clear, the traditional presidential-parliamentary divide is not useful to understand the conditions for executive leadership. The conventional expectation is to find stronger executives in presidential systems than in parliamentary systems, since, in the latter, parliaments appoint the prime minister and can bring down a government through a no-confidence vote. However, it is possible to find presidential systems with a strong legislature (France) and parliamentary systems with a strong executive (United Kingdom). See Arend Lijphart, *Patterns of Democracy: Government Forms and Performance in Thirty-Six*

*Countries* (Yale University Press, 1999), p. 27. Indeed, there is wide variation within parliamentary systems in terms of executive power. Whereas some countries in the Westminster tradition operate under strong prime ministerial leadership, many others are characterized by weak cabinet governments. For these reasons, Helen Milner argues that divided government should be seen as a continuous variable cutting across both presidential and parliamentary systems, and that executive power can be measured by its control over essential legislative powers (agenda setting, amendment, ratification, referendums, and side payments). See Milner, *Interests, Institutions, and Information*, pp. 37–42, 100.

14. Ann Capling, "Can the Democratic Deficit in Treaty-Making be Overcome? Parliament and the Australia-United States Free Trade Agreement," in *The Fluid State: International Law and National Legal Systems*, edited by Hilary Charlesworth and others (Sydney: The Federation Press, 2005), pp. 65–67.

15. I. M. Destler, *American Trade Politics*, 4th ed. (Washington: Institute for International Economics, 2005), pp. 15–17.

16. Mathew D. McCubbins and Thomas Schwartz, "Congressional Oversight Overlooked: Police Patrols versus Fire Alarms," *American Journal of Political Science*, vol. 28, no. 1 (February 1984), pp. 168–69.

17. As Gilbert Winham explains, one of the purposes for Congress to establish the trade advisory committee system was to delegate monitoring of trade negotiations to constituency interests themselves. This is, in essence, a fire alarm device in that affected interest groups will raise the decibel level if disappointed with final negotiation results. See Gilbert R. Winham, *International Trade and the Tokyo Round Negotiation* (Princeton University Press, 1986), p. 313.

18. Perhaps one of the most extreme examples is Mexico's practice of briefing interested lobby groups on-site during FTA negotiations in the so-called room next door (*cuarto de junto*). Moreover, contrary to what happens in the American and Canadian trade advisory systems, the Mexican private sector itself appoints its own delegates. See Carlos Alba and Gustavo Vega, "Trade Advisory Mechanisms in Mexico," in "The Trade Policy-Making Process Level One of the Two Level Game: Country Studies in the Western Hemisphere," INTAL-ITD-STA Occasional Paper 13 (Buenos Aires: Inter-American Development Bank Integration and Regional Trade Department, March 2002) (www .sice.oas.org/ctyindex/ARG/policymaking_e.pdf).

19. For instance, during the NAFTA mock markup sessions, legislators obtained concessions on trademark protection for spirits, looser snapback provisions for import relief, and more stringent monitoring mechanisms to prevent the transshipment of Australian beef through Mexico. See O'Halloran, *American Trade Policy*, pp. 149, 170.

20. Congressional discomfort over ease of access to text and quality of input to trade negotiators are also important and were discussed in chapter 5.

21. Data exclusivity refers to the protection of clinical test data before it is made available to generic producers that seek marketing approval of their products.

With patent linkage authorities notify the patent holder when a generic producer seeks marketing approval of a similar product.

22. "At Impasse with Wyden over TPA Bill, Hatch Calls on Obama to Intervene," *Inside U.S. Trade*, February 27, 2015.

23. "TPA Hung Up over Disapproval Resolution; Ryan Says Talks Close to Deal," *Inside U.S. Trade*, February 20, 2015.

24. "TPA Bill Includes Additional Tool for Stripping 'Fast Track;' Staff Text Access," *Inside U.S. Trade*, April 17, 2015.

25. Terry M. Moe, "The New Economics of Organization," *American Journal of Political Science*, vol. 28, no. 4 (November 1984); John Creighton Campbell, *Contemporary Japanese Budget Politics* (University of California Press, 1977).

26. Graham Allison and Philip Zelikow, *Essence of Decision: Explaining the Cuban Missile Crisis*, 2nd ed. (New York: Longman, 1999), p. 302.

27. Solís, "Market Liberalization in Japan"; Byung-il Choi and Jennifer Seijin Oh, "Asymmetry in Japan and Korea's Agricultural Liberalization in FTA: Domestic Trade Governance Perspective," *Pacific Review*, vol. 24, no. 5 (December 2011).

28. Haruhiro Fukui, "The GATT Tokyo Round: The Bureaucratic Politics of Multilateral Diplomacy," in *The Politics of Trade: U.S. and Japanese Policymaking for the GATT Negotiations*, edited by Michael Blaker (East Asia Institute, Columbia University, 1978). In fact, the number of ministries involved in trade policymaking has increased to include those besides the traditional four ministries—Ministry of Foreign Affairs (MOFA); Ministry of Economy, Trade and Industry (METI); Ministry of Agriculture, Forestry and Fisheries (MAFF); and Ministry of Finance. As a case in point, FTA negotiations where the trade partner demands the incorporation of labor mobility clauses have brought the Ministry of Health, Labour and Welfare into the negotiation process.

29. Fukui, "GATT Tokyo Round"; Michael Blaker, *Japanese International Negotiating Style* (Columbia University Press, 1977).

30. Destler, *American Trade Politics*.

31. Anne H. Rightor-Thornton, "An Analysis of the Office of the Special Representative for Trade Negotiations: The Evolving Role, 1962–1974," in "Appendix H: Case Studies on US Foreign Economic Policy: 1965–1974," report of the Commission on the Organization of the Government for the Conduct of Foreign Policy, Appendices, Volume 3 (Washington: U.S. Government Printing Office, June 1975), pp. 91–92.

32. Destler, *American Trade Politics*; Susan Ariel Aaronson, *Redefining the Terms of Trade Policymaking* (Washington: National Policy Association, 2001), pp. 28–29.

33. Doug Palmer, "U.S. Trade Candidate Zients Faces Heat on Agency Reform Plan," *Reuters*, February 8, 2013 (www.reuters.com/article/us-obama-trade-zients-idUSBRE91712T20130208).

34. Choi and Oh, "Asymmetry."

35. Solís, "South Korea's Fateful Decision."

36. Jeffrey J. Schott, Euijin Jung, and Cathleen Cimino-Isaacs, "An Assessment of the Korea-China Free Trade Agreement," Policy Brief 15-24 (Washington: Peterson Institute for International Economics, December 2015), p. 4 (https://piie.com/sites/default/files/publications/pb/pb15-24.pdf).

37. Jordana and Ramió, "*Diseños Institucionales*," p. 9.

38. Vinod K. Aggarwal, "Corporate Market and Non-Market Strategies in Asia," *Business and Politics*, vol. 3, no. 2 (2001) and David P. Baron, *Business and Its Environment,* 5th ed. (New Jersey: Prentice Hall, 2010).

39. For studies on Latin America, see Ben R. Schneider, *Business Politics and the State in Twentieth-Century Latin America* (Cambridge University Press, 2004). For studies on Asia, see Saori N. Katada and Mireya Solís, "Domestic Sources of Japanese Foreign Policy Activism: Loss Avoidance and Demand Coherence," *International Relations of the Asia-Pacific*, vol. 10, no. 1 (January 2010); and Mireya Solís, "Business Advocacy in Asian PTAs: A Model of Selective Business Lobbying with Evidence from Japan," *Business and Politics*, vol. 15, no. 1 (April 2013).

40. Antonio Postigo, "Institutional Spillovers from the Negotiation and Formulation of East Asian Free Trade Agreements," *Review of International Political Economy*, vol. 23, no. 3 (2016).

41. Cornelia Woll and Alvaro Artigas, "When Trade Liberalization Turns into Regulatory Reform: The Impact on Business–Government Relations in International Trade Politics," *Regulation and Governance*, vol. 1, no. 2 (June 2007).

42. "AFL-CIO Suspends Political Contributions to Lawmakers Ahead of TPA Vote," *Inside U.S. Trade*, March 6, 2015.

43. Edward-Isaac Dovere, "Democrats Recount Labor's Pressure Tactics," *Politico*, May 27, 2015.

44. Robert E. Baldwin and Christopher S. Magee, "Is Trade Policy for Sale? Congressional Voting on Recent Trade Bills," Working Paper 6376 (Cambridge, Mass.: National Bureau of Economic Research, January 1998) (www.nber.org /papers/w6376.pdf).

45. Will Tucker, "Millions Spent by 487 Organizations to Influence TPP Outcome," *OpenSecrets* blog, Center for Responsive Politics, October 6, 2015 (https://www.opensecrets.org/news/2015/10/millions-spent-by-487 -organizations-to-influence-tpp-outcome).

46. Clark Mindock, "Trans-Pacific Partnership Deal Has Mighty Lobbying Power on Its Side," *OpenSecrets* blog, Center for Responsive Politics, April 9, 2015 (www.opensecrets.org/news/2015/04/trans-pacific-partnership-deal-has -mighty-lobbying-power-on-its-side).

47. John S. Odell, *Negotiating Trade: Developing Countries in the WTO and NAFTA* (Cambridge University Press, 2006); Katada and Solís, "Japanese Foreign Policy Activism."

48. Richard Baldwin, "A Domino Theory of Regionalism," in *Expanding Membership of the European Union*, edited by Richard E. Baldwin, Pertti Haapararanta, and Jaakko Kiander (Cambridge University Press, 1995).

49. Thomas Brambor and Johannes Lindvall, "Fiscal Capacity, Domestic Compensation, and Trade Policy: A Long-Term View" (paper under review for publication, 2014) (http://svet.lu.se/en/thomas-brambor/publication/4696391).

50. Brian Burgoon and Michael J. Hiscox, "Trade Openness and Political Compensation: Labor Demands for Adjustment Assistance," paper presented at the Annual Meeting of the American Political Science Association (Washington, September 2000), p. 24.

51. J.F. Hornbeck and Laine Elise Rover, "Trade Adjustment Assistance (TAA) and Its Role in U.S. Trade Policy," Report R41922 (Washington: Congressional Research Service, August 11, 2011), p. 8 (http://fpc.state.gov/documents/organization/171390.pdf).

52. Burgoon and Hiscox, "Trade Openness," p. 25.

53. "Statement by AFL-CIO President Richard Trumka on Introduction of Trade Adjustment Assistance (TAA) Legislation," AFL-CIO press release, February 25, 2015 (www.aflcio.org/Press-Room/Press-Releases/Statement-by-AFL-CIO-President-Richard-Trumka-on-Introduction-of-Trade-Adjustment-Assistance-TAA-Legislation).

54. Hornbeck and Rover, "Trade Adjustment Assistance."

55. Cathleen Cimino-Isaacs, Gary Clyde Hufbauer, and Jeffrey J. Schott, "The New TAA Package Stands on Its Own Merits," *Trade and Investment Policy Watch* blog, Peterson Institute for International Economics, June 22, 2015 (https://piie.com/blogs/trade-investment-policy-watch/new-taa-package-stands-its-own-merits).

56. Yotam Margalit, "Costly Jobs: Trade-Related Layoffs, Government Compensation, and Voting in U.S. Elections," *American Political Science Review*, vol. 105, no. 1 (February 2011).

57. Sean D. Ehrlich, "Who Supports Compensation? Individual Preferences for Trade-Related Unemployment Insurance," *Business and Politics*, vol. 12, no. 1 (2010).

58. The main disagreements were about the exclusion of tobacco from investor-state dispute settlement (ISDS), the exclusion of financial services from the ban on data server localization (although a fix to be applied to subsequent trade agreements was worked out), and the period of exclusivity for biologics test data. Undoubtedly, the last issue was the most challenging.

59. "Seeking to 'Free the Hostage,' Obama says he will not hold up TPA over TAA," *Inside U.S. Trade*, June 19, 2015. More accurately, the link was weakened but not severed, since Democrats in Congress willing to support TPA needed reassurances from the Republican leadership that the TAA bill would come to a vote and be approved.

## CHAPTER 7

1. Top-down decisionmaking means there are fewer hurdles to implementing new policies, but it is not a predictor of the direction of those policies. After all, examples of centralized political systems with little appetite for reform abound.

2. For example, even though NAFTA and the U.S.-Korea Free Trade Agreement were negotiated under fast-track rules (allowing no congressional amendments), the United States reopened negotiations to include side chapters on labor and the environment (NAFTA) and additional concessions in autos with South Korea to pave the way for congressional ratification.

3. Rose J. Spalding, "Civil Society Engagement in Trade Negotiations: CAFTA Opposition Movements in El Salvador," *Latin American Politics and Society*, vol. 49, no. 4 (Winter 2007), p. 86.

4. Andreas Dür and Gemma Mateo, "Gaining Access or Going Public? Interest Group Strategies in Five European Countries," *European Journal of Political Research*, vol. 52, no. 5 (August 2013).

5. Anne Binderkrantz, "Interest Group Strategies: Navigating Between Privileged Access and Strategies of Pressure," *Political Studies*, vol. 53, no. 4 (December 2005), p. 698.

6. Andreas Dür and Gemma Mateo, "Public Opinion and Interest Group Influence: How Citizen Groups Derailed the Anti-Counterfeiting Trade Agreement," *Journal of European Public Policy*, vol. 21, no. 8 (2014).

7. Margaret E. Keck and Kathryn Sikkink, *Advocates Beyond Borders: Advocacy Networks in International Politics* (Cornell University Press, 1998).

8. Dür and Mateo, "Public Opinion and Interest Group Influence."

9. Ibid., pp. 1212–13.

10. Eric Vincent C. Batalla, "Veto Players and State Decisiveness: Negotiating Bilateral Economic Partnership Agreements between Japan and Southeast Asia," *Philippine Political Science Journal*, vol. 33, no. 1 (2012).

11. Ibid., pp. 49–50, 52, 56–57.

12. A more extensive analysis of South Korean trade politics is available in Mireya Solís, "South Korea's Fateful Decision on the Trans-Pacific Partnership," Policy Paper 31 (Foreign Policy Program, Brookings Institution, September 2013).

13. Mi Park, "Framing Free Trade Agreements: The Politics of Nationalism in the Anti-Neoliberal Globalization Movement in South Korea," *Globalizations*, vol. 6, no. 4 (2009), p. 457.

14. Ibid.

15. Yong Cheol Kim and June Woo Kim, "South Korean Democracy in the Digital Age: The Candlelight Protests and the Internet," *Korea Observer*, vol. 40, no. 1 (Spring 2009).

16. Legislators complained that the government only made available one English copy of the KORUS FTA to twenty members of the Korea-U.S. Special Committee in the National Assembly and refused to make more copies or allow wider circulation. See Hyun-Chool Lee, "Ratification of a Free Trade Agreement: The Korean Legislature's Response to Globalisation," *Journal of Contemporary Asia*, vol. 40, no. 2 (May 2010), p. 298.

17. Yong-Shik Lee, "The Beginning of Economic Integration between East Asia and North America? Forming the Third Largest Free Trade Area between

the United States and the Republic of Korea," *Journal of World Trade*, vol. 41, no. 5 (2007), p. 1118.

18. Lee, "Ratification of a Free Trade Agreement," pp. 302–05.

19. Hyun-Seok Yu, "Political Institutions and Protectionism in Korea: The Case of Korea-Chile FTA Ratification Process," *Korea Observer*, vol. 37, no. 4 (Winter 2006), p. 663; Jeong-ju Na and Tae-hoon Lee, "National Assembly Ratifies Korea-EU FTA," *Korea Times*, May 4, 2011.

20. "GNP Railroads KORUS FTA in Surprise Plenary Session," *Hankyoreh* (Seoul), November 23, 2011.

21. Younsik Kim, "The Policy and Institutional Framework for FTA Negotiations in the Republic of Korea," in *The European Union and South Korea*, edited by James Harrison (Edinburgh University Press, 2013).

22. Government Accountability Office, "International Trade: Prior Updates of the Trade Advisory System Offer Insights for Current Review," testimony of Loren Yager, director of International Affairs and Trade, before the Subcommittee on Trade, Committee on Ways and Means, House of Representatives (July 21, 2009).

23. Organisation for Economic Co-operation and Development (OECD), *Trade and Structural Adjustment: Embracing Globalisation* (Paris: OECD Publishing, 2005).

24. Jean-Christophe Maur, "Coping with Trade Liberalization Adjustment," Policy Brief (Paris: *Groupe d'Économie Mondiale de Sciences Po*, December 2006) (http://ssrn.com/abstract=951431).

25. Stephanie J. Rickard, "Trade Openness and the Composition of Government Spending: Further Disentangling the Ties that Bind," paper (2008) (www .researchgate.net/publication/228776827_Trade_Openness_and_the _Composition_of_Government_Spending_Further_Disentangling_the_Ties _that_Bind).

26. Rickard, "Trade Openness," p. 7.

27. Roger Martini, "The Role of Compensation in Policy Reform," OECD Food, Agriculture and Fisheries Papers 5 (Paris: OECD Publishing, August 2007) (http://dx.doi.org/10.1787/125487536033).

28. Maur, "Trade Liberalization Adjustment."

29. The Australian government folded its trade adjustment assistance program in 1976, after only three years of operation, out of concern over the difficulty of certifying the eligibility of workers harmed directly by trade liberalization, the growing demands from other workers to receive special benefits as well, and the estimation that the program hindered mobility. See OECD, *Trade and Structural Adjustment*, p. 102. More recently, the EU launched a program in 2006 to help workers affected by global trade, but the European Globalization Adjustment Fund only provides training benefits with no unemployment payments, and it is capped at 150 million euros. See Zareh Asatryan and others, "Compensating the Losers of Free Trade," Working Paper 63 (Vienna, Austria: WWWforEurope, June 2014), p. 6 (www.foreurope.eu/fileadmin/documents /pdf/Workingpapers/WWWforEurope_WPS_no063_MS6.pdf).

30. Trade-impacted firms have received much lower funding levels for adjustment assistance, with appropriations for FY 2015 at $12.5 million and $13 million in FY 2016, while adjustment assistance for farmers started in 2002 and has averaged $10 million per year. In both cases, technical assistance has been the main form of support. Firms can split the cost of hiring consultants to draft business improvement projects (capped at $75,000) and farmers receive technical assistance to draft a business plan that addresses import competition. See Rachel F. Fefer, "Trade Adjustment Assistance for Firms," Report RS20210 (Washington: Congressional Research Service, September 1, 2016) (www.fas .org/sgp/crs/misc/RS20210.pdf); Howard F. Rosen, "Strengthening Trade Adjustment Assistance," PIIE Policy Brief 08-2 (Washington: Peterson Institute for International Economics, January 2008) (https://piie.com/publications/pb/pb08 -2.pdf); and "Program Benefits," Trade Adjustment Assistance for Firms (www .taacenters.org/benefits.html).

31. General Accounting Office, "Dislocated Workers: Trade Adjustment Assistance Program Flawed," testimony of Linda G. Morra, director of Education and Employment Issues, Human Resources Division, before the Subcommittee on Employment, Housing, and Aviation, Committee on Government Operations, House of Representatives (GAO: October 19, 1993) (www.gao.gov /products/T-HRD-94-4).

32. General Accounting Office, "Trade Adjustment Assistance: Trends, Outcomes, and Management Issues in Dislocated Worker Programs," Report GAO-01-59 (GAO: October 13, 2000) (www.gao.gov/products/GAO-01-59).

33. Cathleen Cimino-Isaacs, Gary Clyde Hufbauer, and Jeffrey J. Schott, "The New TAA Package Stands on Its Own Merits," *Trade and Investment Policy Watch* blog, Peterson Institute for International Economics, June 22, 2015 (https://piie.com/blogs/trade-investment-policy-watch/new-taa-package -stands-its-own-merits).

34. Kara M. Reynold and John S. Palatucci, "Does Trade Adjustment Assistance Make a Difference?" American University, Department of Economics Working Paper no. 2008-12 (August 2008) (w.american.edu/cas/economics /repec/amu/workingpapers/2008-12.pdf).

35. Ronald D'Amico and Peter Z. Schochet, "The Evaluation of the Trade Adjustment Assistance Program: A Synthesis of Major Findings," report prepared for the U.S. Department of Labor (Oakland, Calif.: Social Policy Research Associates; Princeton, N.J.: Mathematica Policy Research, December 2012) (www.mathematica-mpr.com/our-publications-and-findings/publications/the -evaluation-of-the-trade-adjustment-assistance-program-a-synthesis-of-major -findings).

36. Ibid., p. 9.

37. Editorial Board, "Save U.S. Trade Deals by Fixing Job Training," *Bloomberg View,* June 15, 2011.

38. D'Amico and Schochet, "Trade Adjustment Assistance Program," p. 12.

39. David H. Autor, David Dorn, and Gordon H. Hanson, "The China Shock: Learning from Labor Market Adjustment to Large Changes in Trade,"

Working Paper 21906 (Cambridge, Mass.: National Bureau of Economic Research, January 2016), pp. 32–33 (www.nber.org/papers/w21906).

40. Yong Kyu Choi, "Free Trade Agreements of Korea in Agricultural Sector," Working Paper (Organization for Regional and Inter-Regional Studies, Waseda University, November 25, 2011) (www.waseda.jp/inst/oris/assets/uploads/2015 /10/i4-2.pdf).

41. For a more detailed discussion, see Solís, "South Korea's Fateful Decision."

42. Jeongbin Im and Iljeong Jeong, "The Frame of Agricultural Policy and Recent Major Agricultural Policy in Korea," Food and Fertilizer Technology Center for the Asian and Pacific Region, July 10, 2014, p. 8 (http://ap.fftc.agnet .org/ap_db.php?id=265).

43. OECD, "Korea," in *Agricultural Policy Monitoring and Evaluation 2016* (Paris: OECD Publishing, 2016) (http://dx.doi.org/10.1787/agr_pol-2016 -18-en).

44. Jin-ho Myoung and others, "The Decade-Long Journey of Korea's FTAs," IIT Working Paper 14-01 (Seoul: Institute for International Trade, Korea International Trade Association, June 2014), p. 36.

45. Inkyo Cheong and Jungran Cho, "Reforms of Korea's Trade Adjustment Assistance Program for Its Bilateral Free Trade Agreements with the European Union and the United States," *Asian Economic Papers*, vol. 10, no. 1 (Winter/ Spring 2011), pp. 38–39.

46. Yoon Heo, "Institutional Arrangement for FTA Implementation: Trade Adjustment Assistance (TAA) in Korea," *Sogang IIAS Research Series on International Affairs*, vol. 12 (December, 2012).

47. The empirical record shows that trade liberalization benefits can far surpass adjustment costs. In the case of the TPP, Robert Lawrence and Tyler Moran estimate benefit-cost ratios of 3 to 1 in the adjustment period (2017–26) and 18 to 1 in the post-adjustment phase (2027–30) in the worst-case scenario of job displacement and annual wage losses. In the more benign scenario, benefit-cost ratios are 36 to 1 and 357 to 1, respectively. See Robert Z. Lawrence and Tyler Moran, "Adjustment and Income Distribution Impacts of the Trans-Pacific Partnership," Working Paper 16-5 (Washington: Peterson Institute for International Economics, March 2016), p. 15 (https://piie.com/publications/working-papers /adjustment-and-income-distribution-impacts-trans-pacific-partnership).

48. Commission on Growth and Development, "The Growth Report: Strategies for Sustained Growth and Inclusive Development" (Washington: World Bank, 2009), p. 92 (http://siteresources.worldbank.org/EXTPREMNET /Resources/489960-1338997241035/Growth_Commission_Final_Report.pdf).

49. Council of Economic Advisers, "The Long-Term Decline in Prime Aged Male Labor Force Participation" (June 2016) (www.whitehouse.gov/sites/default /files/page/files/20160620_cea_primeage_male_lfp.pdf).

50. Ibid., pp. 5, 13, 26.

51. Bureau of Labor Statistics, "Job Openings and Labor Turnover Survey News Release—July 2016," September 7, 2016.

52. OECD, *OECD Employment Outlook 2015* (Paris: OECD Publishing, 2015), pp. 67, 114.

53. Ibid., p. 133; Jun Nie and Ethan Struby, "Would Active Labor Market Policies Help Combat High U.S. Unemployment?" *Economic Review - Federal Reserve Bank of Kansas City* (Third Quarter 2011), p. 43; Asatryan and others, "Compensating the Losers of Free Trade," p. 24.

54. Robert Maxim, "No Helping Hand: Federal Worker Retraining Policy," in *How America Stacks Up: Economic Competitiveness and U.S. Policy*, by Edward Alden and Rebecca Strauss (New York: Council on Foreign Relations, 2016), p. 118.

55. Lael Brainard, Robert Litan, and Nicholas Warren estimated the cost of a wage insurance program for all workers over forty-five years of age to run in the neighborhood of $3.5 billion per year. See Lael Brainard, Robert Litan, and Nicholas Warren, "Insuring America's Workers in a New Era of Offshoring," Policy Brief 143 (Brookings Institution, July 2005) (www.brookings.edu/wp -content/uploads/2016/06/pb143.pdf). Jun Nie and Ethan Struby estimate the cost of active labor market policies to reduce U.S. unemployment rate by 1 percent to be $79.5 billion. See Nie and Struby, "Active Labor Market Policies."

56. Raj Chetty and others, "The Fading American Dream: Trends in Absolute Income Mobility Since 1940," Working Paper 22910 (Cambridge, Mass.: National Bureau of Economic Research, December 2016) (www.equality-of -opportunity.org/papers/abs_mobility_paper.pdf).

57. Bruce Stokes, "Republicans, Especially Trump Supporters, See Trade Agreements as Bad for the U.S.," FactTank, Pew Research Center, March 16, 2016 (www.pewresearch.org/fact-tank/2016/03/31/republicans-especially-trump -supporters-see-free-trade-deals-as-bad-for-u-s/).

58. Ibid.

59. Dina Smeltz and others, "America in the Age of Uncertainty: American Public Opinion and US Foreign Policy," The Chicago Council on Global Affairs (October 6, 2016) p. 22 (www.thechicagocouncil.org/sites/default/files /ccgasurvey2016_america_age_uncertainty.pdf).

60. For the 2016 election, Hendrix identifies eleven battleground states that hold 137 electoral votes. See Cullen S. Hendrix, "Protectionism in the 2016 Election: Causes and Consequences, Truths and Fictions," Policy Brief 16-20 (Washington: Peterson Institute for International Economics, November 2016), pp. 6–7 (https://piie.com/publications/policy-briefs/protectionism-2016-election-causes -and-consequences-truths-and-fictions).

61. Mark Muro and Sifan Liu, "Another Clinton-Trump Divide: High-Output America versus Low-Output America," *The Avenue* blog, Brookings Institution, November 29, 2016 (www.brookings.edu/blog/the-avenue/2016/11/29/another -clinton-trump-divide-high-output-america-vs-low-output-america).

62. Ronald F. Inglehart and Pippa Norris, "Trump, Brexit, and the Rise of Populism: Economic Have-Nots and Cultural Backlash," HKS Faculty Research Working Paper No. RWP16-026 (Harvard Kennedy School, August 2016) (https://research.hks.harvard.edu/publications/getFile.aspx?Id=1401).

63. Smeltz and others, "America in the Age of Uncertainty," pp. 3, 9.

64. Gary Hufbauer provides the best account of the broad powers the executive enjoys in the areas of trade enforcement and exit from trade agreements. See Gary Clyde Hufbauer, "Could a President Trump Shackle Imports?" in *Assessing Trade Agendas in the US Presidential Campaign*, PIIE Briefing 16-6 (Washington: Peterson Institute for International Economics, September 2016) (https://piie.com/system/files/documents/piieb16-6.pdf).

65. Hendrix, "Protectionism in the 2016 Election," p. 10.

## CHAPTER 8

1. Keidanren, "Towards the Implementation of Strategic Trade Policies" (June 2001) (www.keidanren.or.jp/english/policy/2001/029.html).

2. Mireya Solís and Saori N. Katada, "Unlikely Pivotal States in Competitive Free Trade Agreement Diffusion: The Effect of Japan's Trans-Pacific Partnership Participation on Asia-Pacific Regional Integration," *New Political Economy*, vol. 20, no. 2 (2015).

3. An earlier analysis of FTA diffusion can be found in Mireya Solís, Barbara Stallings, and Saori N. Katada, eds., *Competitive Regionalism: FTA Diffusion in the Pacific Rim* (Basingstoke, U.K.: Palgrave Macmillan, 2009) and Solís and Katada, "Unlikely Pivotal States."

4. Mireya Solís, "Japan's New Regionalism: The Politics of Free Trade Talks with Mexico," *Journal of East Asian Studies*, vol. 3, no. 3 (December 2003); Mireya Solís and Saori N. Katada, "The Japan-Mexico FTA: A Cross-Regional Step in the Path towards Asian Regionalism," *Pacific Affairs*, vol. 80, no. 2 (2007).

5. Mark Manger, "Competition and Bilateralism in Trade Policy: The Case of Japan's Free Trade Agreements," *Review of International Political Economy*, vol. 12, no. 5 (2005).

6. Naoko Munakata, "How Trade Agreements Can Reform Japan," *Globalist*, July 10, 2012 (www.theglobalist.com/how-trade-agreements-can-reform-japan).

7. Interview with former senior METI official, Tokyo, May 2006.

8. Imported pork below a certain price threshold pays a specific charge (in addition to the import duty) to bring its price on par with domestic pork.

9. Keidanren, "ACCJ-Keidanren Joint Statement on Japan/U.S. EPA," July 21, 2009 (www.keidanren.or.jp/english/policy/2009/066.html); Keidanren, "Toward Japan-EU Economic Integration: Second Proposal for Japan-EU Economic Partnership Agreement," April 14, 2009 (www.keidanren.or.jp/english/policy/2009/037.html).

10. Interview with Keidanren (Japan Business Federation) officials, Tokyo, June 2008.

11. Mireya Solís, "Japan and East Asian Economic Regionalism," in *The Routledge Handbook of Japanese Politics*, edited by Alisa Gaunder (New York: Routledge, 2011).

12. China advocated an ASEAN+3 (China, Japan, South Korea) configuration, while Japan pushed for a wider ASEAN+6 framework including Australia, New Zealand, and India.

13. Solís and Katada, "Unlikely Pivotal States."

14. The admission of Japan into the TPP also presented major challenges: protracted negotiations as the negotiators squared off on long-divisive market access issues and a much steeper ratification battle as powerful political actors (for example, the U.S. automobile companies and unions) opposed Japan's inclusion.

15. Patrick Messerlin, "The TPP and the EU Policy in East Asia (China Mainland Excluded)," paper prepared for the French Ministry of Foreign Affairs (May 2012) (www.ecipe.org/media/publication_pdfs/Messerlin_TPP-EU _EN05212.pdf).

16. Solís and Katada, "Unlikely Pivotal States."

17. On the same day the United States and Japan wrapped up their bilateral consultations on Japan's TPP membership, the Japanese government unilaterally announced that no new cancer insurance products from Japan Post would be approved until equivalent conditions of competition existed for private suppliers (and that would require several years). See Office of the United States Trade Representative, "Fact Sheet: Toward the Trans-Pacific Partnership: U.S. Consultations with Japan," April 12, 2013 (https://ustr.gov/about-us/policy -offices/press-office/fact-sheets/2013/april/US-consultations-Japan).

## CHAPTER 9

1. The analysis of this section draws from Mireya Solís, "Can FTAs Deliver Market Liberalization in Japan? A Study on Domestic Political Determinants," *Review of International Political Economy*, vol. 17, no. 2 (May 2010).

2. Gerald L. Curtis, *The Japanese Way of Politics* (Columbia University Press, 1988).

3. Arend Lijphart, *Patterns of Democracy: Government Forms and Performance in Thirty-Six Countries* (Yale University Press, 1999), p. 129.

4. Aurelia George Mulgan, "Japan's 'Un-Westminster' System: Impediments to Reform in a Crisis Economy," *Government and Opposition*, vol. 38, no. 1 (Winter 2003), pp. 77, 84. Party politicians asserted this right for the first time in 1962 and the practice was widely established by the 1970s.

5. On the cabinet's authority to conclude international treaties, see Mitsuo Matsushita, "Japan and the Implementation of the Tokyo Round Results," in *Implementing the Tokyo Round: National Constitutions and International Economic Rules*, edited by John H. Jackson, Jean-Victor Louis, and Mitsuo Matsushita (University of Michigan Press, 1984).

6. MITI changed its name to the Ministry of Economy, Trade and Industry (METI) in 2001. See Haruhiro Fukui, "The GATT Tokyo Round: The Bureaucratic Politics of Multilateral Diplomacy," in *The Politics of Trade: U.S. and Japanese Policymaking for the GATT Negotiations*, edited by Michael Blaker (East Asia Institute, Columbia University, 1978), p. 108; Amy Searight, "MITI and Multilateralism: The Evolution of Japan's Trade Policy in the GATT Regime," PhD dissertation, Stanford University, 1999; Aurelia George Mulgan,

"Where Tradition Meets Change: Japan's Agricultural Politics in Transition," *Journal of Japanese Studies*, vol. 31, no. 2 (Summer 2005).

7. Ellis S. Krauss and Robert J. Pekkanen, "Explaining Party Adaptation to Electoral Reform: The Discreet Charm of the LDP?" *Journal of Japanese Studies*, vol. 30, no. 1 (Winter 2004); Ellis S. Krauss and Benjamin Nyblade, "'Presidentialization' in Japan? The Prime Minister, Media and Elections in Japan," *British Journal of Political Studies*, vol. 35, no. 2 (April 2005).

8. George Mulgan, "Japan's 'Un-Westminster' System," pp. 87–89.

9. George Mulgan, "Where Tradition Meets Change," pp. 276–77.

10. Japan Machinery Center for Trade and Investment, "*Waga Kuni FTA Seisaku e no Teigen: Higashi Ajia Jiyū Bōeki Chiiki no Arikata—Higashi Ajia Jiyū Bijinesu Ken no Kakuritsu ni Mukete*" [Proposal for our Country's FTA Policy: The State of the East Asia Free Trade Zone—Toward the Establishment of an East Asian Free Business Area], October 18, 2004, p. 3 (www.jmcti.org /jmchomepage/naigai_seisaku/toushi/pdf/041018.pdf); Keidanren, "A Call for the Development and Promotion of Proactive External Economic Strategies," October 16, 2007 (www.keidanren.or.jp/english/policy/2007/081.html).

11. Ko Mishima, "Unattainable Mission? The Democratic Party of Japan's Unsuccessful Policymaking System Reform," *Asian Politics and Policy*, vol. 7, no. 3 (July 2015), pp. 436–37.

12. Mishima, "Unattainable Mission?"; Hideyuki Miura, "The Domestic Policy-Making Process under the Democratic Party of Japan Government: Japan's Participation in the Trans-Pacific Partnership Agreement," paper presented at the International Studies Association Annual Conference (San Diego, California, April 2, 2012).

13. Hironori Sasada, "The Impact of Rural Votes in Foreign Policies: The FTA Policies under the DPJ Government in Japan," *Asian Journal of Political Science*, vol. 21, no. 3 (2013), p. 235.

14. Mireya Solís, "Japan and East Asian Economic Regionalism," in *The Routledge Handbook of Japanese Politics*, edited by Alisa Gaunder (New York: Routledge, 2011), p. 307.

15. Hiroko Tabuchi, "Japan's Farmers Oppose Pacific Free-Trade Talks," *New York Times*, November 12, 2010; Jun Hongo and Natsuko Fukue, "Dissent within DPJ Ranks Looks Set to Fester," *Japan Times*, November 12, 2011.

16. Aurelia George Mulgan, "Bringing the Party Back In: How the DPJ Diminished Prospects for Japanese Agricultural Trade Liberalization Under the TPP," *Japanese Journal of Political Science*, vol. 15, no. 1 (March 2014).

17. "Analysis: Noda's Tough TPP Negotiations Start in the DPJ," *Asahi Shimbun,* November 12, 2011.

18. Yakushiji Katsuyuki, "Abe and the Triumph of the Old LDP," The Tokyo Foundation, January 15, 2013 (www.tokyofoundation.org/en/articles/2013/abe -and-triumph-of-old-ldp).

19. Stimulus *sans* reform will leave Japan worse off. The International Monetary Fund did an interesting exercise projecting Japan's growth rate over the next several years under different scenarios of Abenomics. In one of them, just

the first two arrows were launched (only stimulus) and Japan's growth rate by 2020 was negative (–2 percent). In another, all three arrows (stimulus plus reform) were implemented and Japan's growth rate was estimated at 3 percent. Another major conundrum for Abenomics has been which direction to aim the fiscal arrow. Trying to make progress on fiscal consolidation, the government raised the consumption tax to 8 percent in spring 2014 only to see domestic demand and growth take a serious hit. Thereafter, the second consumption tax increase, to 10 percent, was twice postponed. See International Monetary Fund, *World Economic Outlook 2013: Transitions and Tensions* (Washington: International Monetary Fund, October 2013), pp. 49–51 (www.imf.org/external /pubs/ft/weo/2013/02/pdf/text.pdf).

20. Izuru Makihara, "Abe's Enforcer: Suga Yoshihide's Stabilizing Influence on the Cabinet," Nippon.com, September 25, 2014 (www.nippon.com/en /currents/d00135).

21. Ushio Shioda, *"Abe Shushō ni Tsunawatari no Jikaku ga aruka"* [Is Prime Minister Abe aware of the risks that he is running?], *Toyo Keizai*, April 22, 2014 (http://toyokeizai.net/articles/-/35885).

22. Izuru Makihara, "The Role of the Kantei in Making Policy," Nippon .com, August 8, 2013 (www.nippon.com/en/features/c00408); Takashi Terada, "The Abe Effect and Domestic Politics," *Asian Perspective*, vol. 39, no. 3 (July-September 2015).

23. Gregory W. Noble, "Too Little, Too Late? Raising the Consumption Tax to Shore Up Japanese Finances," *Japanese Political Economy*, vol. 40, no. 2 (2014).

24. Takao Toshikawa, "MOF Loses Tax Fight to Abe. Kantei Asserts its Power," *Oriental Economist*, vol. 84, no. 1 (January 2016), p. 4.

25. Shinzo Abe, press conference, Office of the Prime Minister, Tokyo, Japan, March 15, 2013 (http://japan.kantei.go.jp/96_abe/statement/201303 /15kaiken_e.html).

26. William L. Brooks, "Politics and Trade Policy in Japan: Trans-Pacific Partnership Negotiations," Policy Papers series 18 (Washington: Reischauer Center for East Asian Studies, Johns Hopkins University-SAIS, 2015), p. 39 (www.reischauercenter.org/en/wp-content/uploads/2015/02/Final-Brooks1 .pdf).

27. Wendy Cutler, remarks at "The Trans-Pacific Partnership and Beyond," event hosted by the Maureen and Mike Mansfield Foundation and the Embassy of Japan at Evermay (Washington, November 17, 2015).

28. According to NHK opinion polls, support for the Abe cabinet started at a high 64 percent in January 2013 and stayed above 50 percent almost consistently for the next two years. It began to dip in the fall of 2014 (to 44 percent) with a sluggish economy in the aftermath of the consumption tax increase. In the summer of 2015 when the Diet deliberated on controversial security legislation, the rate of disapproval (46 percent) surpassed the rate of approval (37 percent) for the first time. However, a few months later, the Abe cabinet support rate had gone up to 46 percent. See NHK Hōsō Bunken Kenkyujo, *"Seiji ishiki getsurei*

*chōsa*" [Monthly Survey of Political Awareness], 2016 (www.nhk.or.jp/bunken /yoron/political/index.html). This recovery notwithstanding, lackluster economic performance has fueled disenchantment with Abenomics. In a Nikkei/TV Tokyo poll in February 2016, 50 percent of people said they were unhappy with the government's economic policy. See "Half of Japanese Voters Unhappy with Abenomics," *Nikkei Asian Review*, February 29, 2016 (http://asia.nikkei.com /Politics-Economy/Policy-Politics/Half-of-Japanese-voters-unhappy-with -Abenomics). So far, opposition parties have been unable to tap into growing skepticism of Abenomics, while distrust among the public of the DPJ's ability to govern effectively continues unabated. Conventional wisdom among Japan watchers is that the cabinet approval level must dip below 30 percent before an internal challenger is considered viable.

29. Kazuhito Yamashita, "A First Step Toward Reform of Japan's Agricultural Cooperative System," Nippon.com, April 20, 2015 (www.nippon.com/en /currents/d00169).

30. Aurelia George Mulgan, *The Politics of Agriculture in Japan* (New York: Routledge, 2000), p. 223; Robert Bullock, "Nōkyo: A Short Cultural History," Working Paper 41 (Oakland, Calif.: Japan Policy Research Institute, December 1997) (http://www.jpri.org/publications/workingpapers/wp41.html).

31. Yoshihisa Godo, "Financial Liberalization and Japan's Agricultural Cooperatives," paper presented at the International Association of Agricultural Economists Conference, Gold Coast, Australia, August 12–18, 2006, p. 7 (http:// ageconsearch.umn.edu/bitstream/25477/1/pp060793.pdf).

32. Jennifer Amyx, "The Political Economy of Japanese Agriculture," in "A Way Forward for Japanese Agriculture," Pacific Economic Papers 300 (Canberra: Australia-Japan Research Centre, Australia National University, February 2000).

33. Kazuhito Yamashita, *Bōkoku Nōsei no Shūen* [The demise of ruinous agricultural administration] (Tokyo: Bestsellers, 2009), p. 202.

34. Yoshihisa Godo and Daisuke Takahashi, "Evaluation of the Japanese Agricultural Policy Reforms under the WTO Agreement on Agriculture," paper presented at the International Association of Agricultural Economists, Brazil, August 18–24, 2012, p. 8 (http://ageconsearch.umn.edu/bitstream/125102/2 /20120609GodoIAAE_AESPoster.pdf).

35. George Mulgan, *The Politics of Agriculture in Japan;* Ministry of Agriculture, Forestry and Fisheries, Japan (MAFF), "*Kumiaiinsū oyobi kumiaiinkosū*" [Number of Members and Member Households], in "*Heisei 24 Jigyōnendo Sōgō Nōkyo Tōkeihyō*" [Statistics of Agricultural Cooperatives—2012 Business Year], June 16, 2014 (www.e-stat.go.jp/SG1/estat/List.do?lid=0000011 19700).

36. Kazuhito Yamashita, "Agricultural Policy Reform and Free Trade," presentation, Brookings Institution (February 20, 2015) (www.canon-igs.org/event /report/report_150220/presentation/150220_yamashita_presentation.pdf).

37. Aurelia George Mulgan, "Can Abe's Third Arrow Pierce Japan's Agricultural Armour?" *East Asia Forum*, April 6, 2014 (www.eastasiaforum.org/2014

/04/06/can-abes-third-arrow-pierce-japans-agricultural-armour);     Yamashita, "Agricultural Policy Reform."

38. Hironori Sasada, "The 'Third Arrow' or Friendly Fire? The LDP Government's Reform Plan for the Japan Agricultural Cooperatives," *Japanese Political Economy*, vol. 41, no. 1-2 (2015).

39. Yamashita, "First Step Toward Reform."

40. George Mulgan, *The Politics of Agriculture in Japan*, p. 304.

41. Curtis, *The Japanese Way of Politics*.

42. Patricia L. Maclachlan, "The Electoral Power of Japanese Interest Groups: An Organizational Perspective," *Journal of East Asian Studies*, vol. 14, no. 3 (Sept-Dec 2014).

43. George Mulgan, *The Politics of Agriculture in Japan*, p. 396.

44. Christina L. Davis, *Food Fights Over Free Trade: How International Institutions Promote Agricultural Trade Liberalization* (Princeton University Press, 2003), p. 124.

45. The LDP escaped similar electoral punishment when the Japanese government implemented the Uruguay Round's rice liberalization measures in 1994 because the opposition coalition under Morihiro Hosokawa was in power at the time. See George Mulgan, *The Politics of Agriculture in Japan*, p. 454. Soon after, when the LDP returned to office it adopted a generous compensation package.

46. Kay Shimizu, "What the 2012 Lower House Elections Has to Say about Japan's Urban-Rural Divide," in *Japan Decides 2012: The Japanese General Election*, edited by Robert Pekkanen, Steven R. Reed, and Ethan Scheiner (New York: Palgrave Macmillan, 2013), pp. 148–53.

47. Hiroko Tabuchi, "Japanese Begin to Question Protections Given to Homegrown Rice," *New York Times,* January 9, 2014.

48. Ko Maeda, "Has the Electoral-System Reform Made Japanese Elections Party-Centered?" in *Political Change in Japan: Electoral Behavior, Party Realignment, and the Koizumi Reforms*, edited by Steven R. Reed, Kenneth Mori McElwain, and Kay Shimizu (Stanford, Calif.: The Walter H. Shorenstein Asia-Pacific Research Center, 2009), pp. 47–66.

49. Ellis S. Krauss and Robert J. Pekkanen, *The Rise and Fall of Japan's LDP: Political Party Organizations as Historical Institutions* (Cornell University Press, 2011).

50. Krauss and Pekkanen, *The Rise and Fall of Japan's LDP*, p. 253.

51. Steven R. Reed, Ethan Scheiner, and Michael F. Thies, "New Ballgame in Politics: Party-Centered, More Volatile," *Oriental Economist*, vol. 77, no. 10 (October 2009), p. 9.

52. Yoree Koh, "Election Returns Confirm Rural-Urban Voter Divide," *Wall Street Journal*, July 31, 2010.

53. Richard Katz, "LDP Didn't Win; DPJ Lost," *Oriental Economist* vol. 81, no. 1 (January 2013); Patricia L. Maclachlan and Kay Shimizu, "The Kantei vs. the LDP: Agricultural Reform, the Organized Vote, and the 2014 Election," in *Japan Decides 2014: The Japanese General Election*, edited by

Robert J. Pekkanen, Steven R. Reed, and Ethan Scheiner (New York: Palgrave Macmillan, 2016), pp. 170–82.

54. Aurelia George Mulgan, "Farmers, Agricultural Policies, and the Election," in *Japan Decides 2012*, edited by Pekkanen, Reed, and Scheiner, p. 218; Maclachlan and Shimizu, "The Kantei vs. the LDP," p. 177.

55. "Ruling Coalition's Landslide Victory Is By No Means Carte Blanche for Agricultural Policy," *Japan Agri News*, December 16, 2014; "Abe Pick Loses Governor Race in Farm-Heavy Saga," *Japan Times*, January 12, 2015.

56. Ayako Mie, "LDP Election Strategy: Double Farming Income," *Japan Times*, April 25, 2013.

57. Maclachlan and Shimizu, "The Kantei vs. the LDP"; Saori N. Katada and Scott Wilbur, "Japan's Stealth Decision 2014: The Trans-Pacific Partnership," in *Japan Decides 2014*, edited by Pekkanen, Reed, and Scheiner, pp. 247–61.

58. Interview with senior JA officials, Tokyo, August 2005.

59. JA Zenchū (Central Union of Agricultural Cooperatives), "*Kankoku, Tai, Firipin, Marēshia, Indoneshia to no jiyūbōeki kyotei (FTA) ni kansuru JA gurūpu no kihonteki kangaekata*" [JA Group's Basic Thinking on the Free Trade Agreements (FTA) with Korea, Thailand, Philippines, Malaysia, and Indonesia], February 2004, p. 4.

60. Japan External Trade Organization, "Report of the Committee for Closer Economic Relations between Japan and Mexico," 1999.

61. Aurelia George Mulgan, "Agriculture and Political Reform in Japan: The Koizumi Legacy," Pacific Economic Papers 360 (Canberra: Australia-Japan Research Centre, Australia National University, 2006) (https://crawford.anu.edu.au/pdf/pep/pep-360.pdf).

62. This point was made by bureaucrats from both MOFA and MAFF, author interviews, Tokyo, August 2005.

63. Mireya Solís, "Japan's New Regionalism: The Politics of Free Trade Talks with Mexico," *Journal of East Asian Studies*, vol. 3, no. 3 (December 2003), p. 395; Masaki Sakai, "*Nihon o meguru FTA no dōkō to kadai*" [Trends and Topics in Japan's FTAs], *Nōson to Tōshi o Musubu* [Linking Farming Villages and Cities], no. 624 (September 2003), pp. 6–7.

64. Sakai, "*Nihon o meguru FTA no dōkō to kadai*" [Trends and Topics in Japan's FTAs], p. 10.

65. Solís, "Japan's New Regionalism."

66. John H. Barton, and others, *The Evolution of the Trade Regime: Politics, Law, and Economics of the GATT and the WTO* (Princeton University Press, 2006).

67. Takashi Terada, "The Japan-Australia Partnership in the Era of the East Asian Community: Can They Advance Together?" Pacific Economic Papers 352 (Canberra: Australia-Japan Research Centre, Australia National University, 2005).

68. JA Zenchū, "*WTO·Nichi-Gō EPA·kihon nōsei kakuritsu taisaku ni kansuru jūten yōsei*" [Important Demands Concerning WTO-Japan-Australia EPA Measures for the Establishment of Basic Agricultural Policy], Febru-

ary 2007. Negotiations remained inconclusive for several years. It was only under the new policymaking dynamics of the second Abe administration that a breakthrough was achieved. Australia obtained some concessions (reducing the beef tariff from 38.5 percent to 23.5 percent in fifteen years), but no tariff elimination for sensitive products, as JA demanded.

69. JA Zenchū, "*'Kohatsu teki Keizai Renkei ni kansuru Kihon Hoshi' no Kakugi Kettei ni Atatte*" [On the Cabinet Resolution Concerning the Basic Policy for Comprehensive Economic Partnerships], November 2010.

70. JA Zenchū, "Re: Japan's Expression of Interest in the Trans-Pacific Partnership Trade Negotiations," letter from Akira Banzai to Ron Kirk, January 12, 2012 (www.regulations.gov/document?D=USTR-2011-0018-0017).

71. JA Zenchū, "RE: Japan's Participation in the Proposed Trans-Pacific Partnership Trade Agreement," letter from Akira Banzai to the Office of the U.S. Trade Representative, June 7, 2013 (www.zenchu-ja.or.jp/wp-content/uploads/2013/06/up312.pdf).

72. "TPP Jitters Spur Protest Statements," *Japan Times*, January 17, 2011.

73. Aurelia George Mulgan, "To TPP or Not TPP: Interest Groups and Trade Policy," in *The Political Economy of Japanese Trade Policy*, edited by Aurelia George Mulgan and Masayoshi Honma (Basingstoke, U.K.: Palgrave Macmillan, 2015), p. 147.

74. Megumi Naoi and Shujiro Urata, "Free Trade Agreements and Domestic Politics: The Case of the Trans-Pacific Partnership Agreement," *Asian Economic Policy Review*, vol. 8, no. 2 (2013).

75. "JCP Holds Nationwide Action in Concert with Farmers' Anti-TPP Rally," *Japan Press Weekly*, October 26, 2011.

76. For comparison purposes, figure 9-1 also tracks online interest in the TPP in the United States. It is interesting to note that the public of each country were most interested in the TPP at very different times. Even though the United States announced its intention to join the TPP in 2009, online interest in the United States peaked in June 2015 and it was very much driven by the political fight to pass trade promotion authority (TPA) in Congress (critical to the TPP's ratification prospects). As in Japan, however, the conclusion of the talks in October 2015 also generated strong interest in the United States.

77. Takaaki Mitsuhashi, "*TPP no Shōtai*" [TPP's True Character], in *TPP Kaikokuron no Uso* [*The Lie of TPP's Open Country Thesis*], edited by Takeshi Nakano, Satoshi Higashitani, and Takaaki Mitsuhashi (Tokyo: Asukashinsha, 2011).

78. The ban on mixed medical treatments mandated that patients willing to receive new treatments not covered by public health care insurance had to forgo all coverage (even for approved treatments). In a mid-2014 decision unrelated to TPP negotiations, the Abe government decided to expand the availability of mixed medical treatments. Starting in 2016, patients who receive approval will only pay the cost of the new treatment, without losing medical insurance benefits.

79. Mie Yasuda, *Saru de mo wakaru TPP* [*TPP for Dummies*] (Tokyo: Gōdō Shuppan, 2012).

80. JAgrouptpp, "*TPP no [ISD jōkō] ga ataeru eikyō*" [The impact of the TPP's ISD provision], November 30, 2012 (https://www.youtube.com/watch?v=6NXJjnxCigo).

81. In Masayasu Hosaka, Yukio Okamoto, and Takeshi Nakano, "*'Nihon no kibou' ka 'Beikoku no inbou' ka*" [Japan's hope or America's conspiracy?], *Bungei Shunju*, 2012 New Year's Special Edition (December 9, 2011), p. 149.

82. Saori Katada, "*Amerika no TPP Seisaku to Nihon*" [America's TPP Policy and Japan], *Kokusai Mondai*, no. 644 (September 2015), pp. 33–44.

83. "Editorial: Radical Reform Led by Abe Risks Leading the Nation in the Wrong Direction," *Japan Agri News* (Tokyo), November 1, 2013 (http://english.agrinews.co.jp/?p=1210).

84. "*Abe Seiken san nen (Kantei shudo) ga fushin maneku*" [Three Years of Abe Administration (Prime Minister's Office Leadership) Invites Distrust], *Nihon Nōgyō Shimbun* (Tokyo), December 26, 2015.

85. *TPP Kenkyūkai* [TPP Study Group], "*TPP no Ronten*" [TPP Points of Debate], report (Tokyo: Canon Institute for Global Studies, October 26, 2011).

86. Keidanren, "*Hontō ni wakaru TPP—Sekai to tomo ni ikiteiku tame ni*" [Truly Understanding the TPP: Toward Living Together with the World], June 2013, pp. 8–9 (www.keidanren.or.jp/policy/2012/pamphlet201306.pdf).

87. George Mulgan, "To TPP or Not TPP," pp. 129, 140.

88. Mireya Solis, "Business Advocacy in Asian PTAs: A Model of Selective Business Lobbying with Evidence from Japan," *Business and Politics*, vol. 15, no. 1 (April 2013).

89. These summaries and a list of some information dissemination activities appear on MOFA's website. See "4. *TPP kōshō sanka ni muketa kankei-koku to no kyōgi-tō*" [4. Consultations with Member States Toward Participation in the TPP Negotiations], in "*Kantaiheiyō pātonāshippu (TPP) kyōtei kōshō*" [Trans-Pacific Partnership (TPP) Agreement Negotiations], Ministry of Foreign Affairs, Japan (www.mofa.go.jp/mofaj/gaiko/tpp/index.html#section4).

90. See "*Seifu no torikumi*" [Government Initiatives], *Naikaku Kanbō TPP Seifu taisaku honbu* [Governmental Headquarters for the TPP] (www.cas.go.jp/jp/tpp/torikumi/index.html).

91. In March 2016, the DPJ merged with the Japan Innovation Party to form the Democratic Party.

92. Jiji, "Abe Camp Facing TPP-Ratification Headwinds after Ruling Bloc Losses in Farmer-Friendly Tohoku," *Japan Times* (Tokyo), July 25, 2016.

### CHAPTER 10

1. Randall S. Jones, "Income Inequality, Poverty and Social Spending in Japan," OECD Economics Department Working Paper 556 (Paris: OECD Publishing, June 11, 2007).

2. OECD, "Income Distribution and Poverty," OECD Income Distribution Database. In contrast to the United States, Japan does not have an acute con-

centration of wealth in the top 1 percent. As Jacob M. Schlesinger points out, the concentration of income in this bracket (excluding capital gains) has declined since 2008 to 9 percent in 2012. See Jacob M. Schlesinger, "Japan May Be Exception to Piketty's Thesis," *Wall Street Journal,* February 9, 2015.

3. For comparison purposes, the responses in the U.S. survey to these questions were 51 percent (opportunity) and 30 percent (failure). See Global Entrepreneurship Monitor, "Persistently Low Levels of Activity–But High Activity Among Those with Positive Entrepreneurial Attitudes," 2014 (www.gemconsortium.org /country-profile/76).

4. T. J. Pempel, "Between Pork and Productivity: The Collapse of the Liberal Democratic Party," *Journal of Japanese Studies*, vol. 36, no. 2 (Summer 2010).

5. OECD, *OECD Economic Surveys: Japan 2015* (Paris: OECD Publishing, April 2015), p. 106.

6. Pempel, "Between Pork and Productivity."

7. Richard Katz, "Voodoo Abenomics: Japan's Failed Comeback Plan," *Foreign Affairs*, vol. 94, no. 4 (July-August 2014).

8. Among the strongest opponents to Japan's TPP participation were the Big Three U.S. car companies, unions (UAW and AFL-CIO), and some representatives from Congress, many of them hailing from the Midwest. In making their case against Japan in the TPP, they argued that long-standing barriers such as certification standards, unfair distribution practices, government incentives favoring domestic cars, and even the "exclusionary preferences" of Japanese consumers had created a perpetual trade imbalance that had not been addressed in past bilateral trade negotiations, nor could it be addressed effectively in the TPP. Some of their recommendations hailed back to the era of managed trade thinking (which is now clearly resurgent) as they aimed to link U.S. tariff reductions to increased market share in the Japanese market for American car companies. A focal point in their campaign was the charge that Japan has engaged in currency manipulation to generate a pattern of "one-way trade." See "Bicameral Group of Members Raises Alarm on Japan's Possible Interest in Joining TPP Negotiations," Congressman Sandy Levin press release, March 14, 2013 (http://levin.house.gov/press-release/bicameral -group-members-raises-alarm-japan%E2%80%99s-possible-interest-joining -tpp) and "Levin Statement on U.S. Announcement on Japan and TPP," Congressman Sandy Levin, press release, April 20, 2013 (http://levin.house.gov /press-release/levin-statement-announcement-regarding-japan-and-tpp). However, their proposals for a binding currency manipulation clause deviated from IMF principles on the need to demonstrate intent to deliberately lower the value of a currency for the sake of export advantage in determining currency manipulation, and would have doomed the TPP negotiations. See Mireya Solís, "The Answer is Still No On a Currency Manipulation Clause in TPP," *UpFront* blog, Brookings Institution, January 15, 2014 (www.brookings .edu/blogs/up-front/posts/2014/01/15-currency-manipulation-clause-tpp -solis). Instead, the TPP parties issued a joint declaration on macroeconomic

policy pledging to increase transparency and accountability by publicly reporting data on foreign exchange intervention and launching annual macroeconomic policy consultations.

9. Ulrike Schaede, "System Change and Corporate Reorganization in Japan: The Strategic Logic of Business Groups and Main Banks, Revisited," in *Syncretism: The Politics of Economic Restructuring and System Reform in Japan*, edited by Kenji E. Kushida, Kay Shimizu, and Jean C. Oi (Stanford, Calif.: The Walter H. Shorenstein Asia-Pacific Research Center, 2013), pp. 80, 87–89.

10. Schaede, "System Change," pp. 93, 98.

11. Henry Laurence, *Money Rules: The New Politics of Finance in Britain and Japan* (Cornell University Press, 2001).

12. Frances McCall Rosenbluth and Michael F. Thies, *Japan Transformed: Political Change and Economic Restructuring* (Princeton University Press, 2010), p. 131.

13. Kenji E. Kushida, "Foreign Multinational Corporations and Japan's Evolving Syncretic Model of Capitalism," in *Syncretism*, edited by Kushida, Shimizu, and Oi, pp. 199–246. The fate of these corporate alliances varied, even within the same industry. Compare the success of Renault in turning around Nissan with the decision by Chrysler to divest from Mitsubishi Motors in 2005. More recently, Ford sold most of its shares in Mazda, and in January 2016, it announced its exit from the Japanese market. Associated Press, "Ford to Exit Japan, Citing its 'Closed' Market," *Japan Times*, January 26, 2016.

14. Not all regulatory changes in Japan during the "lost decades" worked to ameliorate friction with the United States. One case in point is the uneven process of postal privatization, which, as pointed out by Kenji Kushida and Kay Shimizu, created financial units within Japan Post (banking and insurance) that increasingly were competing with the private sector by entering new profitable markets while enjoying the benefits of state ownership. As state divesture stalled and the obligation to sell government shares was eliminated (in favor of a nonbinding recommendation) in the 2012 revision to the Postal Privatization Bill, this issue came to the fore in Japan's TPP accession negotiations. See Kenji E. Kushida and Kay Shimizu, "The Politics of Syncretism in Japan's Political Economy: Finance and Postal Reforms," in *Syncretism*, edited by Kushida, Shimizu, and Oi, pp. 65–71. As noted before, the Japanese government announced a standstill for new cancer insurance products as part of TPP pre-accession negotiations, and this probably changed the incentives for Japan Post to agree a few months later to a tie-up with the American insurance company Aflac. See "Japan Post, Aflac Forge Insurance Tie Up," Reuters, July 26, 2013.

15. Mireya Solís, *Banking On Multinationals: Public Credit and the Export of Japanese Sunset Industries* (Stanford University Press, 2004); Walter Hatch and Kozo Yamamura, *Asia in Japan's Embrace: Building a Regional Production Alliance* (Cambridge University Press, 1996), p. 185.

16. Japan Bank for International Cooperation (JBIC), "Survey Report on Overseas Business Operations by Japanese Manufacturing Companies—Results of the JBIC FY 2014 Survey: Outlook for Japanese Foreign Direct Investment (26th Annual Survey)," February 25, 2015 (www.jbic.go.jp/wp-content/uploads /reference_en/2015/02/35381/20150224_spot-JBICFDIe.pdf).

17. Kevin C. Cheng and others, "Reaping the Benefits of Global Value Chains," Working Paper 15/204 (Washington: International Monetary Fund, September 2015), p. 6 (www.imf.org/external/pubs/cat/longres.aspx?sk =43311.0). The GVC participation index looks at both forward and backward linkages by including foreign inputs and domestically produced components to be used in third countries' exports as a share of a country's gross exports

18. Mireya Solís, "Japan's Foreign Economic Policies," in *The Oxford Handbook of the International Relations of Asia*, edited by Saadia M. Pekkanen, John Ravenhill, and Rosemary Foot (Oxford University Press, 2014), p. 144.

19. Leonard J. Schoppa, *Bargaining with Japan: What American Pressure Can and Cannot Do* (Columbia University Press, 1997), p. 3.

20. Shujiro Urata, *"Joshō"* [Introduction], in *Nihon keizai no seichō ni mukete. TPP e no sanka to kōzō kaikaku [Facing Japan's Economic Growth. TPP Participation and Structural Reform]*, edited by Shujiro Urata (Tokyo: The 21st Century Public Policy Institute, March 2013).

21. OECD, *OECD Economic Surveys: Japan 2015*, pp. 23, 73.

22. Gary Clyde Hufbauer, "Liberalization of Services Trade," in *Assessing the Trans-Pacific Partnership, Volume 1: Market Access and Sectoral Issues*, PIIE Briefing 16-1 (Washington: Peterson Institute for International Economics, February 2016), p. 83.

23. The services trade restrictiveness index is compiled using information on regulatory transparency, barriers to competition, and restrictions on foreign entry and movement of people, as well as other discriminatory measures.

24. OECD, *OECD Economic Surveys: Japan 2015*, p. 75.

25. European Commission, "Impact Assessment Report on EU-Japan Trade Relations," July 18, 2012 (http://trade.ec.europa.eu/doclib/docs/2012/july /tradoc_149809.pdf); Hikari Ishido, *"Sâbisu bôeki to Nihon no kokunai kôzô kaikaku: TPP wo misueta teigen"* [The Services Trade and Japan's Domestic Structural Reform: Proposals for the TPP], in *Nihon Keizai no Seicho ni Mukete [Facing Japan's Economic Growth]*, edited by Urata, p. 66.

26. European Commission, "Impact Assessment Report," p. 17.

27. OECD, *OECD Economic Surveys: Japan 2015*, p. 76.

28. In a triangular merger, the local affiliate of a foreign company can use a share swap to merge with a Japanese firm. See U.S.-Japan Business Council, "Hitting the Mark: Third Arrow Reforms for Dynamic and Sustainable Growth," May 2015, p. 9 (www.usjbc.org/files/2012/07/Policy-Statement -USJBC_FINAL_5-6-15.pdf?x14756); European Commission, "Impact Assessment Report," p. 17.

29. OECD, *OECD Economic Surveys: Japan 2015*, p. 72.

30. Kazuhito Yamashita, "An Evaluation of the TPP," The Canon Institute for Global Affairs, November 30, 2015 (www.canon-igs.org/en/column /macroeconomics/20151130_3384.html).

31. Cullen Hendrix and Barbara Kotschwar, "Agriculture," in *Assessing the Trans-Pacific Partnership*, p. 51.

32. In its bilateral trade agreements with Mexico, Peru, Chile, and Australia, Japan had used a negative list approach.

33. Hufbauer, "Liberalization of Services Trade," p. 88.

34. Annex II of the TPP text lists permanent nonconforming measures, and in Japan's case these include social services (public health, social security, and insurance), government assets, betting and gambling services, the broadcasting industry, land transactions, primary and secondary educational services, and the energy industry.

35. Office of the U.S. Trade Representative, "Fact Sheet: Toward the Trans-Pacific Partnership: U.S. Consultations with Japan," April 12, 2013 (https://ustr.gov/about-us/policy-offices/press-office/fact-sheets/2013/april /US-consultations-Japan). As noted before, one of the major American concerns on insurance was addressed at the onset of the parallel talks with the standstill on new Japan Post Insurance cancer insurance products until competitive parity could be established. Moreover, Japan's commitments in the parallel talks are in addition to the enforceable obligations for all TPP parties set forth in chapter 11, "Financial Services," of the TPP text, which ensure that no party will give unfair competitive advantage to government postal insurance entities regarding licensing, distribution of products, and regulatory standards.

36. Office of the U.S. Trade Representative, "Japan," in *2013 National Trade Estimate Report on Foreign Trade Barriers*, March 2013.

37. Ibid.

38. Imports of motor vehicles and parts were responsible for 64.9 percent of the American trade deficit in goods with Japan in 2015, and transportation equipment represented 10.8 percent of cumulative Japanese direct investment in the United States in 2015. See TradeStats Express, International Trade Administration, U.S. Department of Commerce (http://tse.export.gov/tse /TSEHome.aspx); U.S. Bureau of Economic Analysis, "Foreign Direct Investment Position in the United States on a Historical-Cost Basis, 2015," Annual Data—Country by Industry Detail from "Foreign Direct Investment in the U.S.: Balance of Payments and Direct Investment Position Data" (www.bea.gov/inter national/di1fdibal.htm).

39. Sarah Oliver, "Auto Sector Liberalization," in *Assessing the Trans-Pacific Partnership,* pp. 60–65.

40. Copenhagen Economics, "Assessment of Barriers to Trade and Investment between the EU and Japan," report prepared for the European Commission, DG Trade, February 3, 2010, p. 226 (http://trade.ec.europa.eu/doclib/docs /2010/february/tradoc_145772.pdf).

41. Japan Automobile Manufacturers Association, "The True Nature of Japan's Automobile Market," 2015 (www.jama.org/media-center/the-true-nature -of-japans-auto-market).

42. "U.S., Japan Auto Dispute Settlement Rules Exceed KORUS in Two Respects," *Inside U.S. Trade*, October 16, 2015.

43. The discussion in this section is based on the TPP-12 agreement. The U.S. withdrawal certainly impacts the viability of the agreement (more on this in chapter 11) as well as the expected economic effects for Japan. An early econometric analysis of a TPP-11 scenario by Kenichi Kawasaki shows that Japan would see its GDP gains from tariff elimination drop significantly from 0.24 percent of GDP to 0.07 percent, but it would retain most of the GDP gains from nontariff liberalization (1.04 percent compared to the original 1.13). Overall, Japan would see its GDP gains reduced, but not in dramatic ways: from 1.37 percent to 1.11 percent of GDP. Moreover, other countries would see larger gains from tariff elimination in a TPP-11 since they would no longer face the same level of competition with U.S. producers (Australia, Chile, Mexico, Peru, New Zealand, and Singapore). These trade diversion effects would represent GDP losses for the United States (0.01 percent), and a bilateral U.S.-Japan FTA would yield inferior gains, both in terms of tariff and nontariff barrier liberalization. See Kenichi Kawasaki, "Emergent Uncertainty in Regional Integration– Economic Impacts of Alternative RTA Scenarios," GRIPS Discussion Paper 16-27 (Tokyo: National Graduate Institute for Policy Studies, January 2017), p. 8 (http://id.nii.ac.jp/1295/00001539/).

44. Peter A. Petri and Michael G. Plummer, "The Economic Effects of the TPP: New Estimates," in *Assessing the Trans-Pacific Partnership*, pp. 6–30. As noted in chapter 2, estimating the income effects of the TPP in complex dynamic economies is an imperfect but useful exercise. The econometric studies by Petri and Plummer, the World Bank, and Japan's Cabinet Secretariat all incorporate the actual market access schedules on tariff reduction/elimination. See Csilla Lakatos and others, "Potential Macroeconomic Implications of the Trans-Pacific Partnership," in *Global Economic Prospects, January 2016: Spillovers Amid Weak Growth* (Washington: World Bank, 2016) and *Naikaku Kanbo TPP Seifu Taisaku Honbu* [Governmental Headquarters for the TPP], "*TPP kyōtei no keizai kōka bunseki ni tsuite*" [On the Analysis of the Economic Effects of the TPP Agreement], December 24, 2015 (www.cas .go.jp/jp/tpp/kouka/pdf/151224/151224_tpp_keizaikoukabunnseki02.pdf). Much harder is the estimate of the impact of reductions in nontariff measures. In this case, these studies must rely on assumptions about the reach of liberalization commitments. For instance, Petri and Plummer assume that 56.3 percent of nontariff measures for goods and 37.5 percent for services can be tackled through TPP commitments (2016, p. 13). For the methodology employed to estimate direct investment effects of the TPP (where they do not rely on the computable general equilibrium model), see the authors' earlier methodology note. See Peter A. Petri, Michael G. Plummer, and Fan Zhai, *The Trans-Pacific Partnership and Asia-Pacific Integration: A Quantitative*

*Assessment* (Washington: Peterson Institute for International Economics, 2012).

45. For example, in absolute terms the increase in the inward FDI stock of the United States will be larger ($128 billion compared to $92 billion in Japan), but in the United States this translates to only a 1.9 percent increase given the much larger stock of inward FDI in the American economy. See Peter A. Petri and Michael G. Plummer, "The Economic Effects of the TPP: New Estimates," in *Assessing the Trans-Pacific Partnership,* pp. 6–30

46. *Naikaku Kanbô TPP Seifu Taisaku Honbu* [Governmental Headquarters for the TPP], *"TPP kyôtei no keizai kôka bunseki ni tsuite"* [On the Analysis of the Economic Effects of the TPP Agreement], December 24, 2015 (www.cas.go.jp/jp/tpp/kouka/pdf/151224/151224_tpp_keizaikoukabunnseki 02.pdf).

47. *Naikaku Kanbō TPP Seifu Taisaku Honbu* [Governmental Headquarters for the TPP], *"TPP kyōteikōshō no oosuji gōi kanren shiryō"* [Materials Related to the Basic Points of Consensus for the TPP Agreement Negotiations], 2015, pp. 15–17 (www.cas.go.jp/jp/tpp/pdf/2015/13/151109_tpp_setsumeikai _siryou.pdf).

48. Sixth industry development refers to programs that increase value added by enabling primary producers to process their products and market them (and move from primary to secondary and tertiary industry: $1 \times 2 \times 3 = 6$).

49. Randall S. Jones and Shingo Kimura, "Reforming Agriculture and Promoting Japan's Integration in the World Economy," Working Paper 1053 (Paris: OECD Publishing, May 27, 2013), p. 6.

50. Yutaka Harada, "Japan's Agriculture and the TPP," Tokyo Foundation, November 21, 2013 (www.tokyofoundation.org/en/articles/2013/japan-agricul ture-tpp).

51. Ministry of Agriculture, Forestry and Fisheries (MAFF), *"2015 nen nōringyō sensasu kekka no gaiyō"* [*Summary of the 2015 Agriculture and Forestry Industries Census Results*], March 25, 2016, p. 9 (www.maff.go.jp/j/tokei /census/afc/2015/attach/pdf/kekka_gaisuuti-2.pdf).

52. Masayoshi Honma, "The TPP and Agricultural Reform in Japan," in *The Political Economy of Japanese Trade Policy,* edited by Aurelia George Mulgan and Masayoshi Honma (Basingstoke, U.K.: Palgrave Macmillan, 2015), p. 103.

53. Yutaka Harada, "Can Japanese Farming Survive Liberalization?" Tokyo Foundation, January 17, 2012 (www.tokyofoundation.org/en/articles/2011 /farming-survive-liberalization).

54. Ibid.

55. Kazuhito Yamashita, "Why are Trade Negotiations Always Blocked by Agriculture in Japan?" Canon Institute for Global Studies, April 11, 2014 (www.canon-igs.org/en/column/macroeconomics/20140411_2498.html).

56. Jones and Kimura, "Reforming Agriculture"; Yamashita, "Why are Trade Negotiations Always Blocked?"; Honma, "TPP and Agricultural Reform in Japan." Consumer spending on agricultural commodities in Japan is esti-

mated to be 1.8 times higher because of government intervention. Jones and Kimura, "Reforming Agriculture," p. 5.

57. Jones and Kimura, "Reforming Agriculture," p. 15.

58. Aurelia George Mulgan, "To TPP or Not TPP: Interest Groups and Trade Policy," in *Political Economy of Japanese Trade Policy.*

59. *Naikaku Kanbō TPP Seifu Taisaku Honbu* [Governmental Headquarters for the TPP], "*Nōrinsuisanbutsu no seisangaku e no eikyō ni tsuite*" [Concerning the Impact on the Output of Agriculture, Forestry, and Fishery Products], December 24, 2015 (www.cas.go.jp/jp/tpp/kouka/pdf/151224/151224_tpp _keizaikoukabunnseki03.pdf); Ministry of Agriculture, Forestry and Fisheries (MAFF), "*Nōsei shinjidai. Doryoku ga mukuwareru nōrinsuisangyō no jitsugen ni mukete*" [A New Era of Agricultural Administration: Toward the Realization of an Agriculture, Forestry, and Fishery Industry where Effort is Rewarded], March 2016 (www.maff.go.jp/j/kanbo/tpp/pdf/nsp_zentai.pdf). Predictions of a collapse in self-sufficiency have long been a battle cry for liberalization foes, although the more meaningful criteria is food security—comprising diversified sources of food supply from abroad.

60. "*Tettei TPP hōdō: 'ketsugi ihan' 69% naikaku shiji 18% seifu to genba ninshiki ni zure honshi nōsei monitā chōsa*" [Thorough TPP Report: "Resolution Violation" 69%, Cabinet Support 18%, A Perception Gap Between Government and the Ground, This Newspaper's Agricultural Administration Monitor's Survey], *Nihon Nōgyō Shimbun*, October 28, 2015.

61. MAFF, "*Nōsei shinjidai*" [New Era of Agricultural Administration], pp. 30–33.

62. Ibid.

63. Aurelia George Mulgan, "Japan's TPP Agriculture Spending a Return to Business as Usual," *East Asia Forum*, January 8, 2016 (http://www .eastasiaforum.org/2016/01/08/japans-tpp-agriculture-spending-a-return-to -business-as-usual/).

64. "*TPP Taisakuhi 3000 oku en kibo de chōsei tochi kairyō ni 1000 oku 15 nendo fukushi*" [300 Billion Yen Range for TPP Countermeasures Expenses, 100 Billion Yen Toward Regulated Land Improvement, FY 2015 Revisions], *Nihon Nōgyō Shimbun*, December 8, 2015.

**CHAPTER 11**

1. For a comprehensive analysis of causes behind the trade slowdown, see International Monetary Fund, "Global Trade: What's Behind the Slowdown?" in *World Economic Outlook 2016: Subdued Demand: Symptoms and Remedies* (Washington: International Monetary Fund, October 2016), pp. 63–119 (www.imf.org/external/pubs/ft/weo/2016/02/pdf/c2.pdf).

2. David Dollar and Edward Alden offer insightful analyses of China's trading and investment practices. See David Dollar, "The Future of U.S.-China Economic Ties," Brookings Big Ideas for America series (Brookings Institution, October 4, 2016) (www.brookings.edu/research/the-future-of-u-s-china-trade

-ties) and Edward Alden, *Failure to Adjust: How Americans Got Left Behind in the Global Economy* (Lanham, Md.: Rowman and Littlefield, 2016). While the Trump administration seemed intent to designate China as a currency manipulator early on, China is no longer intervening to depreciate its currency. As Dollar aptly puts it, "This option is truly fighting the last war."

3. Council of Economic Advisers, "Industries and Jobs at Risk if the Trans-Pacific Partnership Does Not Pass," Issue Brief, November 2016 (https:// obamawhitehouse.archives.gov/sites/default/files/page/files/201611_cost_of _tpp_delay_issue_brief.pdf).

# *Index*